Higher Education Finance and Islamic Endowments

Public debt pressures due to the global economic crisis have impacted higher education in several countries, compelling governments to curtail the funding of higher education institutions (HEIs). Various instruments have been proposed as a platform for the private sector to channel funding to HEIs. This book introduces readers to the issues surrounding the financing of HEIs, especially public universities, which are dependent on government budgets.

It discusses the sources of funding for HEIs, focusing on philanthropic instruments through endowment and *waqf* funds. Since both forms of income are obtained via contributions from third parties, such as alumni, individuals, and business corporations, it is essential that they are managed in such a way to ensure their sustainability and that their benefits can be accessed without interruption. It explains the theory of successful endowment and *waqf* at HEIs, namely appropriate investment planning, superior investment committees, highly skilled investment managers, alumni networks, diversity of income sources, and effective fundraising. These elements have been studied empirically in this book through case studies of several selected Malaysian public universities. The book considers policy implications and offers recommendations of strategies that universities can adopt, such as the appointment of fund managers. No specific guidelines currently exist for appointing fund managers to enable universities to invest in assets such as bonds, equities, and property. Therefore, the book encourages universities to grow endowment and *waqf* funds through proper investment strategies executed by professional fund managers.

The book contributes new knowledge to scholars, students, and researchers, as well as informing university administrators how to collect, manage, and invest funds from endowment and *waqf*.

Nurul Adilah Hasbullah is Senior Lecturer at the Faculty of Economics and Muamalat, Universiti Sains Islam Malaysia, Malaysia.

Asmak Ab Rahman is Associate Professor at the Department of Shariah and Economics, Academy of Islamic Studies, Universiti Malaya, Malaysia.

Islamic Business and Finance Series

Series Editor: Ishaq Bhatti

There is an increasing need for western politicians, financiers, bankers, and indeed the western business community in general to have access to high quality and authoritative texts on Islamic financial and business practices. Drawing on expertise from across the Islamic world, this new series will provide carefully chosen and focused monographs and collections, each authored/edited by an expert in their respective field all over the world.

The series will be pitched at a level to appeal to middle and senior management in both the western and the Islamic business communities. For the manager with a western background the series will provide detailed and up-to-date briefings on important topics; for the academics, postgraduates, business communities, manager with western and an Islamic background the series will provide a guide to best practice in business in Islamic communities around the world, including Muslim minorities in the west and majorities in the rest of the world.

Shariah Governance in Islamic Banking Institutions
Edited by Shafiullah Jan and Muhammad Ismail

The Future of Islamic Banking and Finance in Indonesia
Performance, Risk and Regulation
Romi Adetio Setiawan

Money, Interest and Debt in Monotheistic Religions
An Etymological Approach
Murat Ustaoğlu

Islamic Microeconomics
An Introduction
Lukman Hanif Arbi and M. Ishaq Bhatti

Higher Education Finance and Islamic Endowments
Nurul Adilah Hasbullah and Asmak Ab Rahman

For more information about this series, please visit: www.routledge.com/Islamic-Business-and-Finance-Series/book-series/ISLAMICFINANCE

Higher Education Finance and Islamic Endowments

Nurul Adilah Hasbullah and Asmak Ab Rahman

Routledge
Taylor & Francis Group
LONDON AND NEW YORK

First published 2024
by Routledge
4 Park Square, Milton Park, Abingdon, Oxon OX14 4RN

and by Routledge
605 Third Avenue, New York, NY 10158

Routledge is an imprint of the Taylor & Francis Group, an informa business

British Library Cataloguing-in-Publication Data
A catalogue record for this book is available from the British Library

ISBN: 978-1-032-56527-9 (hbk)
ISBN: 978-1-032-56531-6 (pbk)
ISBN: 978-1-003-43597-6 (ebk)

DOI: 10.4324/9781003435976

Typeset in Times New Roman
by Apex CoVantage, LLC

Contents

Preface

This book discusses the source of higher education finance through endowment and *waqf*. Since both sources are obtained from contributions of third parties (such as alumni, individuals, and business corporations), their sustainability needs to be maintained so that their benefits can be used continuously. In ensuring the sustainability of these sources, this book explains the theory of successful elements of endowment and *waqf* at HEIs consisting of (1) appropriate investment planning, (2) superior investment committees, (3) highly skilled investment managers, (4) alumni networks, (5) diversity of income sources, and 6) effective fundraising. These elements have been studied empirically in this book through several case studies of select Malaysian public universities. These include the Universiti Malaya (UM), Universiti Kebangsaan Malaysia (UKM), and the Universiti Teknologi Malaysia (UTM) representing the endowment fund and Universiti Putra Malaysia (UPM), Universiti Sains Islam Malaysia (USIM) and Universiti Sultan Zainal Abidin (UniSZA), which are the beneficiaries of the *waqf* fund. Based on the empirical study conducted, the following elements were found to contribute towards the successful implementation of endowment and *waqf* at the selected Malaysian public universities: (1) superior investment committees, (2) highly skilled investment managers, (3) alumni networks, (4) diversity of income sources, and (5) effective fundraising. Besides these, the participation of volunteers was found to be another important element in this study. The successful elements are important to investigate and disclose so that they can be used as a reference by other universities in this country, including private universities, on the elements that could help them in driving the successful implementation of these funds at their institutions.

Figures

Tables

Statutes

'Warta Endowmen' Vol. 3. Johor Bahru, 2019
Civil Law Act 1956 (Act 67) (2006) Federal Constitution of Malaysia
Income Tax Act 1967 (ITA)
Trustee Act 1949 (Act 208)
Universities and University Colleges Act 1971 (Act 30)
Wakaf (Melaka) Enactment 2005
Wakaf (Negeri Sembilan) Enactment 2005
Wakaf (Selangor) Enactment 2015
Wakaf (Terengganu) Enactment 2016

Interviews

Ahmad Mustaqim Zolkafali (Assistant Registrar, Chancellor Foundation, UKM, Bangi), in an interview with the authors, 27 March 2020.

Maizatul Yusliana Ab Sofi (Financial Officer, Fund Management & Credit Division, Bursar's Office, University Malaya, Kuala Lumpur), in an interview with the authors, 2 May 2019.

Mohamad Afizal Mehat (Senior Assistant Director, Public HEI Governance Division, Department of Higher Education (Malaysia)), data obtained through email, 9 February 2020.

Mohd Akbal Qamas Abdul Basir (Assistant Bursar, Bursar's Office, UKM, Bangi), in an interview with the authors, 23 March 2020.

Muhammad Faris Zaharudin (Officer, Chancellor Foundation, UKM, Bangi), in an interview with the authors, 8 May 2019.

Noor Mizan Arifin (Assistant Registrar, Office of Waqf & Endowment, UniSZA, Kuala Nerus), in an interview with the authors, 2 March 2020.

Norafitri Buradi (Accountant, Bursar's Office, UTM, Skudai), in an interview with the authors, 27 March 2020.

Nur Asriati Jasmi (Financial Officer, Bursar's Office, UPM, Serdang), in an interview with the authors, 3 April 2020.

Nuruliman Ibrahim (Head, Waqf Management Section, Centre for Management of Waqf, Zakat and Endowment, UPM, Serdang), in an interview with the authors, 31 March 2020.

Rabiatun Adauyah Ishak (Head, Fund Management & Credit Division, Bursar's Office, University Malaya, Kuala Lumpur), in an interview with the authors, 14 May 2019.

Razman Ibrahim (Assistant Registrar, Centre for Awqaf and Zakat, USIM, Nilai) in an interview with the authors, 3 March 2020.

Shaleni a/p S. Muthiah (Financial Officer, Account & Investment Division, Bursar's Office, Universiti Malaya, Kuala Lumpur), in an interview with the authors, 20 March 2020.

Yusof Boon (Associate Professor; Director, Endowment Unit, UTM, Skudai), in an interview with the authors, 23 February 2020.

Yusri Hashim (Deputy Bursar, Central Management Operation Financial Division, Bursar's Office, UPM, Serdang), in an interview with the authors, 18 May 2020.

List of Abbreviations

$:	Dollar
%:	Per cent
ACE:	Access, Certainty, and Efficiency
AED:	United Arab Emirates Dirham
APC:	Anugerah Perkhidmatan Cemerlang
ARB:	Amanah Raya Berhad
BNM:	Bank Negara Malaysia
BoD:	Board of Directors
BoT:	Board of Trustees
CAGR:	Compound Annual Growth Rate
Caltech:	California Institute of Technology
CAQDAS:	Computer Assisted Qualitative Data Analysis Software
CASE:	Council for Advancement and Support of Education
CEO:	Chief Executive Officer
CFO:	Chief Financial Officer
CH:	Switzerland
CN:	China
e.g.:	for example
EFT:	Electronic Fund Transfer
EG:	Egypt
EPFL:	Ecole Polytechnique Federale de Lausanne
et al.:	other people
etc.:	other things
FASB:	Financial Accounting Standard Board
FC:	Finance Committee
GDP:	Gross Domestic Product
GTER:	Gross Tertiary Enrolment Ratio
HE:	Higher Education
HEI:	Higher Educational Institution
HMC:	Harvard Management Company
HR:	Human Resource
i.e.:	stands for the phrase *id est*, which means 'that is'
ICM:	Islamic Capital Market

I-ETF:	Islamic Exchange-Traded Fund
IFMC:	Islamic Fund Management Companies
IQ:	Iraq
I-REIT:	Islamic Real Estate Investment
JAWHAR:	Jabatan Wakaf, Zakat and Haji
JKP:	Jawatankuasa Pengurusan
JO:	Jordan
JV:	Joint Venture
K:	thousands
LB:	Lebanon
LEAP:	Leading Entrepreneur Accelerator Platform
LPU:	Lembaga Pengurusan Universiti
LZS:	Lembaga Zakat Selangor
M:	Masihi
MAIDAM:	Majlis Agama Islam dan Adat Istiadat Melayu
MAIN:	Majlis Agama Islam Negeri
MAINS:	Majlis Agama Islam Negeri Sembilan
MAIS:	Majlis Agama Islam Selangor
MCO:	Movement Control Order
MoE:	Ministry of Education
MoF:	Ministry of Finance
MoHE:	Ministry of Higher Education Malaysia
MoU:	Memorandum of Understanding
MPN:	Majlis Perbandaran Nilai
NACUBO:	National Association of College and University Business Officers
NPO:	Non-Profit Organisation
NTU:	Nanyang Technological University
OECD:	Organisation for Economic Co-Operation and Development
OM:	Oman
p.b.u.h.:	peace be upon him
PNB:	Permodalan Nasional Berhad
PPPW:	Pusat Pembangunan Pembiayaan Wakaf
PTJ:	Responsibility Centre
PWNS:	Perbadanan Wakaf Negeri Sembilan
PWS:	Perbadanan Wakaf Selangor
PWZ:	Pusat Wakaf dan Zakat
QA:	Qatar
QR:	Quick Response
RM:	Ringgit Malaysia
RTM:	Radio Television Malaysia
S.A.:	Saudi Arabia
SAC:	Shariah Advisory Council
SAR:	Sekolah Agama Rakyat
SCM:	Securities Commission Malaysia
SG:	Singapore

SPAC: Special Purpose Acquisition Companies
SRC: Students' Representative Council
SRI: Sustainable and Responsible Investment
TIAA: Teachers Insurance and Annuity Association of America
U.A.E.: United Arab Emirates
UK: United Kingdom
U.S.: United States
UCL: University College London
UIAM: Universiti Islam Antarabangsa Malaysia
UiTM: Universiti Teknologi Mara
UKM: Universiti Kebangsaan Malaysia
UM: Universiti Malaya
UMEF: University Malaya Endowment Fund
UMK: Universiti Malaysia Kelantan
UMP: Universiti Malaysia Pahang
UMS: Universiti Malaysia Sabah
UMT: Universiti Malaysia Terengganu
UniMAP: Universiti Malaysia Perlis
UNIMAS: Universiti Malaysia Sarawak
UniSZA: Universiti Sultan Zainal Abidin
UPM: Universiti Putra Malaysia
UPNM: Universiti Pertahanan Nasional Malaysia
UPSI: Universiti Pendidikan Sultan Idris
USIM: Universiti Sains Islam Malaysia
USM: Universiti Sains Malaysia
UTeM: Universiti Teknikal Malaysia Melaka
UTHM: Universiti Tun Hussein Onn Malaysia
UTM: Universiti Teknologi Malaysia
UUM: Universiti Utara Malaysia
UWB: University *Waqf* Board
VC: Vice-Chancellor
vs: versus
VSE: Voluntary Support of Education
WAQIAH: Pejabat Wakaf dan Infaq
WAZAN: Centre for Management of *Waqf*, *Zakat* and Endowment

List of Appendices

1 Introduction

Background

The public has traditionally been a major source of funding for higher educational institutions (HEIs) worldwide, especially public sector institutions. However, reforms in the higher education finance or funding HEIs occurred after the concept of cost-sharing with the private sector was introduced. Subsequently, various instruments have been proposed as platforms for the private sector to channel funding to HEIs. This book focuses on philanthropic instruments such as endowment and *waqf* funds. Colleges and universities in the U.S. (United States), such as Harvard University and the University of Texas System, have proven that endowment can generate significant funds for institutions. The role of *waqf* in providing funding for HEIs should also be highlighted given the dependence of Islamic universities such as al-Azhar University in Cairo, Egypt, on this fund since their inception.

Both endowment and *waqf* funds are used in Malaysian universities, particularly in public universities. The significance of both these funds for Malaysian public universities is emphasised in this book. Given the belief that the endowment and *waqf* funds could provide permanent funding to Malaysian public universities, their sustainability is prioritised in this book. Therefore, the elements for the successful implementation of these funds are discussed in this book.

The HEI sector is one of the most important sectors for a country, with its benefits accruing not only to the community but also to the country. Ensuring this sector's continuous operation without complete reliance on volatile government funds entails sustainable financing. According to the Organisation for Economic Co-Operation and Development (OECD), to maintain the future productive capacity of HEIs in serving the students and other stakeholders, sustainable finance to cover economic costs and physical, human, and intellectual infrastructure investments is needed.[1] In this regard, long-term planning is essential to create and maintain financial sustainability.

Historically, most HEIs (particularly public universities) globally have relied on funds provided by the public. However, the sources of HEI funding have changed, and the dependency on private sources has increased. Various methods have been proposed, including the implementation of the endowment concept. World-leading universities, such as Harvard University and the University of Texas System in the

DOI: 10.4324/9781003435976-1

U.S., have proven that endowment funds can generate massive funding for universities, with their endowment value reaching $39.43 billion and $30.96 billion, respectively.[2] Notably, endowment is an essential source of funding for universities in other countries, including the UK (United Kingdom) and Singapore.

Similar to an endowment, the role of *waqf* in funding universities is undeniable, as evidenced by popular universities in the Muslim world. For example, Al-Azhar University in Egypt demonstrated that the *waqf* practice established in the 10th century could assist in the provision of free education for many Muslim students, from both within and outside the country. At Al-Azhar University, the use of *waqf* income includes providing funds for students' accommodation, known as *al-bu'uth*, and for all schools that are established under the administration of the university.[3] Al-Azhar University continues to survive with the funding provided by the *waqf*. Other countries that employ the *waqf* income to fund HEIs include Turkey, Morocco, the United Arab Emirates (UAE), and Indonesia.

Public debt pressures in several countries arising from the global economic crisis have impacted higher education, compelling governments to curtail funding of higher education, as illustrated by various scholars such as Peruta and Benson;[4] Rohayati, Najdi, and Williamson;[5] Jacob and Gokbel;[6] and McClure et al.[7] This also applies to Malaysia, as discussed by Ramli and Mohamed.[8] The reduction in funding indicates the government's inability to adequately support higher education because national revenues were adversely affected by the crisis, as illustrated in Figure 1.1. The reduction of the government's budget for the Ministry of Higher

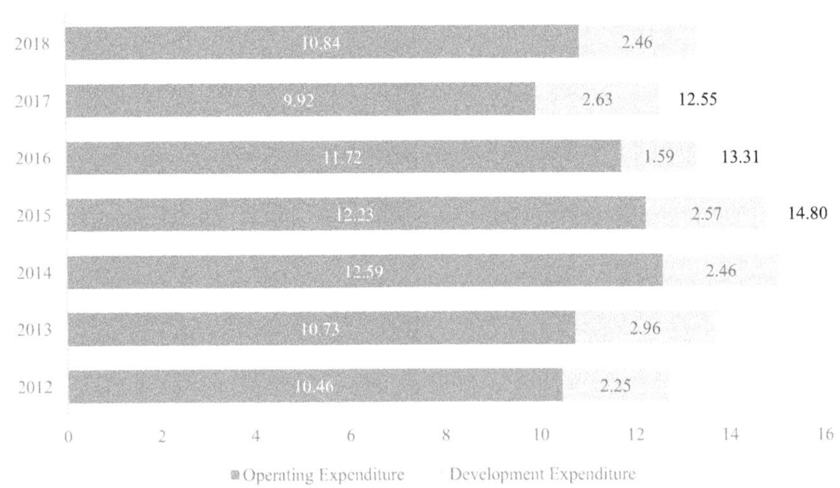

Figure 1.1 Higher Education Ministry's Budget Allocation (2012–2018) in Billion

Note: All figures have been rounded off.

Source: Ministry of Finance, 2020,[9] 2018,[10] and 2015.[11]

Education (MoHE) resulted in the cutdown of operating and development expenditures from RM15.05 billion in 2014 to RM12.55 billion in 2017. Although the budget increased to RM13.30 billion in 2018, the amount was lower compared to the 2014 budget amount. At the same time, this increase did not indicate that the overall needs of higher education were fulfilled, but it reflects the increase in the economic costs of the country as the price of goods and the cost of living increased.

The reduction in the budget for higher education directly impacted the university by forcing them to make drastic cost-saving, such as reducing costs across all university functions (e.g. administrative functions, travel repayments, event management, international faculty recruitment, academic staff mobility, and infrastructure development) and reducing the capacity for conducting research and teaching. This budget reduction had a significant impact particularly on public universities because of their high dependency on government funding. To address the shortage of financial sources, the college tuition fees were increased while a paid system was established to avail of the university facilities, as documented by Che Wan Ismail, Wahid, and Mohd Noor[12] and Ali Hamdan and Mahamood.[13] This tremendously impacted students and changed their spending patterns as a whole. However, despite the increase, the fees imposed on students remained insufficient to fund the operating costs of the universities as economic costs continue to rise.

Given the prediction by various scholars such as Sabri[14] and Mohammad Aslam and Wan Mohar[15] about the continuously increasing education costs, the ability of students and their parents to fund higher education through tuition fees is affected. A further increase in tuition fees to defray higher education costs would reduce students' university enrolment rates. However, if most of the public university provisions originate from the government, the increase in the operating cost of universities would place an additional burden on the government. To reduce the burden on both parties, alternative sources that could provide additional income to universities need to be explored. As suggested by the MoHE, Malaysia,[16] and scholars including Mahamood and Ab Rahman[17] and Mohiddin,[18] endowment and *waqf* funds are among the methods that could be implemented.

This suggestion has received positive responses from all public universities in Malaysia—the endowment fund has been implemented in all the universities and the *waqf* fund in 17 universities. However, based on the data provided by the Public HEI Governance Division, Department of Higher Education (Malaysia),[19] only a few universities have recorded a high collection of these funds. Although this achievement of the universities is not comparable to those of international universities, they are remarkable because they are among the public universities. Furthermore, as these funds are additional sources of income, this achievement is even more noteworthy. As universities are the benchmark in the implementation of endowment and *waqf* funds at HEIs in Malaysia, the elements driving their success are explored in this book to provide key insights for the successful implementation of these funds in other universities, including private universities. Scholars including Mohiddin[20] and Raja Ramli and Abd Hamid[21] discussed the potential of the *waqf* fund to solve the financial problems faced by an institution. We follow this by exploring the elements that can contribute to the successful implementation of this fund and the endowment fund. Thus, through proper implementation, institutions can demonstrate the utility of these funds in solving financial problems.

After the change in the higher education finance, the financial sources provided by the private sector have become increasingly important. Private sector sources obtained through the endowment mechanism, including the *waqf*—as the endowment is known as *waqf* in the Islamic world—are the focus of this book, which also dwells on the application of these funds at Malaysian universities. We narrowed down the universities to public universities that implemented the endowment fund and 17 universities that employed the *waqf* fund. Given our belief that endowment and *waqf* funds could generate various benefits to universities and promote perpetual funding to the university, the sustainability of these funds should be emphasised. Therefore, in this book, we examine the elements that drive the successful implementation of endowment and *waqf* income in funding public universities in Malaysia.

Sources of Funding for HEIs

Empirical studies such as Ozturk,[22] Lin,[23] Mariana,[24] and Wang and Liu[25] have established that higher education has a positive and significant impact on a country's economic growth. Mariana investigated the causal relationship between education (specifically higher education) and economic growth in Romania from 1980 to 2013 using a vector error correction model. Gross domestic product (GDP) per capita was applied as the measure for economic growth, while the number of students enrolled in HEIs and the public spending on education were used as indicators for education. The results indicated that higher education had an important and positive impact on economic growth.[26] Therefore, the governments should ensure that students reap benefits from the public funds allocated for higher education.

Governments in most countries have been providing funding to the education sector, especially higher education. However, large-scale reforms have occurred in the higher education finance worldwide after the introduction of the concept of cost-sharing between the government and private sector—which consists of taxpayers, parents, students, and/or individual or institutional donors—by Johnstone in 1986.[27] The introduction of this concept has been generally accepted worldwide and supported by the World Bank in countries with a distinction in terms of economic level and higher education institutional development, as reported by Johnstone, Arora, and Experton.[28] Another study by Johnstone on the challenges of financial austerity emphasised that revenue diversification in higher education was limited.[29] The funds generated from the implementation of cost-sharing, academic entrepreneurship, and the cultivation of donors should not be assumed as a replacement for the government or taxpayer support but as a supplement, although these sources may be limited.

The transition to cost-sharing directly affected public universities that were previously entirely dependent on government funding. In this context, the proposal for diversification of income has been suggested by many scholars. A global study on higher education practices for sustainable financing by Singh focused on university methods to change trends in financing education and asserted that maintaining university standards entails diversification of funding sources instead of relying entirely on government allocations,[30] an argument that aligns with Ahmed's study for Nigeria.[31] Singh highlighted that almost all countries have become increasingly reliant on households to fund higher education, and the tuition fee has emerged as a large income source, although this remains a politically heated debate.[32]

Hübner investigated the impact of tuition fees on enrolment probability in Germany based on the information obtained from the entire population of high school graduates between 2002 and 2008 and found a negative effect.[33] A study by Neill found similar results for Canada, estimating that a C$1,000 increase in university tuition fees reduces the enrolment rate by 2.5–5 percentage points.[34] Furthermore, Sá investigated the relationship between tuition fees and university applications, focusing on two policy changes—the reduction of tuition fees in Scotland in 2001 and an increase in England in 2012. Using the variation in the university tuition fees over time and counties in the UK, the study revealed that the number of applications reduced in response to higher tuition fees, particularly for courses that led to lower anticipated salaries and employment rates after graduation.[35]

According to Martin, prevailing circumstances, including the prolonged economic slowdown and increase in the state savings on the public funding of goods and services, caused the current generation to largely borrow money to complete higher education despite significantly fewer employment opportunities after graduation.[36] This is confirmed by Mitchell, Leachman, and Masterson, who illustrated that the students borrowed more in response to higher tuition fees.[37] In this regard, Martin argued that distributive justice (students should pay for the education received) and higher education are important in supporting personal autonomy as a central liberal democratic value.[38] However, lending money to students also has risks, such as their inability to repay after graduation, failure to graduate, or defaults on debt.

Webb examined the survival of colleges and universities during challenging economic conditions through the application of revenue diversification. Following the rational arguments on the necessities of income diversification, including portfolio and resource dependence theories, a regression model was developed to evaluate the impact of income diversification and dependency of tuition fees on institutional revenues. The author found that the increase in income diversification during the years before the recession led to a higher total year-to-year income for each student.[39] This shows that income diversification is very important to ensure the survival of colleges and universities during challenging times. Income diversification can be achieved by attracting external funds and developing internal activities. This strategy was considered challenging for institutions and worked as a motivation to enhance national or international competitiveness to provide the best higher education for all.

In the case of external donations or philanthropic instruments in higher education, the history of university development in the U.S. should be an example. Chan applied the resource dependency and institutional theories to provide an overview of historical, sociological, and organisational practices of philanthropy in higher education in the U.S. and presented two arguments. First, the fundraising professional (e.g. board of trustees, the president, and development officers) was highly dependent on the external environment for the sustenance and development of academic institutions. The second argument was presented in the contexts of resource allocation, donor engagement, and fundraising, which also played a role in fostering isomorphism on campus.[40]

McClure et al. examined philanthropy practised by foundations for HEIs in North California based on the social network analysis. In line with the adopted theory, the authors argued that the institutional position in the network led to advantages in terms of competition and procurement of contributions from the foundations; moreover, the highly selective and research-oriented institutions (e.g. Duke, Wake Forest, and University of North California-Chapel Hill) were located at strategic positions in the network, which allowed the competition and contributions from the foundations. Meanwhile, the baccalaureate institutions, which served more students from marginalised racial and financial backgrounds, were less positioned in the network.[41] Therefore, this shows that universities that have been established for a long time and are well known have an advantage in getting contributions compared to those that are not.

Drezner investigated fundraising in higher education based on identity, as it is a factor contributing to donation. In this study, a philanthropic mirroring framework was developed based on social identity and social distance theories, including the identity-based motivation model. Using experiments conducted on the target population, specifically the alumni, the author found that respondents who shared at least one marginalised social identity (e.g. women, racial and ethnic minorities, first-generation college students) with students profiled in fundraising solicitations regarded the cause as more important and were likely to contribute more compared to other respondents.[42] In this regard, the contributions from alumni are relatively easy to obtain if the institution or university intends to collect from them.

A marginalised social identity in the Islamic world does not exist. For instance, women who contribute to society through philanthropy receive recognition. This phenomenon was proven by Souad, Ramdane, and Khan in their historical study of Fātimah al-Fihrī and Religious Fraternity at Al-Qarawiyy University, which predicted that Fātimah al-Fihrī could assist in breaking the negative interpretations about women, especially Muslim women. Additionally, this institution could also illustrate the importance of philanthropy in education as it is an effective instrument in strengthening religion, uniting societies, and building civilisation.[43]

Funding HEIs Through Endowment and *Waqf*

Endowment

An endowment is an investment fund maintained for the benefit of an educational institution, which may also hold cash or property.[44] The income generated from the endowment could be used to cover operating expenses or defray other institutional costs. The use of the fund may be permanently restricted, temporarily restricted, or unrestricted. The most common type of endowment employed by colleges and universities is the true endowment,[45] where the funds specified by the donor should be maintained in perpetuity. Therefore, this fund cannot be used up, expended, or exhausted.

Waqf

Waqf is defined as holding a *Maal* (an asset) and preventing its consumption to repeatedly extract its usufruct for the benefit of an objective representing righteous philanthropy. Based on this definition, *waqf* was identified as involving continuously usufruct-offering properties as long as its principle is preserved, which can be achieved by either its nature (i.e. land or building) or arrangement and conditions prescribed by the *waqf* donors. This definition covers the traditional concept of *waqf* assets (e.g. perpetual) for their beneficial life span and temporary *waqf*, which is allowed by the Maliki schools.[46] There are a few novel forms of *waqf* that are not discussed in the classical literature, such as *waqf* of financial rights and *waqf* of usufruct. Based on the earlier definition, provided that all types of assets may be donated as *waqf*, the concept of *waqf* can be applied not only to a fixed asset (e.g. land or building) but also to other assets, such as cash or shares.

Three unique characteristics of *waqf* were highlighted by Kahf[47] and Mohammad and Mar Iman:[48] perpetuity, irrevocability, and inalienability. All these three features were established based on the *ḥadīth* of the prophet Muhammad peace be upon him (p.b.u.h.) related to the *waqf* land contributed by Umar bin al-Khattab, where the Prophet stated that the property should not be sold, given as a gift, or inherited. Drawing on this *ḥadīth*, the *saqadah* created after the death of the donor is also considered as *al-habs* (holding) as long as the contribution continuously benefits Muslims.[49]

Successful Elements of Endowment and *Waqf*

Appropriate Investment Planning

Investment returns are among the major sources of endowment growth at universities. The shift from fixed income securities, cash, and equities to alternative assets (e.g. hedge funds, private equity, and commodities) as a strategic initiative was adopted by most of the universities to gain a high return, and their allocation to this asset class increased every year (1993–2005). The share of endowments devoted to alternative assets at universities such as those at Ivy League Schools has increased considerably—on average, twice that of other schools. Thus, the best-performing universities in terms of endowment have been increasingly investing in alternative assets. However, the superior endowment performance did not depend solely on the asset class allocation, with the selection of the assets within each class also playing a role.[50]

Barber and Wang[51] and Azlen and Zermati[52] indicated that the top-performing endowment consistently achieved high investment returns with moderate volatility because of exposure to the alternative asset class. Although the performance of the U.S. Endowment Funds was affected by the financial crisis of 2008, the long-term total endowment and risk-adjusted returns at the top-performing endowment remained superior because of significant exposure to this class asset.[53] In this regard, the importance of investing in alternative assets received attention from investors around the world, including universities, perhaps because they have learnt from the financial crisis. This was particularly true for those that were expected to experience an increase in the background income and a decrease in its variability.[54]

However, investors should not blindly increase allocations to alternative investments without considering several risks about inflation, liquidity, and extreme market events,[55] since risk exposure influences endowment returns. To mitigate investment risks, various scholars such as Leković,[56] Jayeola, Ismail, and Sufihani,[57] and Gurrib and Alshahrani[58] highlighted that diversification is an option, while the benefits gained through portfolio diversification for endowments were acknowledged by Azlen and Zermati,[59] Jayeola, Ismail, and Sufahani,[60] and Lord.[61] The higher knowledge and expertise of the investment committee in the diverse asset classes led to greater portfolio diversification.[62]

In *waqf*, the importance of investment diversification strategy is also acknowledged, as illustrated by Sulaiman, Hasan, and Sulaiman–Mohamad,[63] Sulaiman and Hasan,[64] and Oladapo, Oseni, and Mohammed.[65] Nevertheless, it should be managed efficiently so that it could maximise the yield to effectively meet the needs of the community. Simultaneously, the voluntary involvement of financial experts in the *waqf* project also should be considered to ensure the presentation of true opinions related to investment matters.

Superior Investment Committees

The role of the investment committee cannot be overlooked, as demonstrated in the study by Lerner, Schoar, and Wang,[66] which emphasised that endowment funds of more selective universities had access to superior alternative investment opportunities because of superior investment committees. Their involvement is very important to ensure the success of endowment investment in an institution.

The investment committees' roles were recognised generally because of their business or investment credentials and experience as executives or roles on other boards. Moreover, most investment committee members were found to be donors to the university itself,[67] and their presence in the investment committee benefitted the university. Notably, investment decisions were formed with more caution as the invested money was owned by the members. In addition, a stronger presence of donors on the investment committee would promote outsourcing of investment decisions to external fund managers, who had vast experience in managing alternative assets, as a risk management strategy.[68]

Highly Skilled Investment Managers

Although a study found that manager selection did not generate the alpha for top-performing and elite institutions,[69] there are a few studies that found manager selection was an important element for a successful investment, such as the studies of Cejnek et al.[70] and Binfarè et al.[71] This is because they (inside and outside investment managers) have the skills and experience in selecting assets within asset classes over time. At the same time, poor selection could be indirectly avoided. As underlined by Black[72] and by Fishman,[73] investment committees were required for asset selection and evaluating the operational risks of an investment; besides, they served as an informed sounding board. Using the data obtained from GuideStar for schools, Lerner, Schoar, and Wang found that endowment officers were among the five highest-paid employees between 1997 and 2004.[74] Therefore, if institutions need their services, then the cost of their compensation should be considered and allocated.

Alumni Networks

Lee studied the relationships between institutional characteristics and endowment growth by comparing and categorising institutions with endowment market values of over $120 million in 1995 and tracing the pattern of growth for the past decades. The study involved a sample of 147 institutions, comprising 47 public and 100 private institutions. Based on the literature review and discussion, ten variables were identified as possible factors to achieve endowment growth. However, only a few factors, which included alumni giving, were found to have a significant and positive correlation with endowment growth.[75] Alumni giving may be driven by something that motivates them to do so, such as a positive experience or satisfaction with their alma mater.

Given the importance of alumni's role in ensuring endowment growth at a university, building a network with them should be emphasised because of their strong influence on alumni to contribute back to their universities. From the investment aspect, alumni network is beneficial for endowment fund since it has led to improved investments of many selected universities.[76] In this regard, alumni networks should be created and maintained by universities and education providers to benefit the endowment education fund. Additionally, alumni networks became highly relevant after important positions were gained by alumni in organisations and companies.

Diversity of Income Sources

Although universities with large endowment sizes have proven that investments could generate lucrative endowment income, this situation is different in the Malaysian context. Therefore, other sources that could provide income to the endowment fund cannot be overlooked. Munadi conducted a study on the management of endowment funds at one of the universities in Malaysia, Universiti Teknologi Malaysia (UTM). At this institution, the income derived from other projects was found to be higher compared to that from the investment of the endowment fund. The projects implemented in this institution included sales of sponsored books from UTM Publisher, golf tournaments, and recruitment alms during Ramadhan and Idul Fitri among others.[77] This shows that the diversity of income sources is significant in determining the success of non-profit organisations (NPOs), particularly HEIs.

In *waqf*, this strategy was perceived as important, especially for the property that is contributed in the form of land and building. A study reported that Malaysia had 11,091.82 hectares of *waqf* land, with 92.8 per cent still being underdeveloped because of various issues, such as management inefficiencies and lack of funding. Furthermore, the development and utilisation of *waqf* land were not optimised despite the potential to be developed through various instruments. One of the mechanisms proposed in this study was the business model.[78] The importance of diversity of income sources for *waqf* funds should be emphasised to generate continuous income for the benefit of the community. Among the methods that can be implemented to generate the *waqf* income are through rental, fees, agriculture, and sales.

Effective Fundraising

In ensuring that the endowment and *waqf* could provide continuous contributions, the aspect of promotion (e.g. campaign) should be considered as it is an important medium for communicating with people. The significance of this aspect has been examined by various scholars such as Chapman, Masser, and Louis, who specifically analyse peer-to-peer fundraising. The study aimed to investigate the actions leading to the success of peer-to-peer fundraising based on survey and behavioural data from 1,647 online peer-to-peer fundraisers. The strongest predictors in determining peer-to-peer fundraising success were solicitation and high investment in the campaign, and the scholars concluded that fundraisers could achieve more success if more efforts are placed on promoting their charity.[79] One of the efforts that fundraisers can take is to build a strong relationship with their donors or supporters. This is because they can not only provide the contribution but also be an intermediary in promoting the funds to others through campaigns.

At the same time, social media facilities also should be utilised by fundraisers because it is able to reach the potential donors more widely. If social media is used efficiently, then fundraisers will not only receive donations online but also potentially increase the offline donations by word of mouth. There are various social network platforms available, such as Facebook and Twitter, which have emerged in recent years. In the study by Hong, Hu, and Burtch, they found that the buzz on Twitter was a more influential factor in campaigns that tended to produce personal items, given that Twitter was more likely to be used for objective information gathering. Meanwhile, the sharing of activities on Facebook had more influence on campaigns that aimed to distribute public goods as Facebook primarily supports connections.[80] Facebook was also used as a tool for campaigning in fundraising and has been found to be effective in reaching a wide range of constituent groups.[81]

All the aforementioned factors are important for *waqf* because of its need for fundraising. Ismail et al. discussed the operational model of *waqf* education in Malaysia and highlighted that it involved three phases: (1) raising *waqf* funds and assets, (2) *waqf* projects management, and (3) *waqf* benefits distribution. The first phase stated the importance of marketing in developing the *waqf* in HEIs. It needs to be done effectively so that the public will have extensive knowledge about *waqf* projects that were organised by HEIs.

These arguments follow the study conducted by Harun et al., which found that most people were highly keen on the application of the *waqf*; but the low awareness of this instrument prevented them from practising it.[82] This issue not only needs to be left to the university to handle it, but also the authorities need to join hands by promoting the *waqf* fund implemented in the university. Activities such as talk shows, awareness campaigns, and dissemination of information in mass or electronic media should be encouraged more. The promotion could also be channelised through the university website, directly through the students' portal and through printed materials (e.g. posters, banners, flyers, and signboards).

Application of Endowment and *Waqf* at Malaysian Universities

Endowment

Although many studies on endowment in higher education have been conducted, only a few were found in the context of Malaysia. For example, a study by Haneef asserted that the increasingly challenging economic situation led HEIs, especially from the public sector, to seek alternative sources of funding. Despite the provision by the government, this alternative source of funding was crucial to ensure the sustainability of higher education finance. One of the alternative sources proposed was endowment,[83] whose role in Malaysian public universities.

Hassan, Mazlan, and Lahsasna pointed out that the establishment of endowment funds by HEIs in Malaysia at its initial stage had several challenges, including (1) current legislation, (2) limited financial instruments, (3) lack of awareness among corporations or industries on philanthropy, and (4) limited alumni network. Nevertheless, the authors believed that Malaysian universities were ready to implement the endowment concept despite these challenges and that it would be an opportunity for them to prove to the world that endowment is a platform for progress.[84]

In terms of the management aspect of endowment funds, Abdul Hamid, Hassan– Kamarudin, and Abdul Syahid Sowell identified an appropriate mechanism for increasing endowment funds in higher education. Based on interview data, they suggested that Malaysian public universities should focus on three important elements to establish endowment funds: (1) the governance structure for better monitoring of investment activities, (2) alumni networks as the most promising potential source of donor continuity, and (3) appropriate investment planning that matches the risk appetite of the university. The authors also suggested that the Malaysian government should support the universities in creating financial stability, opening new challenges, and allowing a new area of research in the universities. However, the research on endowments, particularly at Malaysian public universities, has not been extensively explored, implying that many aspects of endowments can be further investigated.[85]

Waqf

In the Malaysian context, studies on *waqf* at higher education levels are numerous. Mujani et al. documented the history of *waqf* development in the education system in

Malaysia. Besides explaining the concept, definition, and types of *waqf*, the importance of this instrument for the development of the Malaysian education system was also emphasised. The authors contended that Malaysia had a long history of implementing *waqf* in the education system, with *waqf* properties having the potential to support higher education in Malaysia.[86] This situation illustrates that *waqf* fund had not only successfully upgraded the education system in Malaysia but also provided an opportunity for the poor and needy to access higher learning environments.

Many scholars including Mahamood and Rahman,[87] Dahalan et al.,[88] and Haneef[89] highlighted the requirement of the *waqf* instrument in providing one of the alternative funding sources for higher education in Malaysia. Hamdan and Mahamood's study on *waqf* in higher education based on a legal perspective found that its implementation in higher education had a considerable potential to facilitate income generation for universities.[90] Nowadays, the implementation of *waqf* in Malaysian HEIs is growing rapidly, and there are also innovations being made such as the introduction of cash *waqf*. Cash *waqf* innovation is seen to be increasingly accepted and gaining attention because it is easier to make a contribution and manage due to its liquid nature.

Mujani and Yaakub contended that public universities with a strong *waqf* indicate the ability of universities to obtain revenues through grants or in response to demand.[91] This belief was also in line with that of Fadhilah et al.,[92] although Mujani and Yaakub argued that the implementation of *waqf* at Malaysian universities is not a simple task as it is subject to various restrictions, including legal restrictions and religious principles, and suggested to always bear in mind the challenges that they were likely to face.[93]

Haneef also discussed the various challenges of *waqf* implementation at HEIs in Malaysia and the way forward for its success, which covered several aspects, including administrative framework, management, governance, and investment. He asserted that *waqf* can be successfully developed and implemented in higher education using the '3 Ps': political will, qualified people, and appropriate policies.[94] This statement aligned with the study by Mohamed Nor and Yaakub, who claimed that the development of effective cash management, strong legislation, good governance, marketing efforts, and an appropriate model of *waqf* management could enhance the implementation of *waqf* in higher education.[95]

In terms of legislation, Hussin, Abdul Rashid, and Yaakub argued that the implementation of *waqf* in HEIs in Malaysia should be conducted through Majlis Agama Islam Negeri (MAIN) as the sole trustee of the *waqf* funds in the country. However, if each university implemented different laws, then *waqf* would be practised and implemented differently. Based on the exploration of the implementation of the *waqf* concept in HEIs, they found that public universities did not have enough freedom to implement the *waqf* as they were bound by university rules and regulations. They also praised the *waqf* implementation in Turkey, which is more organised as it is monitored by the same laws provided by their government. This aspect was hoped to be implemented in Malaysia and other Muslim countries worldwide.[96]

Mujani, Mohd Taib, and Rifin examined the use of *waqf* fund in empowering higher education. Applying qualitative analysis, the authors found that taking

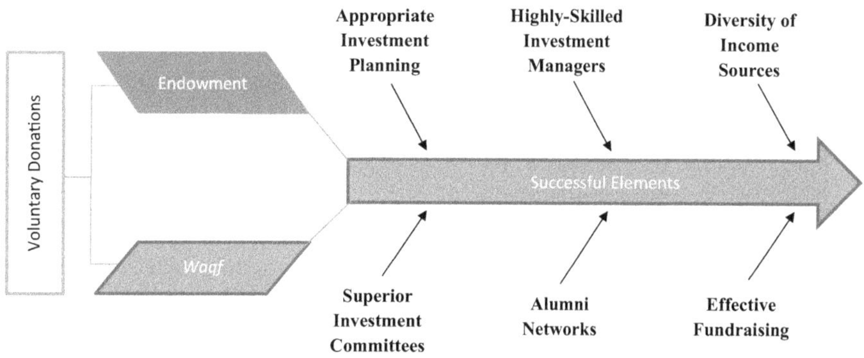

Figure 1.2 Conceptual Framework of the Study

Source: Developed by the authors.

information from the *waqf* institutions, including the exploration and development of *waqf* funds, could be accomplished through the formation of formal organisations at the state and federal levels. They also found that the good quality of HEIs required the rearrangement of the Malaysian educational budget and policy.[97] This finding was confirmed by Harun et al.[98] while Mujani, Mohd Taib, and Rifin suggested that the potential effort of *waqf* in higher education should be demonstrated by the MoHE.[99] However, Hussin argued that the goal of rendering *waqf as* one of the financial instruments for higher education in Malaysia could be achieved if all the stakeholders play their roles.[100]

The vast strand of literature discussed above is fundamental in formulating this study and is followed by a more detailed discussion in the subsequent chapters. However, this book focuses on the successful elements of endowment and *waqf*. The study closest to this was that by Lerner, Schoar, and Wang,[101] who examined the endowment area in the U.S. The results of this study were referred to in the context of Malaysia. Given the value-added in the past study, other elements, such as diversity of income sources and effective fundraising were also explored and used in the *waqf* area. The theoretical framework of this study comprises the exploration of the successful elements of endowment and *waqf* in funding Malaysian universities, especially public universities through a field study, as illustrated in Figure 1.2.

Conclusion

This chapter explained the sources of higher education finance, highlighting endowment and *waqf* as key sources; the successful elements of endowment and *waqf* at HEIs; the application of these funds at Malaysian public universities; and the successful elements for the provision of funding for Malaysian public universities.

Notes

1 Organisation for Economic Co-operation and Development (OECD), *On the Edge: Securing a Sustainable Future for Higher Education* (France: OECD Publications, 2004), 35.
2 "The 20 Richest Colleges in the United States in FY 2019, by Endowment Funds Market Value," *Statista* (2020), accessed on 19 March 2020, www.statista.com/statistics/221147/the-20-richest-colleges-in-the-us/.
3 S. M. Mahamood and A. Ab Rahman, "Financing Universities through Waqf, Pious Endowment: Is It Possible?," *Humanomics* 31, no. 4 (2015): 430–53, 447, https://doi.org/10.1108/H-02-2015-0010.
4 A. Peruta and C. Helm, "Engaging University Alumni through Social Media: Strategies for Creating Community," *The Journal of Social Media in Society* 7, no. 1 (2018): 123–50, 124.
5 M. I. Rohayati, Y. Najdi, and J. C. Williamson, "Philanthropic Fundraising of Higher Education Institutions: A Review of the Malaysian and Australian Perspectives," *Sustainability* 8, no. 541 (2016): 1–20, 1, https://doi.org/10.3390/su8060541.
6 W. J. Jacob and V. Gokbel, "Global Higher Education Learning Outcomes and Financial Trends: Comparative and Innovative Approaches," *International Journal of Educational Development* 58 (2018): 5–17, 7, https://doi.org/10.1016/j.ijedudev.2017.03.001.
7 K. R. McClure et al., "Philanthropic Giving by Foundations to Higher Education Institutions: A State-Level Social Network Analysis," *Philanthropy & Education* 1, no. 1 (2017): 1–28, 4, https://doi.org/10.2979/phileduc.1.1.02.
8 A. Mohd Ramli and M. O. Mohamed, "Cabaran Pembiayaan Sektor Pengajian Tinggi Awam di Malaysia: Potensi Instrumen Wakaf Tunai," in *Sinergisme Wakaf Pendidikan Tinggi di Malaysia*, ed. M. S. Shahruddin et al., 57–73 (Shah Alam: Institut Kajian Zakat Malaysia (IKaZ), UiTM, 2016), 64.
9 Kementerian Kewangan Malaysia, *Anggaran Perbelanjaan Persekutuan* (Kuala Lumpur: Percetakan Nasional Malaysia Berhad, 2020), 25.
10 Kementerian Kewangan Malaysia, *Anggaran Perbelanjaan Persekutuan* (Kuala Lumpur: Percetakan Nasional Malaysia Berhad, 2018), 24.
11 Kementerian Kewangan Malaysia, *Anggaran Perbelanjaan Persekutuan* (Kuala Lumpur: Percetakan Nasional Malaysia Berhad, 2015).
12 C. W. M. Che Wan Ismail, H. Wahid, and M. A. Mohd Noor, "Pola Perbelanjaan dan Cadangan Penentuan Haddul Kifayah Mahasiswa Institusi Pengajian Tinggi: Kajian di Kuala Terengganu, Terengganu," in *Pengurusan Zakat di Malaysia: Isu dan Cabaran Kontemporari*, ed. H. Wahid and M. A. Mohd Noor (Bangi: Pusat Penyelidikan Ekonomi dan Kewangan Islam (EKONIS-UKM), 2018), 29–50, 30–31.
13 S. U. Ali Hamdan and S. M. Mahamood, "Aplikasi Prinsip Berkekalan Wakaf di Institusi Pengajian Tinggi Terpilih: Perspektif Perundangan," *Journal of Shariah Law Research* 1, no. 2 (2016): 229–50, 238.
14 M. F. Sabri, "Geran Permudah Pembiayaan Pendidikan," *Utusan Malaysia*, September 19, 2017.
15 M. M. Mohammad Aslam and W. M. D. H. Wan Mohar, "Kelestarian Program Akademik dan Kewangan dalam Pengajian Tinggi Islam," *Journal of Asian Islamic Higher Institutions (JAIHI)* 1, no. 1 (2015): 1–6.
16 Ministry of Higher Education Malaysia, *University Transformation Programme, Purple Book: Enhancing University Income Generation, Endowment & Waqf* (Putrajaya: Kementerian Pendidikan Tinggi Malaysia, 2016), 3.
17 Mahamood and Ab Rahman, "Financing Universities through Waqf, Pious Endowment: Is It Possible?" 430.
18 M. N. Mohiddin, "Kredibiiti Wakaf dalam Menangani Isu Pembiayaan Pengajian Tinggi," *International Research Journal of Shariah, Muamalat and Islam (IRJSMI)* 2, no. 4 (2020): 9–21, 9, https://doi.org/10.35631/IRJSMI.24002.

19 Mohamad Afizal Mehat. *Senior Assistant Director, Public HEI Governance Division, Department of Higher Education (Malaysia)*, data obtained through email, 9 February 2020.
20 Mohiddin, "Kredibiliti Wakaf dalam Menangani Isu Pembiayaan Pengajian Tinggi," 15.
21 R. N. A. Raja Ramli and N. A. Abd Hamid, "Kelestarian Wakaf dalam Membangunkan Institusi Pendidikan: Kajian Awal," *Paper presented, International Conference on Post-graduate Research*, Kuala Lumpur, 2014, 454–65, 463.
22 I. Ozturk, "The Role of Education in Economic Development: A Theoretical Perspective," *Journal of Rural Development and Administration* XXXIII, no. 1 (2001): 39–47, 39.
23 T. C. Lin, "The Role of Higher Education in Economic Development: An Empirical Study of Taiwan Case," *Journal of Asian Economics* 15, no. 2 (2004): 355–71, 355.
24 D. R. Mariana, "Education as a Determinant of the Economic Growth. The Case of Romania," *Procedia—Social and Behavioral Sciences* 197 (2015): 404–12, 404, https://doi.org/10.1016/j.sbspro.2015.07.156.
25 Y. Wang and S. Liu, "Education, Human Capital and Economic Growth: Empirical Research on 55 Countries and Regions (1960–2009)," *Theoretical Economics Letters* 6 (2016): 347–55, 347, https://doi.org/10.4236/tel.2016.62039.
26 Mariana, "Education as a Determinant of the Economic Growth. The Case of Romania," 404.
27 B. Johnstone, *Sharing the Costs of Higher Education: Student Financial Assistance in the United Kingdom, the Federal Republic of Germany, France, Sweden, and the United States* (New York: The College Board, 1986).
28 D. B. Johnstone, A. Arora, and W. Experton, "The Financing and Management of Higher Education: A Status Report on Worldwide Reforms," in *UNESCO World Conference on Higher Education* (Paris, France: The World Bank, 1998), 1–33, 27, https://c33c6999-a-62cb3a1a-s-sites.googlegroups.com/site/asambleadeestudiantesuc/documentos-sobre-el-eees-/documentos-oficiales/FinanciacionyAdministraciondelaEducacionSuperior(BancoMundial,1998).pdf?attachauth=ANoY7crbn6ZIPhMU3GvkACm8vyisRS-YfwFoybBcchd.
29 B. Johnstone, "Challenges of Financial Austerity: Imperatives and Limitations of Revenue Diversification in Higher Education," *The Welsh Journal of Education* 11, no. 1 (2002): 18–36, 34, https://doi.org/10.16922/wje.11.1.3.
30 S. Singh, "Higher Education Practices Worldwide for Sustainable Financing," *Working Paper Series* (2014): 1–19, 1.
31 S. Ahmed, "Public and Private Higher Education Financing in Nigeria," *European Scientific Journal* 11, no. 7 (2015): 92–109, 101–02.
32 Singh, "Higher Education Practices Worldwide for Sustainable Financing," 1.
33 M. Hübner, "Do Tuition Fees Affect Enrollment Behavior? Evidence from a 'Natural Experiment' in Germany," *Economics of Education Review* 31 (2012): 949–60, 949, https://doi.org/10.1016/j.econedurev.2012.06.006.
34 C. Neill, "Tuition Fees and the Demand for University Places," *Economics of Education Review* 28 (2009): 561–70, 541.
35 F. Sá, "The Effect of Tuition Fees on University Applications: Evidence from the UK," *IZA Discussion Paper*, no. 8364 (2014): 1–26, 949.
36 C. Martin, "Should Students Have to Borrow? Autonomy, Wellbeing and Student Debt," *Journal of Philosophy of Education* (2015): 1–20, 1.
37 M. Mitchell, M. Leachman, and K. Masterson, *Funding Down, Tuition Up: State Cuts to Higher Education Threaten Quality and Affordability at Public Colleges* (Washington, DC: Center on Budget and Policy Priorities, 2016), 24.
38 Martin, "Should Students Have to Borrow? Autonomy, Wellbeing and Student Debt," 1.
39 J. Webb, "A Path to Sustainability: How Revenue Diversification Helps Colleges and Universities Survive Tough Economic Conditions," *Journal of International & Interdisciplinary Business Research* 2, no. 7 (2015): 69–97.

40 R. Y. Chan, "Studying Philanthropy and Fundraising in the Field of Higher Education: A Proposed Conceptual Model," in *Facilitating Higher Education Growth through Fundraising and Philanthropy*, ed. H. C. Alphin et al. (Hershey, PA: Information Science Reference (an imprint of IGI Global), 2016), 1–27, 8–16, https://doi.org/10.4018/978-1-4666-9664-8.ch001.
41 McClure et al., "Philanthropic Giving by Foundations to Higher Education Institutions: A State-Level Social Network Analysis," 2.
42 N. D. Drezner, "Philanthropic Mirroring: Exploring Identity-Based Fundraising in Higher Education," *The Journal of Higher Education* (2017): 1–35, 1, https://doi.org/10.1080/00221546.2017.1368818.
43 M. Souad, T. Ramdane, and M. S. Khan, "Fātimah Al-Fihrīand Religious Fraternity in Al-Qarawiyy in University: A Case Study," *International Journal of Humanities and Social Science* 7, no. 10 (2017): 177–83, 177, https://doi.org/10.1108/17504971211236308.
44 M. F. Sherlock et al., "College and University Endowments: Overview and Tax Policy Options," *Congressional Research Service* (2015): 1–27, 2, http://search.ebscohost.com/login.aspx?direct=true&db=tsh&AN=111387593&site=ehost-live.
45 R. L. S. McElhaney, "The Effects of Higher Education Endowment Management Practices on Endowment Performance," Ph.D. thesis, the University of Southern Mississippi, 2010, 5.
46 M. Kahf, "Financing the Development of Awqaf Property," *Paper presented, Seminar on Development of Awqaf*, Kuala Lumpur, 1998, 4–5.
47 Kahf, "Financing the Development of Awqaf Property," 8.
48 M. T. S. Mohammad and A. H. Mar Iman, "Obstacles of the Current Concept of Waqf to the Development of Waqf Properties and the Recommended Alternative," *Malaysian Journal of Real Estate* 1, no. 1 (2006): 27–38, 28–30, https://doi.org/10.1108/H-02-2015-0010.
49 M. Kahf, "Suwar Mustajida Min Al-Waqf," (2004): 1–75, 5–6, http://monzer.kahf.com/papers/arabic/sowar_mustajida_min_al-waqf.pdf.
50 J. Lerner, A. Schoar, and J. Wang, "Secrets of the Academy: The Drivers of University Endowment Success," *Journal of Economic Perspectives* 22, no. 3 (2008): 207–22, 214–16.
51 B. M. Barber and G. Wang, "Do (Some) University Endowments Earn Alpha?" *Financial Analysts Journal* 69, no. 5 (2013): 26–44, 27.
52 M. W. Azlen and I. Zermati, "Investing Like the Harvard and Yale Endowment Funds," *Alternative Investment Analyst Review* 6, no. 3 (2017): 7–13, 11.
53 Ibid., 11.
54 H. S. Rosen and A. J. W. Sappington, "What Do University Endowment Managers Worry About? An Analysis of Alternative Asset Investments and Background Income," *NBER Working Paper Series*, no. 21271 (2015): 1–34, 27.
55 K. H. Black, "Risk Management for Endowment and Foundation Portfolios," *The Journal of Alternative Investments* 15, no. 4 (2013): 8796, 95.
56 M. Leković, "Investment Diversification as a Strategy for Reducing Investment Risk," *Economic Horizons* 20, no. 2 (2018): 169–84, 169, https://doi.org/10.5937/ekonhor1802173l.
57 D. Jayeola, Z. Ismail, and S. F. Sufahani, "Effects of Diversification of Assets in Optimizing Risk of Portfolio," *Malaysian Journal of Fundamental and Applied Sciences* 13, no. 4 (2017): 584–87, 584, https://doi.org/10.11113/mjfas.v0n0.567.
58 I. Gurrib and S. Alshahrani, "Diversification in Portfolio Risk Management: The Case of the UAE Financial Market," *International Journal of Trade, Economics and Finance* 3, no. 6 (2012): 445–49, 449, https://doi.org/10.7763/ijtef.2012.v3.243.
59 Azlen and Zermati, "Investing Like the Harvard and Yale Endowment Funds," 7.
60 Jayeola, Ismail, and Sufahani, "Effects of Diversification of Assets in Optimizing Risk of Portfolio," 585.
61 M. Lord, "University Endowment Committees: How a Learning Orientation and Knowledge Factors Contribute to Portfolio Diversification and Performance," *The European Journal of Finance* (2014): 1–25, 1, https://doi.org/10.1080/1351847X.2013.879536.
62 Ibid., 1.

63 S. Sulaiman, A. Hasan, and A. A. Sulaiman-Mohamad, "Pembangunan Dan Pelaburan Lestari Harta Wakaf dari Perspektif Islam," *Kanun* 28, no. 1 (2016): 68–100, http://jurnalkanun.dbp.my/wordpress/wp-content/uploads/2016/02/4-Lestari.pdf.
64 S. Sulaiman and A. Hasan, "Strategi Pembangunan dan Pelaburan Wakaf Secara Lestari Menurut Perspektif Syariah," *Jurnal Syariah* 24, no. 2 (2016): 237–70, 237.
65 H. B. Oladapo, R. A. Oseni, and M. O. Mohammed, "A Comparative Analysis of Waqf Institution and Endowment Foundation: Determinants of Sustainability," *International Journal of Novel Research in Humanity and Social Sciences* 3, no. 4 (2016): 151–62.
66 Lerner, Schoar, and Wang, "Secrets of the Academy: The Drivers of University Endowment Success," 208.
67 J. R. Brown et al., "The Governance of University Endowments: Insights from a TIAA-CREF Institute Survey," *Research Dialogue*, no. 102 (2012): 1–15, 1.
68 Ibid., 5.
69 Barber and Wang, "Do (Some) University Endowments Earn Alpha?" 26.
70 G. Cejnek et al., "A Survey of University Endowment Management Research," *SSRN Electronic Journal* (2013): 1–39, 2. https://doi.org/10.2139/ssrn.2205207.
71 M. Binfarè, R. S. Harris, G. W. Brown, and C. T. Lundblad, "How Important Are Investment Committees? Evidence from University Endowments," 1–49.
72 Black, "Risk Management for Endowment and Foundation Portfolios," 95.
73 J. J. Fishman, "What Went Wrong: Prudent Management of Endowment Funds and Imprudent Endowment Investing Policies," *The Journal of College and University Law* 40, no. 2 (2014): 199–246, 236.
74 Lerner, Schoar, and Wang, "Secrets of the Academy: The Drivers of University Endowment Success," 218–19.
75 H. Lee, "The Growth and Stratification of College Endowments in the United States," *International Journal of Educational Advancement* 8, no. 3/4 (2008): 136–51, 136, https://doi.org/10.1057/ijea.2009.10.
76 Lerner, Schoar, and Wang, "Secrets of the Academy: The Drivers of University Endowment Success," 217–18.
77 M. Munadi, "Pengelolaan Endowment Fund Di Perguruan Tinggi Malaysia: Studi Kasus Di Universitas Teknologi Malaysia," *Al-Ulum* 17, no. 2 (2017): 306–31, 306, https://doi.org/10.30603/au.v17i2.199.
78 N. Mohd Ali, R. Ahmad, and N. S. Ahmad Mahdzan, "The Need of an Effective Business Model for Waqf Land Development in Malaysia," *Paper presented, The 20th International Research Conference on Business, Economics, and Social Sciences*, Istanbul, Turkey, 2015, 1–12.
79 C. M. Chapman, B. M. Masser, and W. R. Louis, "The Champion Effect in Peer- to-Peer Giving: Successful Campaigns Highlight Fundraisers More Than Causes," *Nonprofit and Voluntary Sector Quarterly* (2018): 1–21, 1, https://doi.org/10.1177/0899764018805196.
80 Y. Hong, Y. Hu, and G. Burtch, "How Does Social Media Affect Contribution to Public versus Private Goods in Crowdfunding Campaigns?" *Paper presented, Thirty Sixth International Conference on Information Systems*, Fort Worth, 2015, 1.
81 M. J. Zickar, T. H. Ron, and C. Arnold, "Using Facebook Pages to Connect with Students, Faculty, Alumni, and Friends: An Empirical Analysis," *Teaching of Psychology* 45, no. 4 (2018): 358–62, 358, https://doi.org/10.1177/0098628318796923.
82 R. Harun et al., "Promotion as a Determinants for Waqf Awareness Among University Students," *International Academic Research Journal* 2, no. 1 (2016): 95–99, 99.
83 M. A. Haneef, "Funding of Higher Education in Malaysia-The Potential Role of Awqaf and Endowment," in *International Symposium on Waqf and Higher Education (ISWHE 2016)*, ed. S. Kayadibi and S. Alimova (Kuala Lumpur: Centre for Islamic Economics (CIE), IIUM, 2016), 20–25, https://doi.org/10.1017/CBO9781107415324.004.
84 W. Hassan, N. Mazlan, and A. Lahsasna, "Malaysian Higher Education Institutions: Is the Endowment Fund the Way Forward?" *IF HUB* (2017): 16–21, 21, https://ikr.inceif.org/handle/INCEIF/2674.

85 B. Abdul Hamid, W. Hassan-Kamarudin, and S. Abdul Syahid Sowell, "The Endowment Fund as a Source of Sustainability for Higher Education in Malaysia: Maximising Investment Returns." *ISRA Research Paper*, no. 103 (2018): 1–32.

86 W. K. Mujani et al., "The History of the Development of Higher Education Waqf in Malaysia," *International Journal of Civil Engineering and Technology (IJCIET)* 9, no. 3 (2018): 549–57.

87 Mahamood and Ab Rahman, "Financing Universities through Waqf, Pious Endowment: Is It Possible?" 448.

88 N. F. Dahalan et al., "Risiko Pengurusan Dana Wakaf Untuk Institusi Pendidikan Tinggi Di Malaysia: Satu Kerangka Konseptual," *Jurnal 'Ulwan* 1 (2016): 164–78.

89 Haneef, "Funding of Higher Education in Malaysia-The Potential Role of Awqaf and Endowment," 20.

90 Ali Hamdan and Mahamood, "Aplikasi Prinsip Berkekalan Wakaf di Institusi Pengajian Tinggi Terpilih: Perspektif Perundangan," 248.

91 W. K. Mujani and N. I. Yaakub, "Waqf for Higher Education in Malaysia: Overview on Challenges," *European Journal of Multidisciplinary Studies* 5, no. 1 (2017): 455–61.

92 A. A. Fadhilah et al., "The Effort of Selected Public and Private Universities to Develop Awqaf Property in Malaysia," *Pertanika Journal of Social Sciences and Humanities* 25, no. Special Issue (2017): 267–80.

93 Mujani and Yaakub, "Waqf for Higher Education in Malaysia: Overview on Challenges," 455.

94 Haneef, "Funding of Higher Education in Malaysia-The Potential Role of Awqaf and Endowment," 25.

95 S. Mohamed Nor and N. I. Yaakub, "Educational Endowments Governance for Institutions of Higher Education in Malaysia: A Preliminary Study," *Advanced Science Letters* X, no. XXX–XXX (2015): 1–4, https://doi.org/10.1166/asl.2017.7266.

96 R. Hussin, R. Abdul Rashid, and N. I. Yaakub, "Exploratory Study on Waqf Implementation in Malaysian Public and Private Universities: With Special Reference to Turkish Universities," *International Journal of Business, Economics and Law* 9, no. 4 (2016): 16–23.

97 Mujani, W. K., M. S. Mohd Taib, and M. K. I. Rifin, "Waqf Higher Education in Malaysia," *Paper presented, International Conference on Education, E-Learning and Management Technology*, Atlantis Press, 2016, 519–22.

98 F. M. Harun et al., "Issues and Economic Role of Waqf in Higher Education Institution: Malaysian Experience," *Al-Iqtishad: Journal of Islamic Economics* 8, no. 1 (2016): 149–68, https://doi.org/10.15408/aiq.v8i1.2514.

99 Mujani, Mohd Taib, and Rifin, "Waqf Higher Education in Malaysia," 519.

100 R. Hussin, "Waqf Implementation in Malaysian Universities: Overview and Way Forward," *The Social Sciences* 13, no. 1 (2018): 145–49.

101 Lerner, Schoar, and Wang, "Secrets of the Academy: The Drivers of University Endowment Success," 214–16.

2 Theory of Sources of Funding for Higher Educational Institutions

Introduction

As HEIs play an important role in promoting knowledgeable and competitive human capital for a country, their funding system should be examined to ensure smooth operation. Besides the general discussion about HEIs, this chapter provides a detailed discussion about the parties responsible for providing funding to these institutions, the funding initiatives from the Islamic perspective, and the sources of funding for HEIs. These topics are presented in the following four sections that deal on HEIs in general; the parties responsible to fund HEIs; the parties responsible to fund HEIs from the Islamic perspective; and sources of funding for HEIs. The last section presents the conclusion of this chapter.

HEIs

Higher education can be referred to as the tertiary level of education. The institutions providing this level of education are universities, university colleges, polytechnics, academies, and colleges. The basic pattern of higher education comprises four interrelated forms: (1) liberal education, (2) professional education, (3) graduate study and research, and (4) public services. Although each form generally contributes to the individual and society, the establishment of HEIs primarily aims to produce trained and professional manpower in various disciplines at the diploma, degree, and postgraduate levels since HEIs offer excellent research, training, and cultural and civic experience.

Although a national university is present in several countries including Japan and Singapore, universities in developed and developing countries can be generally categorised into two types, public and private universities. A public university is mainly funded by the public through a national or subnational government, whereas a private university is not operated by the government despite receiving tax breaks, public student loans, and grants. This sector differs from the public sector as it consists of both non-profit and profit institutions.

The number of public and private universities differs across countries. For instance, in the U.S., the latest numbers of public and private universities are 1,985 and 4,775, respectively (non-profit and profit).[1] Meanwhile, Japan has 86 national

DOI: 10.4324/9781003435976-2

universities, 89 public universities, and 604 private universities.[2] Based on the latest statistics provided by the Ministry of Education (MoE) Malaysia, 20 public universities[3] and 426 private universities[4] are present in the country.

Who Is Responsible for Funding HEIs?

Higher education can be perceived in two ways, namely as a social need and as an individual need. If the first view is adopted, the government should provide educational opportunities to everyone who needs it. If the second view is adopted, people would have to pay for education provided. In this case, two parties are involved in providing higher education, namely the government and society. This issue is discussed in the subsequent subsections.

Government

The government is a party with the authority to govern a country or state. The authority is derived from the people's mandate and includes enacting, administrating, and implementing the laws. Parallelly, the authority also collects taxes from people as a source of funding for public goods and services, such as education, social care, and support for housing costs, in the country. Although education is categorised as a private good, as elaborated by Buchanan and Flowers,[5] strong qualitative arguments highlight that the benefits gained by individuals also benefit society as a whole in terms of growth, social unity, and the transmission of values, as reported by Bynner and Egerton[6] and Bynner et al.[7] Based on these arguments, it is suggested that subsidies from government funds should be a permanent source of higher education finance.

Economists recognised the public expenditure on this sector as a country's investment in the form of human capital since it can assist in the development of national productivity for both individuals and communities as a whole. This view was aligned with that of Ozturk, who claimed that sustainable economic development could not be achieved in a country without any substantial investment in human capital.[8] In relation to that, countries should invest in human capital if they intend to develop and improve the well-being of their citizens. Examples of developed countries include Norway and Denmark, which spent 96 per cent and 92.3 per cent of their higher education spending, as shown in Figure 2.1. The employment rate of these two countries was 89.2 per cent and 87.6 per cent, respectively (citizens aged between 25 and 64 years), above the average of 68.6 per cent in 2020, as shown in Figure 2.2.[9] This shows that the expenditure incurred by the government is not a disadvantage. But providing equal higher education opportunities for all, including those who are poor, enables individuals to become highly competitive human capital for the country as well as improves their standard of living.

Besides, the government also plays a vital role in providing education to people as individuals have various constraints and cannot adequately avail themselves of the facilities provided by the government. This was recognised by Bray, who

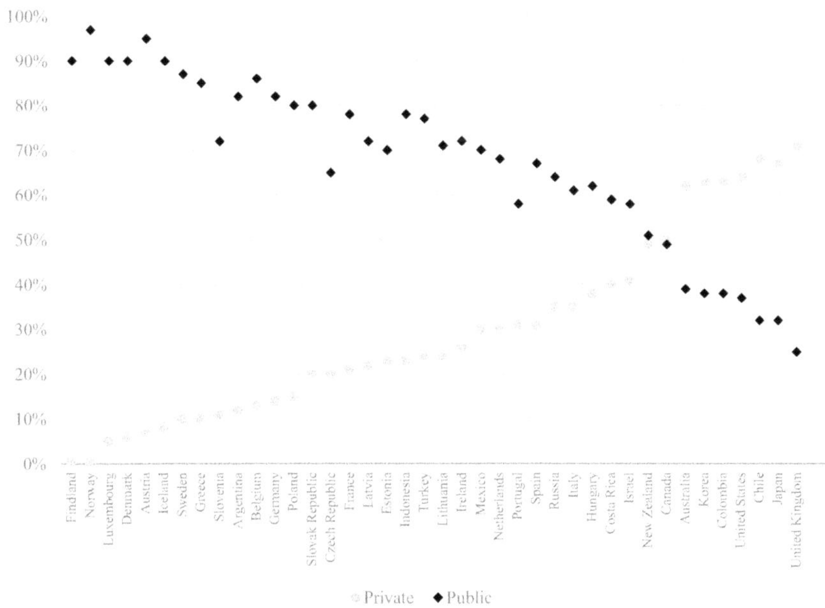

Figure 2.1 Spending on Tertiary Education Based on Latest Available Data (2016)

Source: OECD.[10]

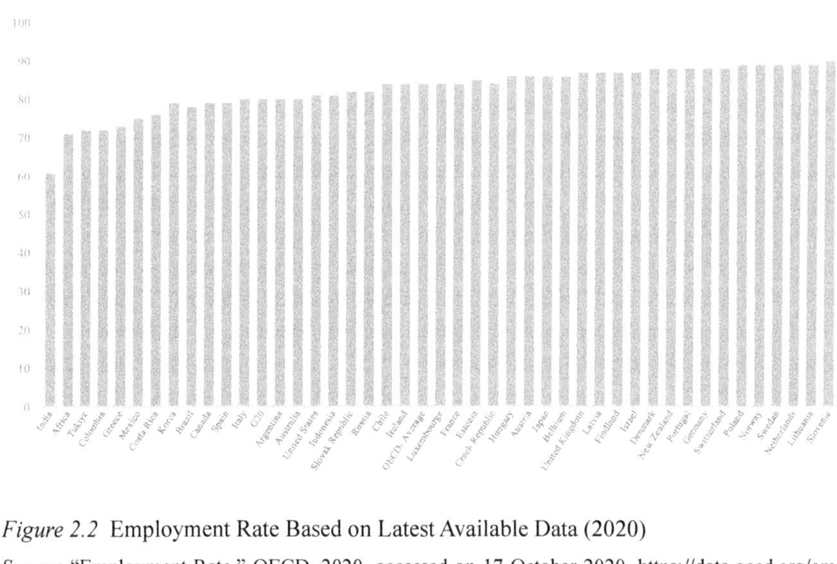

Figure 2.2 Employment Rate Based on Latest Available Data (2020)

Source: "Employment Rate," OECD, 2020, accessed on 17 October 2020, https://data.oecd.org/emp/employment-rate.htm.[11]

identified the situation as 'bridge the gap'.[12] Government expenditure on education could lead to equal opportunity for all, including the poor, and reap the benefits of the higher education system. If education opportunity is provided to the poor, a country can obtain the returns through the income tax paid by them. People can also change their lives and that of their next generation for a better future, which also indirectly reduces the gap between the rich and the poor in a country. This has been demonstrated by the success in Denmark and Norway, which ranked among the top five countries in the equality ranking, as reported by the Commitment to Reducing Inequality Index 2017.[13]

Society

Society implies a group of people who live together. One of the factors that distinguish one person from another is education as it creates knowledgeable and competitive individuals. As mentioned earlier, the government is responsible for providing education to people. However, as higher education is an individual investment, providing such support to them is not necessary, as contended by Terry and Macy[14] and Bray.[15] These views led to a shift in the funding for this sector by private sources. This situation goes back to the 19th century when the private sector provided more funds for education despite public consideration. This shift of the funding is known as cost-sharing, which was developed by Johnstone from 1986 until 2006.[16] It refers to the sharing of the cost of higher education borne by the government with the students and their parents.

According to Johnstone, the transition from public sources to private sources was caused by three rationale reasons, namely: (1) the sheer need for other than government revenue; (2) the cost of education should be shared by parties who have gained from education; and (3) imposing a price on valuable and highly demanded goods and services, such as higher education.[17] The first reason (i.e. the sheer need for other than government revenue) is to respond to the high demand for higher education. The increase in demand for higher education created strong pressures on the portion of higher education expenditure funded by the government. According to Tulip, this situation was caused by inadequate government expenditure to meet the increasing demand despite the increase in the annual budget,[18] as demonstrated in the data provided by the World Bank and depicted in Figure 2.3. The data illustrate that the worldwide gross tertiary enrolment ratio (GTER) has been increasing annually starting from 1970. In 2021, the worldwide GTER reached 40 per cent which is higher than the GTER in the previous years. This condition might be because of state policies, economic development, aspirations for social position, credentialism, or global factors.

For the second rationale reason (i.e. the cost of education should be shared by parties who have gained from education) noted by Johnstone,[19] although higher education provides benefits to society and is important for the national well-being, students are obligated to pay back to society. It is as return for the educational opportunity offered to them. One of the instruments that could be used by students to share the cost of higher education is tuition fee. This is supported by Johnstone's earlier argument, which highlighted the observation from market-oriented

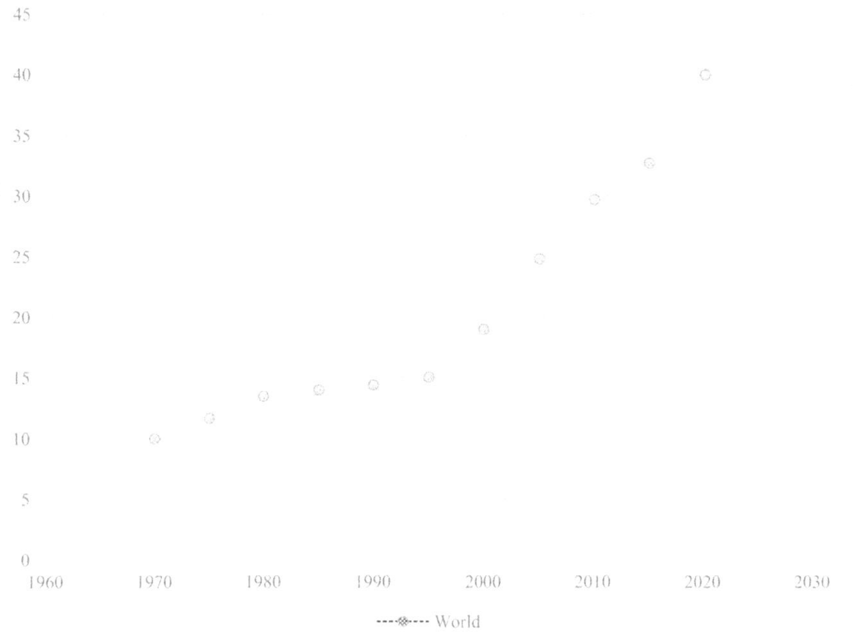

Figure 2.3 School Enrolment, Tertiary (% Gross)

Source: The World Bank.[20]

neoliberal economists that the rapid growth of higher education depended on tuition fees.[21] For students, tuition fees imposed could contribute to a positive value for them as Rolfe noted that tuition fees encourage a 'consumerist' attitude among students towards their university.[22] This means that students are more appreciative of the money spent by them by studying hard so that it is worthwhile. This belief was also supported by theoretical and empirical evidence presented by Beneito, Bosca, and Ferri, who found that an increase in tuition fees could foster students' academic efforts in universities.[23] In line with that, it is suggested that graduates need to bear some of the costs of higher education considering that the institution provides substantial private returns to them. One of the instruments that governments can use is a graduate tax (a tax levied on a graduate's income for a specified time). Parents can also play a vital role in assisting their children to bear the costs of higher education.

Imposing a price on valuable and highly demanded goods and services, such as higher education, which contribute to some virtues (e.g. higher efficiency, producer's responsiveness to individual and societal needs) of the market is necessary.[24] The benefits derived from higher education are not only related to the economy but also intangible and have less immediate value. In this regard, the discovered knowledge might be seen as free, but the acquisition or creation of new knowledge is highly expensive and those who benefit from it need to reimburse the expenses.

Islamic Perspective on Who Is Responsible to Fund HEIs

Islam obligates satisfaction of the basic needs of all people, which is known as *daruriyyah*. Al-Shāṭibī illustrated that *daruriyyah* is a basic need for people to address public interest (*maslahah*) in this world and thereafter.[25] Without *daruriyyah*, the human system will be broken, which could lead to a setback either at the individual or at the country level. *Daruriyyah* involves five core things of human's basic needs, namely 1) religion, 2) soul, 3) intellect, 4) descendant (*nasab*), and 5) property. Given that intellect is a basic human need, Islam encourages humans to often maintain a healthy mind and strive to develop their intellectual potential through activities such as thinking about Allah's creations and greatness, reading, and studying. Imam Ghazali (1058–1111 M) found that 1,404 verses in the al-Qur'an are related to education, constituting approximately 25 per cent of the number of verses, as stated by Salamon.[26] Therefore, education is crucial in the view of Islam. The following is the *ḥadīth* from Prophet Muhammad (p.b.u.h.), as narrated by Anas bin Malik in Sunan Ibn Mājah:[27]

((طلب العلم فريضة على كل مسلم. وواضع العلم عند غير أهله كمقلد الخنازير الجوهر واللؤلؤ والذهب))

> *Seeking knowledge is a duty upon every Muslim, and he who imparts knowledge to those who do not deserve it is like one who puts a necklace of jewels, pearls and gold around the neck of swines.*

As indicated by the *ḥadīth*, Muslims are obliged to seek and disseminate knowledge or education to others who are relatively poor in terms of educational opportunities. Since education could provide the necessary knowledge for change in current practices and the skills for an improved application of available services, it is viewed as important for fulfilling other 'core' basic needs, such as adequate nutrition, clean drinking water, and primary healthcare. Furthermore, the basic or religious education offers more benefits to the public compared to the benefits accrued to individuals who receive it. Therefore, education is not only perceived as satisfying the basic needs of the individual but also regarded as satisfying the social needs from the Islamic perspective.

Public goods refer to public sources and expenditures. One of the most important sources of income for the government is *zakat*. As every Muslim must pay *zakat*, it can also help improve the social status of people who are entitled to receive it. Eight categories of people are exclusively mentioned in the statement of Allah Almighty in Surah at-Taubah, verse 60: 1) the poor, 2) the needy, 3) those employed to collect *zakat*, 4) those whose hearts are inclined towards Islam, 5) slaves, 6) debtors, 7) for the path of Allah, and 8) the wayfarer. Given that *zakat* can be received solely by people from these categories, other instruments to fund the education needs should be adopted to ensure that the benefits from education could be reaped by the community, regardless of the income level, race, and religion.

According to Siddiqi, the expenditures covered by the government in the Islamic economy include (1) defence, (2) law and order, (3) justice, (4) need fulfilment, (5) *da'wah* (e.g. communicating the message of Allah to mankind), (6) enjoining right conduct and forbidding wrong conduct (*al-amr bi al-ma'ruf wa al-nahy 'an-munkar*), (7) civil administration, and 8) fulfilment of social obligations (*fard kifayah*) that the private sector fails to fulfil.[28] Given that education has been categorised as *fard kifayah*[29] by many economists, funding education is not the responsibility of the government alone. The private sector should also play a role in providing funding for education in cases when the government does not provide the required funds.

Sources of Funding for HEIs

As discussed in the previous section, HEIs have two main sources of funding which are public and private sources. The degree of dependence of an institution on these sources varies according to their type of sector. Specifically, the level of dependency of public universities on public (e.g. government) sources is high compared to private universities. However, the requirement for private (e.g. student) sources has also become increasingly important. Besides funding, which is provided by the government and students, other sources, such as sales and contract research, of university income are categorised as private sources. Another private-based source provided voluntarily is donation. Each of these sources is further explained in the following subsections.

Public Fund

As mentioned earlier, public sources refer to the funds provided by the government (e.g. federal, state, or local). The source of revenues earned by the government normally originates from taxes (e.g. personal income, corporate) and non-tax (e.g. administrative revenue, profit from state enterprises, gifts and grants). In the early Islamic period, the government had several revenue sources, such as *zakat* (an obligatory form of giving), *kharaj* (individual Islamic tax on agricultural land), *jizya* (poll tax historically levied on all 'able-bodied' non-Muslims), *ghanimah* (spoils of war) or *khums* (the proportion (one-fifth) of the spoils to be used by the state), *fay* (properties acquired without fighting or heir or claim), customs duties, and taxes on mines and treasure troves. The sources from *zakat* and taxes remain relevant until now, while other additional sources, such as borrowings and human resources, have emerged.

From the government's perspective, several resources such as the education sector, especially higher education, are highly critical for governing and managing the country properly. The dependency of the higher education sector, particularly public universities, on government funds is high as the government is the sector's main stakeholder. At the same time, the government also provides funding to universities from the private sector to cover their operating costs.

The government transfers the funds to HEIs through two main channels, direct and indirect transfers. A direct transfer implies that the government pays directly to HEIs, while indirect transfer refers to the transfer of public funds by the government to HEIs through students or purchase services provided by these institutions. According to the Asian Development Bank, grants are one of the instruments used in most countries to transfer public funds directly.[30] In Malaysia, more than 90 per cent of government grants are provided to public HEIs, while the remainder is provided to polytechnics and community colleges.[31]

Private Funds

Besides public funds, the role of private funds in providing funding to HEIs (especially from the public sector) has become increasingly important as the trend has changed. The sources of private funding for higher education include tuition fees, the sale or lease of university assets, and contract research. Tuition fees are one of the cost-sharing methods suggested to fund the public cost of higher education. Originating from students or their parents who pay the university for the courses, Johnstone and Marcucci[32] highlighted that tuition fees could have a substantial financial impact on universities because of several reasons such as helping meet the cost of rebates of some aggregate income (i.e. grants or discounts) to preserve accessibility. In addition, tuition fees can be both financially significant and ongoing and can even be designed to regularly increase as the cost of teaching per student keeps rising. Accordingly, by charging tuition fees to students can help the university to focus on the core teaching responsibilities.

Apart from tuition fees, universities can also generate income to achieve a strong financial status. One of the proposed methods is the selling or leasing of university assets. According to Johnstone, universities usually have large amounts of desirable land or other assets that are not utilised.[33] Notably, not using the assets or land leads to a wasted opportunity for the institution. In this regard, the sale or lease of university assets to other parties is suggested as a method to ensure extra cash or money earning for universities.

Universities can also earn income through contract research, which refers to the funds sponsored by external parties to support research activities. Such funds are provided by either a corporation or a foundation. When this type of source is provided, the corporation may imply, express, or hope for a reciprocation of the financial support provided. Even so, this source can still help absorb institutional overhead burdens, provide additional income to the faculty, and install the equipment and facilities required in the teaching process. Johnstone also suggested that this source could contribute to general institutional and administrative costs.[34]

Voluntary Donations

Apart from the aforementioned two sources, third parties also provide funding for higher education. These include foundations, business corporations, individuals, religious organisations, and alumni. The funding provided by them is categorised as voluntary donations and is based on the values, goals, and performance of the university. The existence of element values, including other existing elements, particularly belief, was confirmed by Drezner.[35] The practice of voluntary donations for charity and the benefit of others is a universal culture embraced by humanity and encouraged by all religions and cultures. The practice of giving to those in need is a fundamental belief not only in Islam but also in Christianity. Jews also encourage the practice of giving as this type of charity represents the right of the poor or a just claim on the community. Therefore, not only can the needs of the poor be fulfilled but the balance and order in society can also be maintained through the practice of giving. Cascione stated that 'giving to higher education institutions is best understood as philanthropic since it is most often indirect and programmatic and the institution is expected to deliver the means for the instruction of other benefits of an education'.[36]

Pérez-Esparrells and Torre Perez asserted that this voluntary donation is the main fundraising income stream for most institutions.[37] As an example, in the U.S., this type of support, which contributes significantly to their HEIs, reached $49.60 billion in 2019, increasing by 6.1 per cent over 2018. Based on the Voluntary Support of Education (VSE) Survey, the contribution from the Council for Advancement and Support of Education (CASE) was the highest.[38] Foundations contributed the most in 2019, with their total amounting to $17.00 billion (34.3%), followed by alumni with $11.20 billion (22.6%). Other major contributors were non-alumni individuals, corporations, and other organisations. The amount contributed by each party is presented in Figure 2.4.

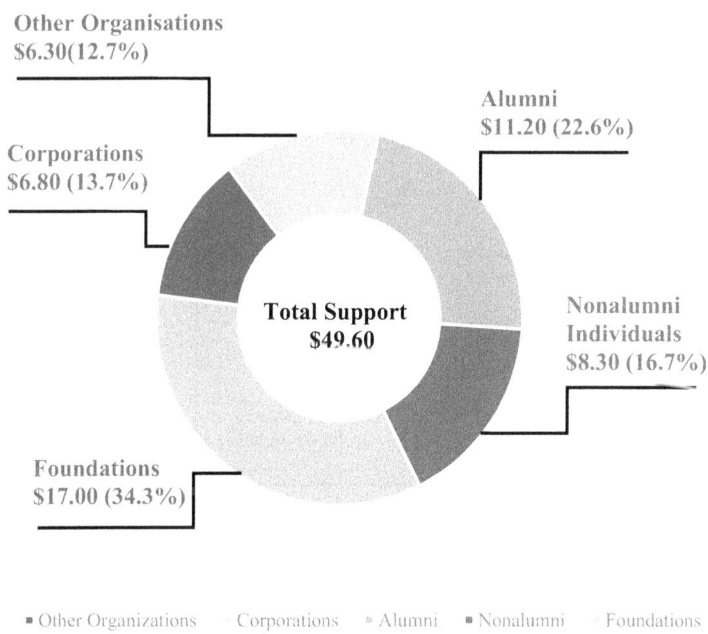

Figure 2.4 Voluntary Support of Higher Education by Source, 2019 ($ billion)

Source: CASE.[39]

In Islam, the practice of voluntary donation is also highlighted, which is in line with the command of Allah to His servants to help each other towards goodness. The command is found in verse 2 in Surah al-Mā'idah, which is as follows:

وَتَعَاوَنُوا عَلَى الْبِرِّ وَالتَّقْوَىٰ ۖ وَلَا تَعَاوَنُوا عَلَى الْإِثْمِ وَالْعُدْوَانِ ۚ﴿2﴾
Al-Mā'idah 5:2

Help you one another in al-Birr and at-Taqwā; but do not help one another in sin and transgression.

Based on this verse, Ibn Kathīr in his *tafsir* stated that Allah commands His believing servants to help one another to perform righteous, good deeds, as reflected by al-Birr (الْبِرِّ). The servants are also commanded to avoid sins, as indicated by At-Taqwa (التَّقْوَى).[40] In Islam, this voluntary action is driven by religious motives for the sake of Allah's blessing as the aforementioned verse which encourages to do so. It has been practised in various aspects of life, including education. The voluntary contribution to educational activities has existed since the beginning of Islam in the early 7th century. Moreover, it was the largest source of funding for public expenditure in early Islamic history and can be an important source of funding if managed suitably.

Mediums for channelling funds through this type of source include endowment, current gifts, or tuition fee redistribution (some students or parents could pay less as the surplus of money is paid to wealthier parents). This book focuses on voluntary contributions in the form of an endowment, which is known as *waqf* in the Islamic financial system. Despite their similarities, the two instruments differ, and their concepts are explored and further explained in the next chapter. The discussions in this chapter are graphically summarised in Figure 2.5.

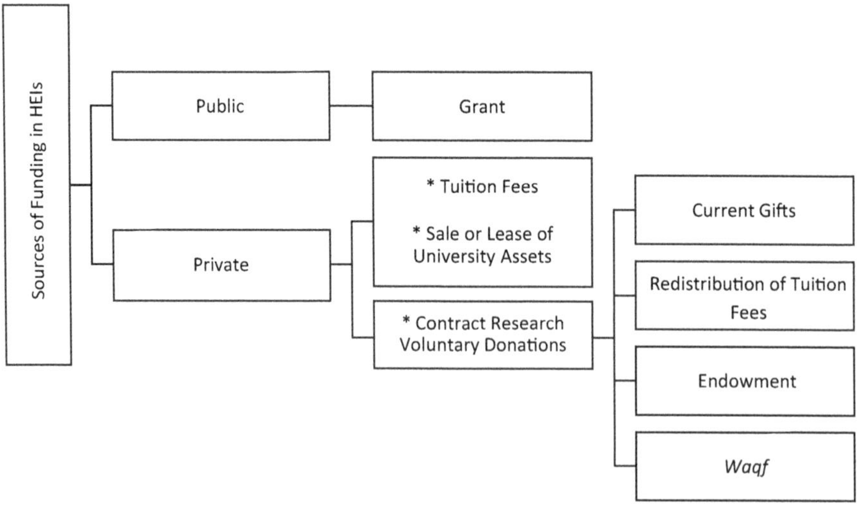

Figure 2.5 Sources of Funding in Public University

Source: Developed by the authors.

Conclusion

In conclusion, the public and private sectors are responsible for providing funding to HEIs. The funds provided by them are crucial in ensuring the financial sustainability of HEIs. Furthermore, various mediums are provided so that all the involved parties can seamlessly channel funds to HEIs. In terms of the private sector, the funds can be channelled through tuition fees, sale or lease of university assets, and contract research. Other sources provided by external parties in financing HEIs are based on voluntary donations. Notably, various mediums are provided to individuals who are keen to donate in the form of a current gift, redistribution of tuition fees, endowment, or *waqf*. This book focuses on endowment and *waqf*, which are discussed further in the following chapters.

Notes

1 D. Lederman, "The Culling of Higher Ed Begins," *Inside Higher Ed*, July 19, 2017, accessed on 26 October 2020, www.insidehighered.com/news/2017/07/19/number-colleges-and-universities-drops-sharply-amid-economic-turmoil.
2 Kyodo, "Japan's Public and Private Universities Face Major Shake-Ups and Mergers as Student Numbers Fall," *The Japan Times*, April 12, 2016, accessed on 25 October 2020, www.japantimes.co.jp/news/2016/04/12/national/japans-public-private- universities-face-major-shakeup-mergers-student-numbers-fall/#.W6xHcUBMTIU.
3 "Direktori Universiti Awam," *Kementerian Pendidikan Malaysia* (Jabatan Pendidikan Tinggi) (2017), accessed on 27 September 2018, http://jpt.mohe.gov.my/index.php/ipta/institusi-pendidikan-tinggi-awam/direktori-universiti-awam.
4 "Statistik Institusi Pendidikan Tinggi Swasta (IPTS) Sehingga 31 Ogos 2018," *Kementerian Pendidikan Malaysia (Jabatan Pendidikan Tinggi)* (2018), accessed on 27 September 2018, https://drive.google.com/drive/folders/18w0PWQnD7DV2W1Dspio3zHm5Up5-AC3l.
5 J. M. Buchanan and M. R. Flowers, *The Public Finance: An Introductory Textbook*, 5th ed. (Homewood, IL: Richard D. Irwin, Inc., 1980).
6 J. Bynner and M. Egerton, *The Wider Benefits of Higher Education* (London: Higher Education Funding Council for England, 2001), 6.
7 J. Bynner et al., *Revisiting the Benefits of Higher Education* (London: Bedford Group for Lifecourse and Statistical Studies, Institute of Education, 2003), iii.
8 I. Ozturk, "The Role of Education in Economic Development: A Theoretical Perspective," *Journal of Rural Development and Administration* XXXIII, no. 1 (2001): 39–47, 39, 1.
9 "Employment Rate," *OECD*, 2020, accessed on 17 October 2020, https://data.oecd.org/emp/employment-rate.htm.
10 "Spending on Tertiary Education," *OECD*, 2018, accessed on 3 October 2018, https://doi.org/10.1787/a3523185-en.
11 "Employment Rate," *OECD*, 2020, accessed on 17 October 2020, https://data.oecd.org/emp/employment-rate.htm.
12 M. Bray, *New Resources for Education: Community Management and Financing of Schools in Less Developed Countries* (London: Commonwealth Secretariat, 1987), 15.
13 M. Lawson and M. Martin, *The Commitment to Reducing Inequality Index* (Oxford: Oxfam International and Development Finance International, 2017), 8.
14 N. Terry and A. Macy, "Determinants of Alumni Giving Rates," *Journal of Economics and Economic Education Research* 8, no. 3 (2007): 3–17, 5.
15 Bray, *New Resources for Education: Community Management and Financing of Schools in Less Developed Countries*, 15.
16 D. B. Johnstone, *Financing Higher Education: Cost-Sharing in International Perspective* (Rotterdam: Sense Publishers, 2006), https://doi.org/10.4324/9780203321515.

17 Johnstone, *Financing Higher Education: Cost-Sharing in International Perspective*, 5–8.
18 Peter Tulip, "Financing Higher Education in the United States," *OECD Economics Department Working Papers*, no. 584 (2007): 1–38, 26, http://search.proquest.com/docview/56601248?accountid=17248.
19 Johnstone, *Financing Higher Education: Cost-Sharing in International Perspective*, 5–8.
20 "School Enrolment, Tertiary (% Gross)," *The World Bank*, 2018, accessed on 19 March 2020, https://data.worldbank.org/indicator/SE.TER.ENRR.
21 D. Bruce Johnstone, "The Economics and Politics of Cost Sharing in Higher Education: Comparative Perspectives," *Economics of Education Review* 23, no. 4 (2004): 403–10, 6, https://doi.org/10.1016/j.econedurev.2003.09.004.
22 H. Rolfe, "The Effect of Tuition Fees on Students' Demands and Expectations: Evidence from Case Studies of Four Universities,"*Discussion Paper*, no. 190 (2001): 1–24, 1.
23 P. Beneito, J. E. Bosca, and J. Ferri, "Tuition Fees and Students' Effort at University," *Economics of Education Review* 64 (2018): 114–28, 28
24 Johnstone, *Financing Higher Education: Cost-Sharing in International Perspective*, 5–8.
25 Al-Shāṭibī, Abī Isḥāq Ibrāhim Ibn Mūsā Ibn Muḥammad al-Lakhmī, *al-Muwāfaqāt*, vol. 2 (Bayrūt: Dār al-Kutub al-'Ilmiyah, 2005), 7.
26 S. Salamon, *Ekonomi Islam: Pengenalan Sistem Dan Kemungkinan* (Petaling Jaya: al-Rahmaniah, 1989), 61.
27 Ibn Mājah, Abū 'Abd Allāh Muḥammad Ibn Yazid al-Qazwinī, *Sunan Ibn Mājah*, vol. 1 (N.p.: Dār Ihyā' al-Kutub al-'Arabiyah, 2009), 81, "Bab Fadl al-'Ilmaa' wa al-Has 'ala Tolib al-'Ilm, No. *ḥadīth*, 224, 81.
28 M. N. Siddiqi, *Teaching Economics in Islamic Perspective*, 1st ed. (Jeddah: Scientific Publishing Centre, 1996), 88.
29 An obligatory duty, the fulfilment of which is a joint responsibility of all members of the community. If someone performs it, it is considered to have been fulfilled, otherwise, all members of the community are considered defaulters.
30 Asian Development Bank, *Good Practice in Cost Sharing and Financing in Higher Education* (Metro Manila: ADB, 2009), 6, www.adb.org/sites/default/files/publication/28623/good-practice-cost-sharing-financing-educ.pdf.
31 Ministry of Higher Education Malaysia, *University Transformation Programme, Purple Book: Enhancing University Income Generation, Endowment & Waqf* (Putrajaya: Kementerian Pendidikan Tinggi Malaysia, 2016), 16.
32 D. B. Johnstone and P. N. Marcucci, "Worldwide Trends in Higher Education Finance: Cost-Sharing, Student Loans, and the Support of Academic Research," in *UNESCO Forum on Higher Education, Research and Knowledge* (N.p: UNESCO, 2007), 1–36, 16.
33 Johnstone, *Financing Higher Education: Cost-Sharing in International Perspective*, 6.
34 Ibid., 41.
35 N. D. Drezner, "Philanthropic Mirroring: Exploring Identity-Based Fundraising in Higher Education," *The Journal of Higher Education* (2017): 1–35, 24.
36 G. L. Cascione, *Philanthropists in Higher Education: Institutional, Biographical, and Religious Motivations for Giving* (New York: Routledge Falmer, 2003), 5.
37 C. Pérez-Esparrells and E. M. Torre, "The Challenge of Fundraising in Universities in Europe," *International Journal of Higher Education* 1, no. 2 (2012): 55–66, 57.
38 A. E. Kaplan, *Voluntary Support of Education* (London, Mexico City, Singapore and Washington, DC: Council for Advancement and Support of Education (CASE), 2020), 4.
39 *Voluntary Support of Education*, 5.
40 Ibn Kathīr, Abū Fidā' Ismā'il Ibn 'Umar, al-Qurshī al-Damashqī, *Tafsīr al-Qur'ān al-'Aẓīm. Tafsir Al-Qur'an Al-'Azmi*, 1st ed., vol. 2 (Qāhirah: Dār al-Ghad al-Gadīd, 2007), 6.

3 Theory of Endowment and *Waqf* as Sources of Funding for Higher Educational Institutions

Introduction

Endowment and *waqf* are among the key private philanthropic sources of higher education finance. Although these instruments may look similar, several elements differentiate them. To identify these differences, in this chapter, the theory of each instrument is discussed in detail, thus helping contribute to further the understanding of endowment and *waqf* implementation in HEIs. The theoretical discourse of these two instruments is explained, which begins with a discussion of the endowment theory in the second section of the chapter and includes the definition, philosophy, types, and elements. The third section presents the theory of *waqf*, where the scope of discussion is similar to that of endowment, followed by the pillars of *waqf*. The fourth and fifth sections discuss the endowment experiences in Western countries and *waqf* experiences in some Islamic countries. Finally, the sixth section presents the chapter conclusion.

Theory of Endowment

Definition

The word 'endow' refers to bestowing a permanent fund or income[1] while the word endowment refers to a certain amount of money that an individual pays to a school, college, or other institutions, or the act of providing this money.[2] In other words, it refers to money or property provided for the permanent use of an institution, person, or object.[3] From the perspective of scholars including Wolanin, endowment refers to donations from private sources (e.g. individuals, businesses, and foundations), which are then invested, and the annual returns acquired by the institution are used to fund the operating expenses or for other purposes.[4] This definition is similar to that provided by Sazonov et al., according to which donors are legal entities and individuals who contribute voluntarily. The donations also consist of a sacrosanct portion that should be invested in financial assets to secure monetary assets in future, with the income generated from the investment of the main sum of the target capital available for use.[5]

Ehrenberg defined endowment from the education institution standpoint by describing it as a stock of financial and real estate that is held by universities to generate income for both current and future operations.[6] From the NPO perspective,

DOI: 10.4324/9781003435976-3

endowment comprises an established fund of cash, securities, or other assets to provide income for the maintenance of an NPO as defined by the FASB, Statement of Accounting Standard No. 117, and Financial Statement of NPOs.[7] Based on the definitions given here, endowment can be understood as a financial instrument that can provide perpetuity income for an institution as the money contributed by the donors could be invested. Getz also pointed out that the purpose of the endowment fund is to generate perpetuity income for its owners.[8]

Philosophy

In strengthening the social economy of a nation, philanthropic funds, including endowments, play a crucial role in providing sources of income. In the education sector, this fund is also important for supporting HEIs financially to produce human capital, which is an asset for a nation. However, motivations and expectations exist from both donors and recipients in shaping charitable actions. These elements indicate the existence of love values, that is, a person performs charity because of the value of love among mankind. In this regard, charity can be understood as an activity not only to fulfil the needs of beneficiaries but also to improve humanity. In other words, philanthropy can establish relationships among humans through the process of giving and receiving. However, Jews and Christians encourage their followers to give instead of receive, which is in line with the following statement by Jesus:

> It is more blessed to give than to receive.[9]

Besides humanity, another aspect influencing a person to contribute to philanthropic funds is generosity. Generosity exists in every culture and religion in this world. Generosity also exists in people's intentions to help the underprivileged because of emphatic concern, helpfulness, and social value orientations. The generosity to give is attributed to a high emphatic disposition and a strong awareness of charitable organisations as well. From the perspective of charitable giving to the education sector, especially higher education, Cascione asserted in his study on philanthropists in higher education that:

> Giving to higher education institutions is best understood as philanthropic since it is most often indirect and programmatic, and the institution is expected to deliver the means for the instruction of other benefits of education.[10]

Types

Endowments in HEIs can be of three types, true endowment, term endowment, and quasi-endowment. The explanation of these three types of endowment is as follows.

True Endowment

True endowment refers to the fund specified by the donor to be retained permanently. Such endowment is commonly restricted to being used as the principal and/

or as an income. Therefore, it is frequently referred to as a permanently restricted endowment, which should be constantly maintained instead of being used up, expended, or otherwise exhausted. Commonly, a true endowment is designed either to fund a scholarship or to provide financial support to universities.

Term Endowment

Term endowment refers to the fund restricted by the donor for a certain time. After the passing of a set time, unused funds or the principal may become unrestricted. This implies that the funds may be expended after the expiration of a stated time depending on donors' wishes. Therefore, it is classified as a temporarily restricted endowment.

Quasi Endowment

Quasi endowment refers to unrestricted funds that function in some cases and are treated as endowments that could be spent if selected. Quasi endowment is subject to voting by the Board of Trustees for any relevant purposes or when instructed by the donors.

Among the three types of endowment, the most common type of endowment applied in HEIs is true endowment. This is consistent with NACUBO's 2017 report, in which true endowment was the largest factor of endowment funds for 809 U.S. colleges and universities amounting to $255.30 billion compared to term endowment and quasi-endowment of $12.26 billion and $135.36 billion, respectively.[11] True endowment also dominated the market value of endowment in the previous year's report as well.

Elements

Based on the definitions of endowment discussed at the beginning of this chapter, a few elements of this fund are discussed in the following subsections.

Perpetuity

Endowment presents an element of perpetuity and could be viewed from the perspective of its principle, where the contributed amount must be invested to generate income. This investment is undertaken to fund the operating expenses and activities of the institution that implements the endowment fund. Therefore, the management of an endowment fund can last for more than one generation. Examples of investment activities involved are equities or bonds or other investment instruments.

Flexible Ownership

In terms of the rights of ownership, endowment has flexible ownership. The funds of true endowment and term endowment are donated as gifts or bequests. This is consistent with the FASB guidelines, which state that 'endowment funds generally are established by donor-restricted gifts and bequests to provide a permanent endowment or term endowment'.[12] These types of funds are owned by the institutions.[13] Nevertheless, an institution can change the owner under certain circumstances and can itself claim ownership despite the funds not being initially donated as gift. Therefore, in quasi-endowment, which is also known as unrestricted funds, the funds do not belong to the institution. With the presence of surplus money for the long term, the institution treats it as a gift, and the fund functions as a true endowment. Therefore, quasi-endowment can also be defined as a fund functioning as an endowment.

Theory of *Waqf*

Definition

In Islam, the fund created for perpetual usage is also available as *waqf*, which originates from the Arabic word, *waqafa*. The term *waqf* refers to holding (*al-habs*) or preventing (*al- man'*) while the plural of *waqf* is *awqaf and wuquf*. Although *waqf* has two literal meanings, *Fiqh* scholars have collectively agreed to define *waqf* according to the term *al-habs*, as this definition is closest to the *Syarak* definition, by referring to al-Nawawī,[14] Ibn Qudāmah,[15] and Ibn 'Abidīn.[16] The term *al-habs* has been widely spoken by Prophet Muhammad (p.b.u.h.) in some of his *ḥadīth*s, with one of the *ḥadīth*s narrated by Umar:[17]

حبس الأصل وسبل الثمرة

Restrain the property and distribute its benefits in Allah's cause.

Legally, the views regarding the *waqf* definition among *Fiqh* scholars have three differences. In the first definition, *waqf* holds the *'ayn* (physical) of *waqf* property owned by *waqf* donors, followed by *ṣadaqah* of the benefits from the *waqf* property for charity purposes. This definition is presented by Abu Hanifah.[18] Based on this definition, there is a possibility of the donor repossessing and selling the property that has undergone *waqf*.[19]

In the second definition, *waqf* holds a property that could be benefitted from the preserved *'ayn*. When a donor donates their property to the *waqf* fund, their ownership of the *waqf* property ceases. In this case, a person practices *waqf* not only for charity but also for the sake of Allah. This definition is presented by *jumhūr*, including al-Hammām[20] from *madhhab* of Hanafi, al-Sharbīnī[21] from *madhhab* of al-Syafie, and al-Rahaybānī[22] from *madhhab* of Hanbali. Based on this definition, the property donated as *waqf* is no longer owned by the *waqf* donor. However, it remains on the *hukum* of Allah, with its benefits being distributed to the charity for *waqf* purposes.[23] According to Nazīḥ Ḥammād, this second definition captures more of its meaning, which is to restrain the property and distribute its benefits in Allah's cause (تحبيس لأصل وتسبيل المنفعة).[24] However, the *waqf* donor's right to use the benefits from the *waqf* property remains if it is donated as *waqf am*. This type of *waqf* is further explained in the section on the types of endowment and *waqf* funds.

The third definition of *waqf* is the act of *ṣadaqah* on the benefits of the *waqf* property as long as the property exists and is owned by the *waqf* donor via an *aqad* (utterance of *ijab*) according to the wishes of the *waqf* donor, as stated by al-Dardīr.[25] This definition was supported by al-Dussūqī, al-Dardīr, and Alish, who contended that the ownership of property is not only through *tahqiq* (true) but also through *taqdiri* (assumption).[26] Based on this definition, the *waqf* donor refrains from performing *tasarruf tamliki* against the *'ayn* of property that has been donated as *waqf*, and the donor's ownership of the *waqf* property remains for a certain time.[27]

Among the three legal definitions of *waqf* that have been discussed, this chapter applies the second definition as it is based on *jumhūr* opinions.

Philosophy

Similar to endowment or other philanthropic funds, *waqf* is another philanthropic fund used to strengthen the socio-economic conditions, especially for Muslims. The values of humanity and generosity in helping those in need are the foundations that result in Muslim donors contributing their properties to this fund. One of the motivations encouraging donors to practise *waqf* is the provision of benefits in terms of the Muslim community's public interest (*maslaha*). However, another factor that becomes a catalyst for donors to perform this action is the fulfilment of the religious obligation to safeguard wealth (*mal*), which is one of the categories under *Maqasid Shariah*. Muslims who contribute their property to this fund demonstrate that they are obliged servants of the religion. However, this fact contradicts the endowment fund, implementation of which varies according to donors' wishes as permitted by the law. Given that *waqf* is one of the methods to perform *ṣadaqah jāriyah*, various verses in the al-Quran could be quoted as support towards this practice, although the term *waqf* is not explicitly mentioned. An example of the verse is as follows:

لَن تَنَالُوا الْبِرَّ حَتَّىٰ تُنفِقُوا مِمَّا تُحِبُّونَ ۚ وَمَا تُنفِقُوا مِن شَيْءٍ فَإِنَّ اللَّهَ بِهِ عَلِيمٌ
﴿92﴾
Ali-Imran 3: 92

Never will you attain the good [reward] until you spend [in the way of Allah] from that which you love. And whatever you spend—indeed, Allah is Knowing of it.

Based on this verse, Allah indicates the necessity to sacrifice the property that one loves through *ṣadaqah jāriyah* as this practice could help a servant to achieve the essence of perfect welfare and goodness. The act of sacrificing the property for the path of Allah demonstrates the confidence of a servant towards the rewards promised by Him. Ibn Kathīr in his *tafsir* stated that Syarik, Abi Ishak, and 'Amru bin Maimun have interpreted the meaning of *al-birr* (الْبِرَّ) as heaven, where servants will not enter until they perform *ṣadaqah* or *infaq* of what they love the most.[28] Besides referring to heaven, *al-birr* is defined as a reward from Allah or good deeds (*'amal soleh*), which deserve to be rewarded, as stated by al-Qurṭūbī in his *tafsir*.[29]

According to al-Ṭabarī, the word *tunfiquu* (تنفقوا) refers to providing anything that one loves and dissuading themself from loving the property.[30] Anas bin Malik narrated that when the verse was revealed, a wealthy companion of Prophet Muhammad named Abu Talhah approached Him to perform *waqf* on the land that he loved most in Bairaha', Madinah. This land was located in front of the Prophet's mosque, which the Prophet often visited and drank water there. Abu Talhah aimed to reap goodness and reward from his *waqf*,[31] which also indicates that the *waqf* practice not only encompasses the obedience of a servant in the religion but also focuses on the ultimate reward from Allah, including heaven. In another verse in al-Quran, Allah reminds His servants:

يَا أَيُّهَا الَّذِينَ آمَنُوا أَنْفِقُوا مِمَّا رَزَقْنَاكُمْ مِنْ قَبْلِ أَنْ يَأْتِيَ يَوْمٌ لَا بَيْعٌ فِيهِ وَلَا خُلَّةٌ وَلَا شَفَاعَةٌ وَالْكَافِرُونَ هُمُ الظَّالِمُونَ ﴿254﴾

Al-Baqarah 2: 254

O you who have believed, spend from that which We have provided for you before there comes a Day in which there is no exchange and no friendship and no intercession. And the disbelievers—they are the wrongdoers.

This verse elaborates on Allah's command to His servants to form *ṣadaqah* from their sustenance for charitable purposes. This act could grant the believers salvation in the hereafter, where they will receive help from no one except what has been performed in the path of charity for the sake of Allah, as mentioned by Ibn Kathīr.[32] Allah reminds His servants about greater rewards provided for those who spend their wealth in the way of Allah, as shown in the following verse:

مَثَلُ الَّذِينَ يُنْفِقُونَ أَمْوَالَهُمْ فِي سَبِيلِ اللَّهِ كَمَثَلِ حَبَّةٍ أَنْبَتَتْ سَبْعَ سَنَابِلَ فِي كُلِّ سُنْبُلَةٍ مِائَةُ حَبَّةٍ وَاللَّهُ يُضَاعِفُ لِمَنْ يَشَاءُ وَاللَّهُ وَاسِعٌ عَلِيمٌ ﴿261﴾

Al-Baqarah 2: 261

The example of those who spend their wealth in the way of Allah is like a seed [of grain] which grows seven spikes; in each spike is a hundred grains. And Allah multiplies [His reward] for whom He wills. And Allah is all-Encompassing and Knowing.

The verse illustrates that Allah is the most gracious as He doubles the reward to those who sacrifice or spend their wealth in His path. Every good practice will be rewarded by 10 until 700 folds, which is equivalent to a grain of wheat growing seven stalks while each stalk produces 100 seeds. For every *ṣadaqah*, Allah will double as much as 700 rewards of goodness, as stated by Ibn Kathīr.[33] According to Said bin Jubair, *infaq* in the way of Allah is offering the wealth in any form of obedience to Allah, and *waqf* is included in the scope of the aforementioned verse.[34]

*Ṣaḥīḥ ḥadīth*s encouraging the *waqf* practice have been presented; for instance, as the following *ḥadīth* narrated by Abu Hurayrah in Ṣaḥīḥ Muslim,[35] Sunan al-Tirmidhī,[36] Sunan Abū Dāwud,[37] and Sunan al-Nasā'ī:[38]

عن أبي هريرة: أنّ رسول الله صلى الله عليه وسلم قال: ((إذا مات الإنسان انقطع|عنه| عمله، إلاّ من ثلاثة: إلا من صدقة جارية، أو علمٍ ينتفع به، أو ولد صالحٍ يدعو له)).

When a man dies, all his good deeds come to an end except for three things: ṣadaqah jāriyah (ongoing charity), beneficial knowledge and a righteous son who prays for him.

According to al-Nawawī, this *ḥadīth* describes the encouragement of *waqf* practice through the *ṣaḥīḥ* reward.[39] *Jumhūr ulamā'* has also interpreted the word *ṣadaqah jāriyah* in this *ḥadīth* as *waqf* as the reward of *ṣadaqah jāriyah* continuously flows to the person who performs it even after their death while the reward of other charities does not constantly flow similarly as *ṣadaqah jāriyah* or *waqf*.[40]

Among the stories of best-known companions in the practice of *waqf* include that by Saidina Umar al-Khattab as he followed the Prophet's advice of performing *waqf* on his treasured land in Khaibar to seek the blessing of Allah. The event was recorded in a *ḥadīth* from Ibn Umar, which is as follows (al-Bukhārī,[41] al-Tirmidhī,[42] al-Nasā'ī',[43] al-Nawawī,[44] and Ibn Mājah):[45]

أنّ عمر بن الخطّاب أصاب أرضا بخيبر، فأتى النّبيّ صلّى الله عليه وسلّم يستأمره فيها، فقال: يا رسول الله! إنّي أصبت أرضا بخيبر، لم أصب مالا قطّ هو أنفس عندي منه، فما تأمرني به؟ قال: ((إن شئت حبست أصلها وتصدّقت بها))، قال: فتصدّق بها عمر: أنّه لا يباع أصلها، ولا يبتاع/، ولا تورث، ولا توهب، قال: فتصدّق عمر فى الفقراء، وفى القربى، وفى الرّقاب، وفى سبيل الله، وابن السّبيل، والضّيف، لا جناح على من وليها أن يأكل منها بالمعروف، أو يطعم صديقا، غير متموّل فيه.

Umar bin al-Khattab acquired a plot of land in Khaibar, then he went to the Prophet (p.b.u.h.) to consult him about it saying: O Allah's Messenger! I have a plot of land in Khaibar, better than I have ever had. What do you suggest that I do with it? The Prophet said: (If you like, you can give the land as a waqf and give its fruit in charity), so Umar gave it in charity as waqf on the condition that it would not be sold or given to anyone as a present, nor was it to be inherited. Its yield would be given in charity to the poor people, kith and kin, slaves, persons in the way of Allah, Ibn Sabil, and guests, there would be no harm if the guardian of the endowment ate from it according to his need with good intention, and he could feed others without storing it for the future.

Besides 'Umar, another companion who practised *waqf* was 'Uthman bin 'Affan, with one of the *waqfs* practices related to the well (*Bi'r Rumah*). As recorded by al-Tirmidhī[46] and al-Nasā'ī,[47] when Prophet Muhammad (p.b.u.h.) arrived in

Madinah, He realised that except for the water of *Bi'r Rumah*, the city was provided with too little drinking water. He then asked, 'Who will purchase Bi'r Rumah to equally share the water drawn from there with his fellow Muslims? Shall be rewarded with a better well in the Paradise?' 'Uthman bought half of the water from its owner, who was a Jew, with his money on the condition that the Jew would draw water for a day and the Muslims would draw it for the next day. This agreement continued for two days when the Jew visited and pointed out that the water was polluted by the Muslims. He then asked 'Uthman to fully purchase the well, who purchased it and formed it a *waqf* for the use of the Muslims.

This *ḥadīth* demonstrates that the Messenger of Allah greatly encouraged His companion to perform charity by sacrificing the property for the benefit of the people, which was appreciated by the companion by practising *waqf*. The practice of *waqf* had been common among the companions of the Prophet (p.b.u.h.) until Jabir narrated that no excess property should exist among the companions unless with the *waqf* of their wealth for Allah's pleasure.[48] The *waqf* practice was shown as being famous and well-known among the companions.

Types

Waqf involves two types of funds, *waqf am* and *waqf khas*. These two types of *waqf* are elaborated here.

Waqf Am

The *waqf am* refers to the *waqf* practice dedicated to general charitable purposes without stipulating any special beneficiaries (individuals or any organisations/ institutions) and specific purposes. *Waqf am* could be utilised for general charitable purposes and could benefit the whole *ummah*; for example, when a person donates their land generally for the use of charity. In *waqf am*, the donor does not impose any specific condition on the property, and it is free to be managed in any way as long as Shariah rules and principles are not violated, and the benefits of the property are enjoyed by the beneficiaries.

Waqf Khas

The purposes and beneficiaries of *waqf khas* are specified by the *waqf* donor or *wāqif*. The *wāqif* determines the recipients of *waqf* and its specific purpose. One of the examples of *waqf khas* in HEIs is the land donated as a *waqf* to build relevant facilities, such as hostels, cafeterias, and students' activity centres. Furthermore, the *waqf* related to *waqf musytarak* and *waqf irsad* is also present. Specifically, *Waqf musytarak* is a combination of *waqf khayrī* (general welfare) and *waqf zurri* (family), which also means a *waqf* partly beneficial to families and partly to the general public. This type of *waqf* is created through *istibdal* and *waqf* share, whereas *waqf irsad* is formed by the government that performs *waqf* on the property owned by the *Baitulmal*. It can be either a movable or an immovable property and is based on public interest. The application of *waqf* funds owned by the *Baitulmal* could be viewed, for example, from its contribution to the educational sector. Some types of *waqf* contemporaries include the additions to the existing forms of traditional *waqf*, such as cash *waqf*, share *waqf*, and *waqf* share.

A type of *waqf* known as *waqf mu'aqqat* also exists, through which the *waqf* donor can perform *waqf* on their property for a limited time. This type of *waqf* is contrary to the real concept of *waqf*, which has a perpetual element. The majority of scholars, including Hanafi, Syafie, and Hanbali, argued that perpetuity is the main feature of *waqf*,[49] and the absence of this feature will result in an invalid *waqf*. Therefore, most scholars did not approve of this type of *waqf*, although it is allowed by the *madhhab* of Maliki. According to this *madhhab*, provided that the conditions for the validity of a *waqf* do not include permanent transfers,[50] *waqf* donor is permitted to perform *waqf* on their property for a certain period. The ownership of the property is returned to the *waqf* donor after the period has expired. The *waqf* donor performs *waqf* on a house for a month, followed by the return of the house ownership to the *waqf* donor after the expiration. In this case, Abu Yusuf from the *madhhab* of Hanafi agreed with Maliki's opinion, in which a temporary *waqf* is permissible, as mentioned by Niẓām.[51]

Pillars

The four pillars of *waqf* are *al-wāqif*, *al-mawqūf*, *al-mawqūf 'alayh*, and *ṣighah*. Each pillar presents certain conditions, which should be followed to ensure that the *waqf* created is valid and accepted. The explanation for each pillar is presented here.

Al-Wāqif

The contributor or donor of the *waqf* fund is known as *al-wāqif*. The conditions for *al-wāqif* are set to ensure that the *waqf* formed is valid and accepted: they must be free citizens, a major (*baligh*), sane, fully responsible, and become *waqf* volunteers.

Al-Mawqūf

Al-mawqūf is the wealth or possession designated for *waqf*. *Al-mawqūf* has to fulfil the following four conditions:

1) The *waqf* property must be certain physically tangible items, such as a house or land.
2) The *waqf* property must be legally owned by the *waqif*, the ownership must be transferable, and it should provide benefits to the community.
3) The benefits of the *waqf* property should be continuous.
4) The benefits of the *waqf* property should be permissible and legal in Islamic law.

The two categories of property for creating *waqf* are immovable and movable properties. The *waqf* of immovable property is widely practised since the era of Prophet Muhammad (p.b.u.h.) and His companions. Scholars including Ibn Qudāmah stated that in the era of Prophet (p.b.u.h.), no *waqf* was performed except in the form of land and house,[52] which shows that the *waqf* property must be permanent and offer continuous benefits.

In terms of movable property, *waqf* is permissible according to *Hanafiyyah* based on three exceptions: 1) any movable property attached with its original property (immovable property), such as a building/trees/well on a piece of land, 2) evidence from Islamic sources that allows some properties for *waqf*, such as weapons and animals for riding in battle, and 3) the implementation of *waqf* through movable properties based on *uruf* (custom tradition) including books, al-Quran, and clothes.[53] This second exemption was supported by al-Shawkānī because of the evidence permitting *waqf* to be created from these properties.[54] In support of this statement, the *ḥadīth* of Prophet Muhammad (p.b.u.h.) narrated by al-Bukhārī is presented as follows:[55]

من احتبس فرسًا فى سبيل الله، إيمانًا بالله، وتصديقًا بوعده، فإنّ شبعه وريّه وروثه وبوله فى ميزانه يوم القيامة

If somebody keeps a horse in Allah's Cause motivated by his faith in Allah and his belief in His Promise, then he will be rewarded on the Day of Resurrection for what the horse has eaten or drunk and for its dung and urine.

In conclusion, the movable property could also be a *waqf*, which is consistent with the views of *jumhūr* (Shafi'iyyah, Malikiyyah, and Hanabilah) that similar to immovable property, movable property is permissible for *waqf*.

Al-Mawqūf 'Alayh

The recipients or beneficiaries of the *waqf* are known as *al-mawqūf 'alayh* and are determined by the *wāqif* in either a specific or a general form. The specific beneficiaries could be assigned to individuals or groups while the general beneficiaries do not require the *wāqif* to set the specific beneficiary, for instance, *waqf* to certain groups (e.g. the poor).

Ṣighah

Ṣighah is an *aqad* containing an offer and acceptance and may also include writing to the *waqf*, either *waqf am* or *waqf khas*. Two types of *aqad* could be classified as *waqf*, which are as follows:

1) *Sarih* (clear direct words): The utterance that brings only one meaning, such as 'I am *waqf* my house is for the poor people'. This type of utterance does not require the *wāqif* to confirm whether they formed *waqf* as the intention to perform *waqf* on the property is clear through the utterance of the *wāqif*.
2) *Kinayah* (indirect word): The utterance that conveys numerous meanings, such as 'my property is *ṣadaqah* to the poor people'. This type of utterance requires the

wāqif to confirm whether the *waqf* has been created. The same is the case with other symbolic *aqads*, which should be confirmed through the *wāqif*'s intention.

Elements

Based on the *waqf* definitions, a few elements of *waqf* include *al-Mu'tamad*, *al-Ta'bid*, and *al-Ilzam*. These elements are discussed as follows:

Al-Ta'bid

As an endowment, *waqf* also contains an element of perpetuity, which is known as *al-ta'bid*. The element of *al-ta'bid* in this fund is viewed from its principal perspective, which should preserve the property that has been contributed. Therefore, *waqf* is often associated with the contribution of lands and houses with an assumption that these assets are permanent and durable. The non-permanent properties or those with a short life span, such as foods and drinks, cannot be used as a *waqf*. It was agreed upon by the majority of scholars who mentioned that perpetuity is among the key *waqf* features.[56]

Al-Mu'tamad

The ownership of the *waqf* fund consists of the *al-mu'tamad* or irrevocable property element, indicating that the *waqf* process is in force when the property is declared as *waqf* by the *waqf* donor. The *waqf* is effective and valid when the *waqf donor* makes the declaration, and the property no longer belongs to him, and it is transferred from the *waqf* donor's possession to the possession of Allah for the use of beneficiaries or *al-mawqūf 'alayh*; thus it cannot be revoked.[57] It was accepted by the majority of scholars from the four Islamic schools of thought.[58]

Al-Ilzam

The *waqf* includes an element of *al-ilzam* or inalienability, which is almost similar to the principle of perpetuity although with some differences. The *waqf* property cannot be transferred in any form for sale, collateral, inheritance, or *hibah* (gift) by the *wāqif* (*waqf* donor), *mutawalli* (*waqf* manager), or beneficiaries. This criterion is in line with a *ḥadīth* where the Prophet explained that the *waqf* property should not be sold, offered as a present, and inherited as previously discussed. However, a legal exemption is applied in this principle if the *waqf* property is exchanged (*ibdal*) or replaced (*istibdal*) with another appropriate property. According to Hanafiyyah, *ibdal* or *istibdal* of the *waqf* property is permissible by *al-Qadhi* (judge/ruler) if *maslahah* (public interest) is accrued by applying this option.[59]

The theory of endowment and *waqf* discussed in this section (i.e. *waqf*) and the previous section (i.e. endowment) demonstrated similarities and differences between the two funds and is summarised in Table 3.1. In terms of similarities, endowment and *waqf* funds have the same purpose, which is to provide permanent funding and create an element of perpetuity. General and specific endowments also

Table 3.1 Similarities and Differences Between Endowment and *Waqf*

	Aspect		*Endowment*	Waqf
Similarities	**Purpose**		Perpetual usage	
	Types		Both instruments have a general (quasi-endowment and *Waqf am)* and specific (true endowment and *Waqf khas)* product.	
	Specific Product		Bound by the conditions set by the donors.	
	Perpetuity		Both instruments have a perpetuity element.	
	Partial Restricted Product		Both instruments have this type of fund known as term endowment and *waqf mu'aqqat*, respectively.	
Differences	**Philosophy**		Humanity and generosity.	To fulfil the religious obligation to safeguarding wealth (*mal*) instead of humanity and generosity.
	General Product		Funds that the university treats as an endowment.	Funds donated as *waqf* for general purposes.
	Pillars		Not applicable.	To fulfil four elements (al-*wāqif*, *al-mawqūf*, *al-mawqūf 'alayh* and *ṣighah*).
	Element	**Perpetuity**	Need to be invested.	Need to be preserved.
		Rights of Ownership	Flexible.	Allah.
		Inalienable	–	*Waqf* has this element.

Source: Developed by the authors.

exist, where the specific type of endowment and *waqf* is bound by the conditions set by their donors. Furthermore, both funds comprise a partially restricted product known as term endowment and *waqf mu'aqqat*, respectively. Although the *waqf mu'aqqat* is absent from the perpetual element, it is allowed by the *madhhab* of Maliki. In terms of differences between these funds, the philosophy of contributing to the endowment includes humanity and generosity while this philosophy to *waqf* features safeguarding of wealth as one of the *Maqasid Shariah*. In an endowment, the general product refers to the funds functioning as endowments, which are not initially donated as gifts (i.e. true and term endowment). As for *waqf*, the general product refers to the fund that can be used for general purposes. Moreover, unlike endowment, *waqf* consists of four elements, namely *al-wāqif*, *al- mawqūf*, *al-mawqūf 'alayh*, and *ṣighah*. The element of perpetuity in endowment is reflected in the need for the fund to be invested while the fund for *waqf* should be preserved. In terms of ownership, endowment comprises flexible ownership, where the donors can determine whether the fund belongs to the university or should be returned. The fund contributed from *waqf* solely belongs to Allah. The endowment fund has no inalienability element, unlike the *waqf*. The fund cannot be transferred to someone else when it is donated to the *waqf* fund.

Endowment's Experiences in Western Countries

The data presented in Table 3.2 based on QS World University Rankings shows that half of the top 20 universities in the world in 2023 were in the U.S. Notably, these universities belong to the private sector, demonstrating that private universities, especially in the U.S., are highly reputable while the quality of education is in line with the higher tuition fees charged compared to public universities. However, lower tuition fees charged by public universities do not indicate that these universities provide lower quality education. On the contrary, public universities such as the University of Cambridge, University of Oxford, Imperial College London, University College London (UCL), and the University of Edinburgh in the UK; ETH Zurich—Swiss Federal Institute of Technology and Ecole Polytechnique Federale de Lausanne (EPFL) in Switzerland; National University of Singapore and Nanyang Technological University (NTU), Singapore; and Peking University and Tsinghua University in China are ranked high. However, a public university is possibly the ideal choice for individuals who need to save money.

Almost all the universities listed in Table 3.2 are the richest in the U.S. since the establishment of the endowment fund at their institutions. To illustrate, the endowment

Table 3.2 Top 20 Universities in the World 2023

World Rank	*University*	*Country*	*Sector*
1	Massachusetts Institute of Technology	U.S.	Private
2	University of Cambridge	UK	Public
3	Stanford University	U.S.	Private
4	University of Oxford	UK	Public
5	Harvard University	U.S.	Private
=6	California Institute of Technology (Caltech)	U.S.	Private
=6	Imperial College London	UK	Public
8	University College London (UCL)	UK	Public
9	ETH Zurich—Swiss Federal Institute of Technology	CH	Public
10	The University of Chicago	U.S.	Private
11	National University of Singapore	SG	Public
12	Peking University	CN	Public
13	University of Pennsylvania	U.S.	Private
14	Tsinghua University	CN	Public
15	The University of Edinburgh	UK	Public
=16	Ecole Polytechnique Federale de Lausanne (EPFL)	CH	Public
=16	Princeton University	U.S.	Private
18	Yale University	U.S.	Private
19	Nanyang Technological University, Singapore (NTU)	SG	Public
20	Cornell University	U.S.	Private

Source: QS World University Rankings.[60]

fund's market value at Harvard University and Yale University amounted to $51.9 billion and $42.28 billion, positioning them as the first- and third-ranked, respectively. This shows that the universities in the U.S. rely heavily on endowments for income. The list of the 20 richest universities in the U.S. is presented in Figure 3.1.

The experience of Harvard University, Yale University, and seven other universities (i.e. Stanford University, Princeton University, Massachusetts Institute of Technology, University of Pennsylvania, University of Notre Dame, Northwestern University, and Colombia University) demonstrates that a private university is highly reliant on endowment fund to survive. The dependency of the U.S. universities on endowment funds was validated by the data provided by

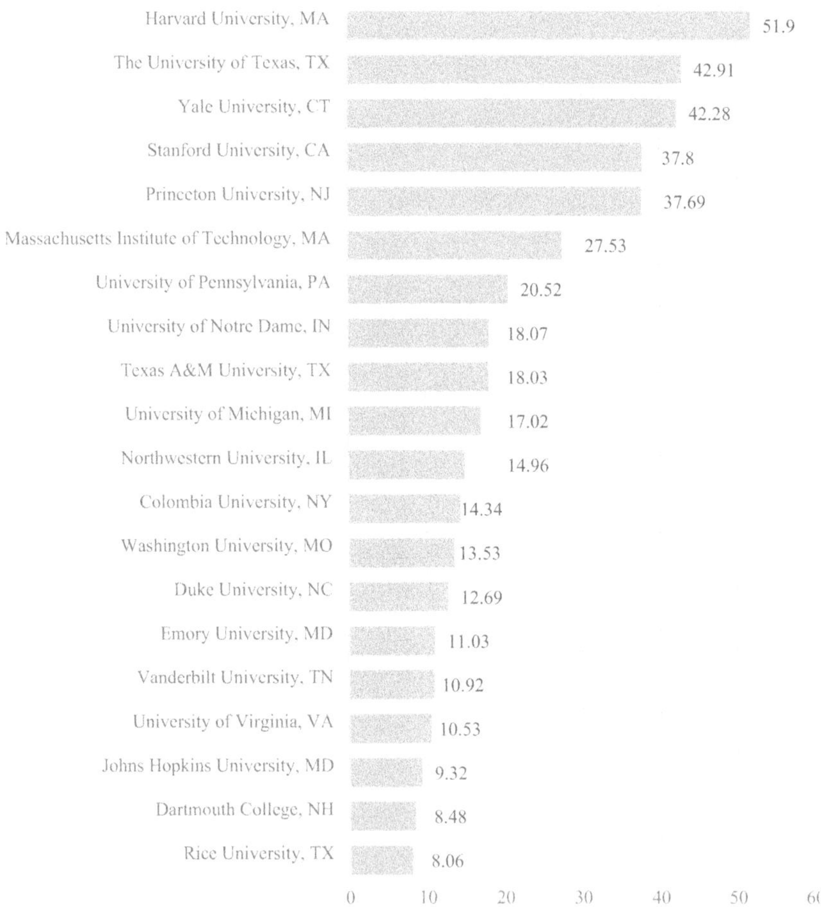

Figure 3.1 20 Richest Universities in the U.S. in 2021 (in billion U.S. dollars)

Source: Statista.[61]

the NACUBO–Teachers Insurance and Annuity Association of America (TIAA) Study of Endowments, which illustrated that the total endowment assets of 678 surveyed institutions amounted to $807 billion as at the end of fiscal year 2022.[62] The average endowment size in that survey was $1.2 billion and the median endowment size was $203.4 million. At the same time, 84% of total market value was held by endowments with more than $1 billion in assets. The experience of universities in the U.S. proves that endowment funds can secure the availability or perpetuity of income for an institution through asset investments to fund current and future operations.

Waqf's Experiences in Some Islamic Countries

As discussed, half of the world's best universities are private universities. However, based on the data provided by the QS Arab Region University Rankings, over half (14) of the top 20 universities in the Arab region in 2020 were from the public sector. The universities were King Abdulaziz University, King Fahd University of Petroleum and Minerals, and King Saud University in Saudi Arabia (SA); UAE University, Khalifa University of Science and Technology, and Zayed University in the UAE; Cairo University, Ain Shams University, and Alexandria University in Egypt; University of Jordan and Jordan University of Science and Technology in Jordan; Qatar University in Qatar, Sultan Qaboos University in Oman; and the University of Baghdad in Iraq. Notably, public universities in the Arab region are highly prestigious and offer better quality education than private universities. Additionally, the cost of education is low which is the reason this sector becomes students' choice for pursuing higher education.

As discussed in Chapter 2, public educational institutions obtain funds from the public. However, these institutions are not entirely dependent on this source because of the presence of other sources of funding for their operation. One of the sources of funding is a *waqf* fund. To illustrate, the top three public universities in Saudi Arabia in Table 3.3 implement *waqf* funds. Besides the public sector, private universities in Saudi Arabia, such as King Abdullah University of Science and Technology (KAUST), also benefit from *waqf* funds. Compared to the three universities, KAUST is the richest university in Saudi Arabia with a *waqf* value of $20 billion[63] donated by the king (King Abdullah bin Abdulaziz al-Saud)[64] as a founder of the King Faisal Foundation. The money donated to KAUST significantly contributed to *waqf* in funding their university operating costs. These universities have also been ranked 11 among the world's richest universities, as reported by Nonprofit Colleges Online.[65]

Besides Saudi Arabia, other Arab countries with large *waqf* funds include Bahrain, Jordan, Kuwait, Morocco, Oman, Qatar, and the UAE.[66] Specifically, the *waqf* funds in the UAE are applied to educational institutions. To illustrate, a multibillionaire businessman from the UAE launched the Arab world's largest education fund of $1.14 billion in 2016.[67] The *waqf* fund in the UAE was managed by the *Awqaf* and Minors Affairs Foundation, whose asset value in 2017 exceeded AED2.8

Table 3.3 Top 20 Universities in the Arab Region in 2023

Arab Region Rank	*World Rank*	*University*	*Country*	*Sector*
1	=106	King Abdulaziz University	SA	Public
2	=208	Qatar University	QA	Public
3	160	King Fahd University of Petroleum and Minerals	SA	Public
4	=237	King Saud University	SA	Public
5	252	American University of Beirut	LB	Private
6	=296	United Arab Emirates University	UAE	Public
7	=181	Khalifa University	UAE	Public
8	=384	Sultan Qaboos University	OM	Public
9	=369	American University of Sharjah	UAE	Private
10	591–600	University of Jordan	JO	Public
11	=416	The American University in Cairo	EG	Private
12	551–560	Cairo University	EG	Public
13	601–650	Lebanese University	LB	Private
14	801–1000	Ain Shams University	EG	Public
15	601–650	University of Sharjah	UAE	Private
16	801–1000	Jordan University of Science and Technology	JO	Public
17	=449	Umm al-Qura University	SA	Public
18	651–700	Prince Mohammad Bin Fahd University	SA	Private
19	561–570	Applied Science University	BH	Private
20	701–750	Zayed University	UAE	Public

Source: QS Arab Region University Rankings[68] and QS World University Rankings.[69]

billion (an increase of 7% over the previous year), where the *waqf* accounted for the highest share with a value of over AED1.4 billion, as reported by Albawaba Business.[70] The revenues of this foundation increased by 2 per cent in 2017, with the *waqf* being the largest contributor with a value of AED121 million (an increase of 9% compared to 2016). The total investment profit amounted to AED140 million (11% until 2016) while the endowment fund had the highest gain of AED93 million (9% until 2016). Besides the UAE University, the experience of other public universities in the UAE, such as Zayed University, proves that the *waqf* fund was crucial in enhancing the existing funding.

Egypt is another country in the Arab region that implements the *waqf* fund in educational institutions. Although Egypt is not included in the list of Arab countries with the largest *waqf* funds, its discussion is necessary as the oldest Islamic educational institution funded by the *waqf* funds, Al-Azhar University, is located there. The implementation of *waqf* in Al-Azhar University allows the provision of free education to its students inside or outside of the country. The success of Al-Azhar University in utilising the *waqf* funds encouraged the Egyptian government to apply *waqf* as one of its sources of income.[71] The university is linked to thousands of educational institutions, including schools and universities, in Egypt and outside the country. Therefore, it is responsible for channelling the funds to those institutions. In addition, the university has also funded many other educational institutions since its establishment.[72] Until now, Al-Azhar University is still surviving with the income from *waqf* funds since its establishment in the 10th century.

Turkey is another Islamic country that has demonstrated that educational institutions, including HEIs, can be funded by *waqf*. The highest stage of the *waqf* implementation in Turkey was achieved during the Ottoman Empire, from the middle of the 8th century until the end of the 19th century. Cash *waqf* was established by generous individuals during this period to finance various pious objectives of society, including education.[73] Considering that cash *waqf* played a significant role in financing the education system, it can be concluded that it was one of the success factors of the Ottoman civilisation. Until 2015, there were 68 *Vakif Üniversitesi* financed by *waqf* fund in Turkey, and this number continues to increase. These *Vakif Üniversitesi* are supported by the governing foundation, which is owned by wealthy Turkish entrepreneurs and philanthropists who own large and prestigious companies, as mandated by the law.[74] It could become another factor contributing to the success of Turkey in applying a well-organised *waqf* system at HEIs.

Similar to endowment, the implementation of *waqf* in educational institutions in Islamic countries has proven its potential to guarantee the financial sustainability of an institution. This is aligned with the *waqf* definition of *al-habs*, which is to 'restrain the property and distribute its benefits in Allah's cause', as narrated by Umar.[75] Given that *waqf* also comprises the elements of *al-ta'bid* (i.e. perpetuity), *al-mu'tamad* (irrevocability), and *al-ilzam* (inalienability), these have been the factors for the existence of *waqf* fund from its inception until the current time.

Conclusion

The endowment and *waqf* theories discussed in this chapter illustrated that both these funds have similarities and differences. The similarities include the purpose of the funds, the existence of perpetuity elements, and their common types (e.g. general, specific, and partial restricted products). In contrast, their differences are in terms of the philosophy of giving, general product meaning, the existence of pillars that should be fulfilled in the *waqf* practice, and some other elements (e.g. perpetuity, rights of ownership, and inalienability). However, each element has its advantage in the provision of funding to an institution, including HEIs, as proven through experience and the success achieved by universities worldwide in applying these two concepts.

Notes

1 *The New International Webster's Comprehensive Dictionary of The English Language*, Deluxe Enc (Naples, FL: Trident Press International, 1996), 419, entry "endow".

2 *Longman Dictionary of Contemporary English*, 4th ed. (London: Pearson Education Limited, 2003), 516, entry "endowment".
3 *The New International Webster's Comprehensive Dictionary of the English Language*, 419, entry "endowment".
4 T. R. Wolanin, "Financing Higher Education in the United States: An Overview," *International Higher Education*, no. 19 (2015): 8–10, 9, https://ejournals.bc.edu/ojs/index.php/ihe/article/download/6875/6092.
5 S. Sazonov et al., "Mechanism of Determination of Effectiveness of Spending Assets of Endowment Funds on the Basis of Mathematical Models," *International Journal of Educational Management* 31, no. 1 (2017): 21–29, 22, https://doi.org/10.1108/IJEM-02-2016-0040.
6 R. G. Ehrenberg, "Demystifying Endowments," *School of Industrial and Labor Relations, Cornell University*, no. 132 (2009): 1–13, 2, http://digitalcommons.ilr.cornell.edu/workingpapers/132/%0ARequired.
7 Financial Accounting Standards Board (FASB), *Statement of Financial Accounting Standards No. 117, Financial Statements of Not-for-Profit Organizations*, accessed on 21 July 2020, https://tinyurl.com/53stdk3u, 48.
8 Malcolm Getz, "Endowment," *The Bottom Line* 4, no. 2 (2007): 37–41, 7, https://doi.org/10.1108/eb025286.
9 "Acts 20:35," *Bible Hub*, accessed 21 July 2020, https://biblehub.com/acts/20-35.htm.
10 G. L. Cascione, *Philanthropists in Higher Education: Institutional, Biographical, and Religious Motivations for Giving* (New York: Routledge Falmer, 2003), 5.
11 National Association of College and University Business Officers (NACUBO) and Commonfund Institute, *NACUBO—Commonfund Study of Endowments* (Washington, DC: NACUBO, 2017), 100.
12 *Statement of Financial Accounting Standards No. 117, Financial Statements of Not-for-Profit Organizations*, 48.
13 H. Kazemi and K. Wilkens, "A Simple Approach to the Management of Endowments," *All About Alpha*, 2017, accessed on 19 October 2018, www.allaboutalpha.com/blog/2017/08/07/a-simple-approach-to-the-management-of-endowments/
14 Al-Nawawī, Abī Zakariyyā Maḥy al-Dīn Ibn Sharf, *al-Majmū' Sharḥ al-Muhadhdhab li al-Shirāzī*, vol. 16 (Jeddah: Maktabah al-Irshād, 1980), 241.
15 Ibn Qudāmah, Abī Muḥammad 'Abd Allāh Ibn Aḥmad Ibn Muḥammad al-Maqdisī, *Mughnī*, vol. 8 (Qāhirah: Hajr, 1992), 184.
16 Ibn 'Ābidīn, Muḥammad Amīn, *Radd al-Muḥtār 'ala al-Durr al-Mukhtār Sharḥ Tanwīr al-Abṣār*, vol. 6 (Bayrūt: Dār al-Ma'rifah, 2000), 516–17.
17 Al-Nawawī, Abī Zakariyyā Maḥy al-Dīn Ibn Sharf, *al-Majmū' Sharḥ al-Muhadhdhab li al-Shirāzī*, vol. 16, 241.
18 Ibn 'Ābidīn, Muḥammad Amīn, *Radd al-Muḥtār 'ala al-Durr al-Mukhtār Sharḥ Tanwīr al-Abṣār*, vol. 6, 516–17.
19 Wahbah al-Zuḥaylī, *al-Fiqh al-Islāmī wa Adillatuh*, vol. 8 (Dimashq: Dār al-Fikr, 2010), 152.
20 K. D. Al-Hammām, *Sharḥ Fatḥ al-Qadīr 'ala al-Hidāyah Sharḥ Bidāyah al-Mubtadi'*, 1st ed., vol. 6 (Bayrūt: Dār al-Kutub al-'Ilmiyyah, 2003), 91.
21 Al-Sharbīnī, Shams al-Dīn Muḥammad Ibn Muḥammad al-Khāṭib, *Mughnī al-Muḥtāj ilā Ma'rifātī Ma'ānī Alfāẓ al-Minhāj*, vol. 2 (Bayrūt: Dār al-Ma'rifah, 1997), 485.
22 M. S. Al-Rahaybānī, *Maṭālib Uli al-Nuhā fī Sharḥ Ghāyah al-Muntahā*, 3rd ed., vol. 6 (N.p.: N.p., 2000), 6.
23 Wahbah al-Zuḥaylī, *al-Fiqh al-Islāmī wa Adillatuh*, vol. 8, 153.
24 Nazīḥ Ḥammād, *Mu'jam al-Muṣṭalaḥāt al-Iqtiṣādiyyah fī Lughah al-Fuqahā'*, 3rd ed. (Riyāḍ: Dār al-'Alamiyyah li al-Kitāb al- Islāmī, 1995), 353.
25 M. A. Al-Dardīr, *Al-Sharḥ al-Ṣaghīr 'ala Aqrab al-Masālik ila Madhhab al-Imām Mālik*, vol. 4 (United Arabic Emirates: Wizārah al-'Adl wa al-Shu'ūn al-Islāmiyyah wa al-Awqāf, 1989), 97.

26 M. A. Al-Dussūqī, A. Al-Dardīr, and M. Alish, *Hāshiyah al-Dussūqī 'ala al-Sharḥ al-Kabīr*, vol. 4 (Qāhirah: Dār Ihyā' al-Kutub al-'Arabiyyah, n.d.), 76.
27 Wahbah al-Zuḥaylī, *al-Fiqh al-Islāmī wa Adillatuh*, vol. 8, 154.
28 Ibn Kathīr, Abū Fidā' Ismā'il Ibn 'Umar, al-Qurshī al-Damashqī, *Tafsīr al-Qur'ān al-'Aẓīm*, vol. 2 (Riyāḍ: Dār Taybah li al- Nashr wa al-Tawzī', 2009), 73.
29 Al-Qurṭūbī, Abī Wālid Muḥammad Ibn Aḥmad Ibn Muḥammad Ibn Aḥmad Ibn Rushd, *al-Jāmi 'li Aḥkām al-Qur'ān*, vol. 5 (Bayrūt: Al-Risālah Publishers, 2006), 201.
30 M. J. Al-Ṭabarī, *Jamī' al-Bayān 'an Ta'wīl al-Qur'ān*, vol. 3 (N.p.: Maktabah Muṣṭafā al-Bābī al-Ḥalābī, 1968), 347.
31 Ibn Kathīr, Abū Fidā' Ismā'il Ibn 'Umar, al-Qurshī al-Damashqī, *Tafsīr al-Qur'ān al-'Aẓīm*, vol. 2, 73.
32 Ibn Kathīr, Abū Fidā' Ismā'il Ibn 'Umar, al-Qurshī al-Damashqī, *Tafsīr al-Qur'ān al-'Aẓīm*, vol. 1, 675.
33 Ibid., 695
34 Ibid.
35 Al-Nawawī, Abī Zakariyyā Maḥy al-Dīn Ibn Sharf, *Sharḥ Ṣaḥīḥ Muslim*, vol. 11 (Bayrūt: Dār al-Ma'rifah, 2005), 87, "Kitāb al-Waṣiyyah, Bāb Ma Yalḥaq al-Insān Min al-Thawab ba'da Wafātih," No. *ḥadīth* 4199.
36 Al-Tirmidhī, *al-Jāmi' al-Ṣaḥīḥ wa Huwa Sunan al-Tirmidhī*, vol. 3 (Bayrūt: Dār al-Kitāb al-'Alamiyah, n.d.), 660, "Kitāb al- Aḥkām, Bāb fī al-Waqf," No. *ḥadīth* 1376.
37 Abū Dāwud, *Sunan Abū Dāwud*, vol. 4 (Bayrūt: Dār al-Risālah al-'Alamiyah, 2009), 506, "Kitāb al-Waṣāyā, Bāb fī al-Ṣadaqah 'an al-Mayyit," No. *ḥadīth* 2880, 506.
38 Al-Nasā'ī, *Sunan al-Nasā'ī: Bi Sharḥ al-Ḥafīẓ Jalāl al-Dīn al-Ṣuyūṭī*, vol. 5 (Bayrūt: Dār al-Kitāb al-'Alamiyah, n.d.), 251, "Kitāb al-Waṣāyā, Bāb fī al-Ṣadaqah 'an al-Mayyit," No. *ḥadīth* 3651.
39 Al-Nawawī, Abī Zakariyyā Maḥy al-Dīn Ibn Sharf. *Sharḥ Ṣaḥīḥ Muslim*, vol. 11, 88.
40 Al-Sharbīnī, Shams al-Dīn Muḥammad Ibn Muḥammad al-Khāṭib, *Mughnī al-Muḥtāj ilā Ma'rifātī Ma'ānī Alfāẓ al-Minhāj*, vol. 2, 485.
41 M. I. Al-Bukhārī, *Ṣaḥīḥ al-Bukhārī* (Riyāḍ: Dār al-Salām, 1999), 451, "Kitāb al-Shurūṭ, Bāb al-Shurūṭ fī al-Waqf," No. *ḥadīth* 2737.
42 Al-Tirmidhī, *al-Jāmi' al-Ṣaḥīḥ wa Huwa Sunan al-Tirmidhī*, vol. 3, 659, No. *ḥadīth* 1375.
43 Al-Nasā'ī, *Sunan al-Nasā'ī: Bi Sharḥ al-Ḥafīẓ Jalāl al-Dīn al-Ṣuyūṭī*, vol. 5, 232, "Kitāb al-Aḥbās, Bāb Ḥabs al-Mashā'," No. *ḥadīth* 3604.
44 Al-Nawawī, Abī Zakariyyā Maḥy al-Dīn Ibn Sharf. *Sharḥ Ṣaḥīḥ Muslim*, vol. 11, 88, "Kitāb al-Waṣiyyah, Bāb al-Waqf," No. *ḥadīth* 4200.
45 Ibn Mājah, Abū 'Abd Allāh Muḥammad Ibn Yazid al-Qazwinī, *Sunan Ibn Mājah*, vol. 2 (Bayrūt: Dār Iḥyā' al-Turāth al-'Arabī, 1975), 801, "Kitāb al-Ṣadaqāt, Bāb min al-Waqf," No. *ḥadīth* 2396.
46 Al-Tirmidhī, *al-Jāmi 'al-Ṣaḥīḥ wa Huwa Sunan al-Tirmidhī*, vol. 5 (Riyāḍ: al-Maktabah al-Islāmiyyah, 1938), 627, "Kitāb al-Manāqib, Bāb fī Manāqib 'Uthmān bin 'Affān Radiy Allāh 'anhu," No. *ḥadīth* 3703.
47 Al-Nasā'ī, *Sunan al-Nasā'ī: Bi Sharḥ al-Ḥafīẓ Jalāl al-Dīn al-Ṣuyūṭī*, vol. 5, 235, "Kitāb al-Aḥbās, Bāb Waqf al-Masājid," *ḥadīth* no. 3608.
48 Ibn Qudāmah, Abī Muḥammad 'Abd Allāh Ibn Aḥmad Ibn Muḥammad al-Maqdisī, *Mughnī*, vol. 8, 185.
49 Niẓām, *al-Fatawā al-Hindiyah*, 1st ed., vol. 2 (Bayrūt: Dār al-Kutub al-'Ilmiyyah, 2000), 361.
50 M. A. Al-Dardīr, *Al-Sharḥ al-Ṣaghīr 'ala Aqrab al-Masālik ila Madhhab al-Imām Mālik*, vol. 4 (Qāhirah: Dār al-Ma'ārif, 1986), 106.
51 Niẓām, *al-Fatawā al-Hindiyah*, vol. 2, 361.
52 Ibn Qudāmah, Abī Muḥammad 'Abd Allāh Ibn Aḥmad Ibn Muḥammad al-Maqdisī, *Mughnī*, vol. 8, 231.
53 I. S. Ṣabrī, *al-Waqf al-Islāmī bayna al-Naẓariyyah wa al-Taṭbīq*, 1st ed. (al-'Urdūn: Dār al-Nafā'is, 2008), 229–30.

54 Muḥammad Ibn ʻAlī Ibn Muḥammad Al-Shawkānī, *Fatḥ al-Qādir*, vol. 5 (Qāhirah: Dār al-Ḥadīth, 2007), 37.
55 M. I. Al-Bukhārī, *Ṣaḥīḥ al-Bukhārī*, 5th ed., vol. 3 (Bayrūt: Dār Ibn Kathīr, 1993), 1048, Kitāb al-Jihād, Bāb Manih Tabasa Farasan, No. 2698.
56 Niẓām, *al-Fatawā al-Hindiyah*, vol. 2, 361.
57 Abū Bakr Muḥammad Shams al-Dīn Al-Sarakhsī, *al-Mabsūṭ*, vol. 12 (Bayrūt: Dār al-Maʻrifah, 1989), 41.
58 Abū Bakr Ibn Masʻūd al-Ḥanāfī Al-Kasānī, *Baḍā'iʻ al-Ṣana'iʻ fī Tartīb al-Sharā'iʻ*, vol. 8 (Bayrūt: Dār al-Kutub al-ʻIlmiyyah, 2003), 383.
59 Muḥammad Amīn Ibn ʻĀbidīn, *Radd al-Muḥtār 'ala al-Durr al-Mukhtār Sharḥ Tanwīr al-Abṣār*, vol. 6 (Riyāḍ: Dār ʻAlīm al- Kutub, 2003), 584.
60 "QS World University Rankings 2023," *QS Quacquarelli Symonds Limited*, 2023, accessed on 24 March 2023, www.topuniversities.com/university-rankings/world-university-rankings/2023.
61 "The 20 Richest Colleges in the United States in FY 2021, by Endowment Funds Market Value."
62 National Association of College and University Business Officers (NACUBO) and Teachers Insurance and Annuity Association of America (TIAA), *NACUBO–TIAA Study of Endowments: Summary Observations from the 2022 NACUBO–TIAA Study of Endowments* (n.p.: NACUBO and TIAA, 2023), 2.
63 UK Science & Innovation Network, *Kingdom of Saudi Arabia* (n.p.: UK Science & Innovation Network, 2018), 2.
64 I. Rose-Smith, "KAUST's Edgar Nehme Said to Leave for a Bass Family Office," *Institutional Investors*, 2017, accessed on 25 October 2020, www.institutionalinvestor.com/article/b1505qcns6p6jw/kausts-edgar-nehme-said-to-leave-for-a-bass- family-office.
65 "50 Richest Universities in the World: University Endowment Rankings," *Nonprofit Colleges Online*, n.d., accessed on 29 March 2023, www.nonprofitcollegesonline.com/wealthiest-universities-in-the-world/.
66 M. Jalbout, "The Case for Engaging Arab Donors in Financing Global Education," *Global Economy & Development*, no. 80 (2014): 1–25, 11.
67 A. Batrawy, "UAE Tycoon Launches Largest Arab Education Fund with $1.14B," *The San Diego Union-Tribune*, April 20, 2016, accessed on 25 October 2020, www.sandiegouniontribune.com/sdut-uae-tycoon-launches-largest-arab-education-fund-2016apr20-story.html.
68 "QS Arab Region University Rankings 2023," *QS Quacquarelli Symonds Limited*, 2023, accessed on 29 March 2023, www.topuniversities.com/university-rankings/arab-region-university-rankings/2023.
69 "QS World University Rankings 2023," *QS Quacquarelli Symonds Limited*, 2023, www.topuniversities.com/university-rankings/world-university-rankings/2023.
70 "Awqaf and Minors Affairs Foundation Raises Asset Value to Dh2.8 Billion, Increase Profits by 11 Per Cent," *Albawaba Business*, 2018, accessed on 25 October 2020, https://www.albawaba.com/business/pr/awqaf-and-minors-affairs-foundation-raises-asset-value-dh28-billion-increases-profits-11.
71 S.M.Mahamood and A. Ab Rahman, "Financing Universities through Waqf, Pious Endowment Is It Possible?" *Humanomics* 31, no. 4 (2015): 430–53, 432, https://doi.org/10.1108/H-02-2015-0010.
72 Jalbout, "The Case for Engaging Arab Donors in Financing Global Education," 4.
73 M. Cizakca, "Waqf in History and Its Implications for Modern Islamic Economies," in *Essential Readings in Contemporary Waqf Issues*, ed. M. Kahf and S. M. Mahamood (Kuala Lumpur: CERT Publications Sdn. Bhd., 2011), 3–42, 25.
74 Mahamood and Ab Rahman, "Financing Universities through Waqf, Pious Endowment: Is It Possible?" 443.
75 Al-Nawawī, *al-Majmū ʻSharḥ al-Muhadhdhab li al-Shirāzī*, vol. 16, 241.

4 Theoretical Perspectives on the Successful Elements of Endowment and *Waqf* in Higher Educational Institutions

Introduction

This chapter discusses the theoretical aspects of the successful elements required to finance HEIs in Malaysia.

Successful Elements

The successful elements of endowment, especially in the university context, have been examined by previous scholars. There are several elements that can drive the success of endowment. For example, asset allocation in alternative assets influence endowment performance. Elements that were found to result in successful investments in this asset were highly skilled investment managers, superior investment committees, and alumni networks. However, as these findings represented those based on top endowment funds, the achievement of similar results by ordinary endowments was assumed to be unlikely.[1] Therefore, besides these elements, other elements were also investigated. To ensure that the study was comprehensive in the Malaysian context, many other strands of literature were also reviewed.

There are several elements contributing to the success of *waqf* in higher education, especially in Malaysia, which have been highlighted by previous scholars. However, as the study was based only on a preliminary survey and was not an empirical study, the topic needs to be explored in more detail. Given the empirical study on endowments, their findings were adopted for *waqf* because the two instruments are conceptually similar. Notably, the preliminary findings became the basis for the next empirical study. All these elements are discussed in the following subsections.

Appropriate Investment Planning

Investment is a strategy used for an endowment to expand its funds. The performance of an endowment depends on the allocation decision made between asset classes with different risk and return characteristics. An endowment can invest in five main asset classes, equities (stocks), fixed income (bonds), real estate,

DOI: 10.4324/9781003435976-4

alternatives (e.g. hedge funds, commodities, and private equity), and cash. Historically, the endowment was largely invested in bonds and high-dividend stocks. Between the 1970s and 1980s, a shift in the endowment investment from the traditional asset class (i.e. bonds and stocks) to alternatives occurred.

Investment allocations to alternative assets have become increasingly popular with the development of the Endowment Model by David Swensen at the Yale University.[2] This model suggests that sophisticated institutional investors allocate a more significant amount of their portfolios to alternative assets. From 1993 to 2005, many universities increased their allocation to this type of asset class. The Ivy League Schools allocated a large proportion of their portfolio to this asset class—which is significantly higher compared to other schools (9.3 vs 1.1% in 1993; 37.1 vs 8.1% in 2005).[3] This finding was consistent with the findings of the World Economic Forum, which illustrated that alternative investments have become the choice among wealthy institutional investors, including endowments, as depicted in Figure 4.1. In addition, the endowments were found to be the third largest investor in alternative investments.

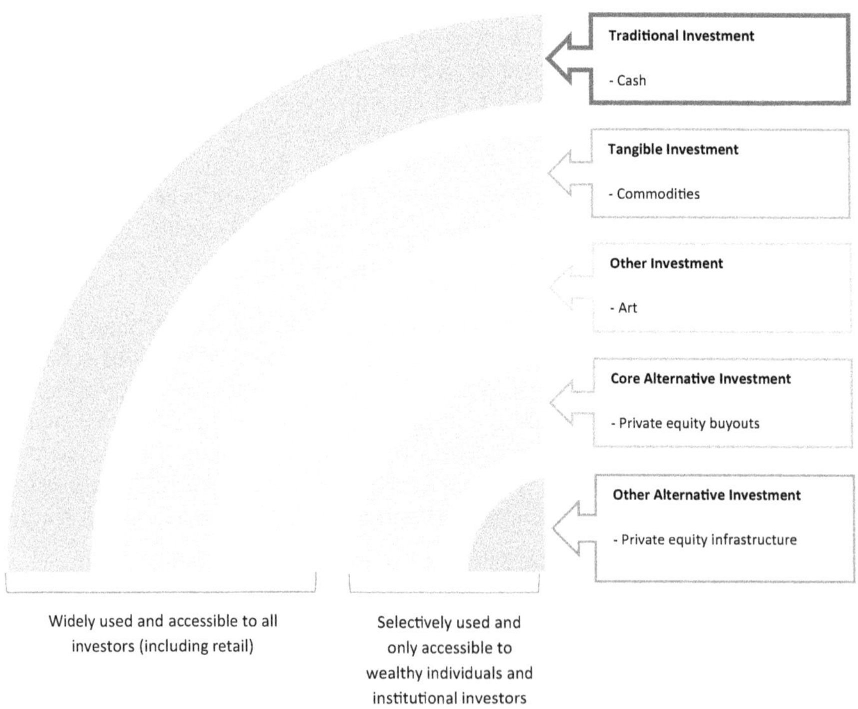

Figure 4.1 Different Types of Investment

Source: World Economic Forum.[4]

As a pioneer in alternative investments, the Ivy League Schools achieved higher returns in this asset class despite the control over the percentage of allocation to alternative assets.[5] The alternative investments offer the following benefits:[6]

1) Exposure to a broader range of investment opportunities and strategies;
2) Potential for improved risk-adjusted returns;
3) Less-extreme market cycle peaks and troughs;
4) Access to less efficient markets, which could create investment opportunities; and
5) Historically lower correlation, where their response to market conditions may differ from those of traditional investments.

Nevertheless, the selection of managers for alternative investments should be prioritised. A skilled and experienced manager for alternative investments is critical because of their ability to interpret unclear data in decision-making for fund selection within the asset class. This may be a major factor contributing to the continuous success that was achieved by the Ivy League Schools.[7] This is discussed in detail in a later subsection of this chapter.

Investments in alternative assets are riskier and more illiquid than traditional assets; therefore, the selection of appropriate time to invest in these assets should be emphasised. Investing in alternative assets at an inappropriate time adversely impacts the return on investment. This was evident in the financial crisis of 2008, when universities were unable to obtain cash as their funds were illiquid.[8] It also affected the largest endowment universities, such as Harvard and Stanford, which had to bear substantial costs because of the illiquidity of the portfolio.[9] Therefore, an appropriate time for investment in alternative assets is important.

The risks of inflation, liquidity, and extreme market events should be considered by endowment investors for investment in alternative assets. To avoid losses in alternative investments, investment diversification as a strategy should be considered. The investment diversification referred to here is the process of spreading an investment across assets where investment portfolios consist of not only highly risky assets but also low-risk assets, stocks, and bonds. Furthermore, asset diversification helps improve the risk-adjusted returns of a portfolio as it is able to determine whether the risk taken is worth the expected return.

Therefore, the appropriate proportion of each asset class needs to be ascertained by endowment investors. This is an important factor in the investment philosophy of the endowment funds at Harvard University and Yale University and is the basis on which the endowment investment portfolios are built.[10] For universities with large endowments, such as the aforementioned universities, a diversified portfolio indicates that the total number of funds managers should be 100 or more, with several different investment styles. Therefore, the discussion about the endowment fund investments, including the *waqf* fund, does not focus on investments in alternative assets only. This chapter adopts the term 'appropriate investment planning' to present a discussion about the balanced investment of these funds.

The Malaysian context should be considered in endowment investments involving public institutions. The principles of halal and haram should not be overlooked when managing the money contributed by the public, especially Muslims. These principles are a priority among Muslims for managing every matter in their daily lives. Furthermore, the principles apply not only to the physical form of items but also to the process of obtaining them. Determining the halal status is compulsory according to the order from Allah. Numerous verses in the al-Quran present the order to prioritise the halal status compared to the haram status, for example, verse 618 of Surah al-Baqarah:

يَا أَيُّهَا النَّاسُ كُلُوا مِمَّا فِي الْأَرْضِ حَلَالًا طَيِّبًا وَلَا تَتَّبِعُوا خُطُوَاتِ الشَّيْطَانِ ۚ إِنَّهُ لَكُمْ عَدُوٌّ مُبِينٌ ﴿168﴾

Al-Baqarah 2: 168

O mankind, eat from whatever is on earth [that is] lawful and good and do not follow the footsteps of Satan. Indeed, he is to you a clear enemy.

If endowments in Malaysia seek to emphasise the contributions of Muslims, the issues of halal and haram should not be overlooked, especially in investment activities, given the income earned from interest payments, dividends, and capital gains. In Islam, interest (*riba*) is one of the prohibited elements that is classified as haram and should be avoided, as illustrated in numerous verses in the al-Quran. This is established by the following verse 275 of surah al-Baqarah:

وَأَحَلَّ اللَّهُ الْبَيْعَ وَحَرَّمَ الرِّبَا ۚ﴿275﴾

Al-Baqarah 2: 275

But Allah has permitted trade and has forbidden interest.

As an alternative to conventional investment, Islamic investment comprises two types of investments, fundamental and standard, known as *mudharabah* and *musyarakah*. Both types of investments are rendered as halal because of the profit which is gained by the capital provider (*rabbul mal*) based on a ratio instead of the value of money as it is considered as *riba*. Any element prohibited in Islam (e.g. *riba*) must be avoided in investment activities to ensure that investments comply with the Shariah rules and principles. These rules and principles are also applied to banking institutions. According to the former Governor of Bank Negara Malaysia (BNM), Dr Zeti Akhtar Aziz, 'this is crucial in instilling confidence in the purity of the operations'.[11]

Today, various capital market products are available for Muslims who seek to invest and transact only in the Islamic Capital Market (ICM), namely Shariah-compliant securities, *Sukuk* (Islamic bond), Islamic unit trusts, Shariah indices, warrants/call warrants, and crude palm oil futures contract. In terms of security, to determine its compliance with Shariah or vice versa, the Shariah Advisory Council (SAC) of the Securities Commission Malaysia (SCM), which functions as the reference body and advisor to BNM on Shariah matters in the ICM, adopts a two-tier quantitative approach, business activity benchmarks, and financial ratio benchmarks. The securities are considered Shariah-compliant if the business activities and financial ratios meet these benchmarks. The details of each benchmark are presented in Table 4.1. Until May 2019, 689 or 76 per cent of Shariah-compliant securities were linked in Bursa Malaysia by the SAC. This list originates from various sectors in the industry, as shown in Table 4.2. The list of companies for each sector is presented in Appendix II. Besides, seven securities listed on the Leading Entrepreneur Accelerator Platform (LEAP) market were classified as Shariah-compliant securities by the SAC, as shown in Appendix III.

Table 4.1 Business Activity and Financial Ratio Benchmarks

Benchmark	*Category*	*Details*
Business Activity Benchmark	**The 5 per cent benchmark**. It is applicable for the following activities: • Conventional banking; • Conventional insurance; • Gambling; • Liquor and liquor-related activities; • Pork and pork-related activities; • Non-halal food and beverages; • Shariah non-compliant entertainment; • Tobacco and tobacco-related activities; • Interest income from conventional accounts and instruments (including interest income arising from a court judgement or arbitrator); • Dividends from Shariah non-compliant investments; and • Other activities deemed non-compliant according to Shariah	The contribution of Shariah non-compliant activities to the Group revenue or Group profit before taxation of the company must be less than 5 per cent.
	The 20-per cent benchmark. It is applicable for the following activities: • Share trading; • Stockbroking business; • Rental received from Shariah non-compliant activities; and • Other activities deemed non-compliant according to Shariah	The contribution of Shariah non-compliant activities to the Group revenue or Group profit before taxation of the company must be less than 20 per cent.
Financial Ratio Benchmark	**Cash over total assets**. • Cash includes only cash placed in conventional accounts and instruments, whereas cash placed in Islamic accounts and instruments is excluded from the calculation. **Debt over total assets**. • Debt includes only interest-bearing debt, whereas Islamic financing or *Sukuk* is excluded from the calculation.	Each ratio, which is intended to measure *riba* and *riba*-based elements within a company's statements of financial position, must be less than 33 per cent.

Source: SCM.[12]

Table 4.2 Numbers and Percentage of Shariah-Compliant Securities

Main Market/ACE Market	*Number of Shariah-Compliant Securities*	*Total Securities**	*Percentage of Shariah-Compliant Securities (%)*
Consumer Products and Services	133	195	68
Industrial Products and Services	209	251	83
Energy	28	32	88
Construction	50	53	94
Transportation and Logistics	28	35	80
Property	77	100	77
Plantation	35	44	80
Technology	77	88	88
Utilities	10	13	77
Financial Services	3	34	9
Healthcare	16	17	94
Telecommunications and Media	23	33	70
Special Purpose Acquisition Companies (SPAC)	Nil	1	Nil
Closed-End Fund	Nil	1	Nil
Total	**689**	**897**	**77**

Source: SCM.[13]

* As on 27 May 2019.

To fulfil the market demand for diversification strategies, other Shariah-compliant capital market instruments are also structured, such as the Islamic Real Estate Investment (I- REIT) and Islamic Exchange-Traded Fund (I-ETF), which could be alternatives to conventional products for Muslims. Until May 2019, four types of I-REITs and six types of I-ETFs were present, as shown in Appendices IV and V. All these products in the ICM are highly important, especially to Malaysia, because of their ability to spur economic growth. The total size of the ICM amounted to RM2.28 billion until May 2022, which accounted for 63.9 per cent of the total market capitalisation in the country.[14] The ICM has a high potential to expand and develop by leveraging the concept of sustainable and responsible investment (SRI), which can help enhance Shariah-compliant Islamic products. This was evident in 2016 when 34 per cent of the total sustainable investment assets ($17.9 billion) were Shariah-compliant.[15] To facilitate the financing of SRI initiatives, the SCM has launched the SRI-*Sukuk* framework in terms of the utilisation of proceeds, eligibility, and disclosure/reporting requirement.

Despite various ICM products being previously discussed, rules and regulations are implemented in universities, especially public universities through the Investment Guidelines for public universities issued by the MoE Malaysia. Based on this guideline, public universities can invest only in low-risk assets, such as fixed deposits, shares, direct investments in convertible securities, and property investments.

As *waqf*'s purpose is similar to that of endowments, which is to preserve the funds over a long period, the methods used in endowments to generate income through investment activities should be considered in *waqf*. Given that *waqf* cannot achieve financial sustainability by depending entirely on donations, the involvement of *waqf* in investment activities is one of the alternatives. Although this involvement has existed especially in Malaysia, growth has not been observed. Therefore, efforts that can expand the *waqf* fund through involvement in investment activities should be emphasised to maximise returns.

Similar to the endowment findings, the diversification in investment portfolios was among the important factors to maximise returns from the *waqf* fund, which could be effectively leveraged to fulfil the needs of the community. There are four potential investment instruments that could be used to generate income from the *waqf* funds in HEIs, namely *Sukuk musyarakah*, corporate *waqf*, *Sukuk ijarah*, and I-REIT.[16] Through these Islamic instruments, the *waqf* funds can be invested swiftly as these are compliant with Shariah rules and principles.

Superior Investment Committees

For endowment, universities can have two structures of endowment governance, either as a part of the university itself or as a separate legal entity. Despite the presence of these two governance structures, most universities delegate the responsibility to govern the endowment funds to the investment committee. This committee also exists for *waqf*, as investment activities of *waqf* should be managed and developed. The investment committee is responsible for determining the asset allocation (e.g. stocks, bonds, alternatives) and manager selection (e.g. active vs passive). In this regard, they play an important role in determining the success of an organisation. At the same time, having a superior investment committee can provide oversight and guidance for endowment management.

Superior investment committees are perceived as active investment committees, and top-performing endowments have active investment committees.[17] The role of the investment committee is highly important for the endowment as it not only controls every minute part of the decisions of the investment staff but also sets a broad policy framework and serves as an informed sounding board. However, the evaluation of whether the endowment has a superior investment committee or vice versa is a question to be answered.

An investigation of endowment teams revealed several characteristics, which were categorised into those belonging to top-performing and low-performing endowments. The characteristics of top-performing endowments included higher investment expertise, efficacy, decision-making independence, and learning commitment.[18] The best practices for investment committees are related to size, expertise, and diversity where they were the basic elements needed for an investment committee's success.[19]

A greater number of investment committee members indicated that the endowment had larger collective wisdom and wider knowledge compared to a committee with a lower number of members. However, this number should not be too high as it leads to inefficient decision-making. An opinion stated that the most effective committee size ranges from five to nine members[20] while another opinion specified the number to range from six to nine members by contending that this range was large enough to ensure diversity (e.g. experience, expertise, and opinion) and small enough for members to provide meaningful contributions while still achieving acceptable decision speed.[21] This argument was consistent with the findings in the 2017 NACUBO Endowment Study, in which the committee size ranged from an average of 6.7 to 9.2. The largest endowments with assets of over $1 billion comprised an average of 9.2 voting members while those with assets under $25 million included, on average, 6.7 voting members.[22] The study also illustrated that the investment committee size was influenced by the endowment size. However, the standard set by the NACUBO in Malaysia does not apply to public universities. Besides, the Malaysian government has issued Investment Guidelines on the number of committee members required in an endowment fund, including the *waqf* fund. Regardless of the size of the fund being large or small, six committee members are required, comprising the following:

1) Vice-chancellor or representative as a chairperson
2) A member of the university Board of Directors
3) Two representatives from a professional body
4) Bursar as a member
5) Special unit of university business as the secretariat

Expertise is another fundamental element in determining the success of an investment committee. An endowment's intention to invest in a certain asset class necessitates having experts in that field to derive positive returns. For instance, for an endowment to directly reap benefits from alternative investments requires the presence of experts on alternative investment instruments in their investment committee. The presence of experts in diverse asset classes could offer more benefits to an endowment as they could engender higher portfolio diversification.[23] Similar to the *waqf*, endowment investments conducted based on Shariah rules and principles require investment committee members to have expertise in Shariah to verify whether or not an investment is legally allowed in Islam. Notably, the appointment of the Shariah experts in the endowment and *waqf* investment committee is not uncommon in Malaysia, as it has been practised in banking institutions to comply with the Shariah governance framework in the country. This is typically practised through the appointment of the Shariah Committee or Shariah Panel. Siddiqi clarified the role of Shariah experts as follows:[24]

> Shariah experts do care for maqasid al-Shariah. As I have argued elsewhere, there are numerous recent examples of fatawa given based on maqasid. The problem in my opinion is not willingness to take maqasid into account. The challenge comes from the nature of the task in the new environment. These are tasks calling for not only economic analysis but drawing upon the latest developments in other social sciences like sociology, psychology, political science and management. Lacking proper institutional arrangements for training to do the task, with its necessary backup in terms of fundamental research, instances of malfunction have been increasing in recent years,

causing anxieties in the market and raising the possibility of a backlash in terms of consumer rejection.

Diversity is another basic criterion determining whether or not an investment committee is successful. A committee with diverse members in terms of professional and committee experiences, education, gender, age, and race could make better decisions compared to less diverse committees because of issues related to group dynamics, such as groupthink and confirmation bias, and group polarisation can be limited.[25] It also offers the best opportunity to enhance the effectiveness of committees by diversifying their membership. At the same time, the diversity is also able to be more relevant and important in measuring the performance of an organisation.[26] Harjoto, Laksmana, and Yang examined the relationship between board diversity (e.g. gender, race, age, tenure, and expertise) and board performance in corporate investment oversight and found that gender, race, age, and board performance were not related, whereas tenure and expertise were negatively associated with suboptimal investments. Therefore, the authors suggested that diverse experiential boards adopt better investment decisions than homogenous experiential boards.[27]

Highly Skilled Investment Managers

An endowment fund involves an asset that should be invested to generate a stable income stream for an institution. This income-generation mechanism is also applied in *waqf* to ensure the generation of long-term benefits. One of the parties that play a significant role in ensuring that the endowment investment is suitably managed and succeeds is its manager. In *waqf*, this party is known as *mutawalli*. With the oversight and guidance from the investment committees, the investment managers decide how the funds should be invested to ensure guaranteed future returns because risk and return characteristics of each asset class (e.g. cash, fixed interest, property, alternative investments, and shares) differ, leading each asset class to behave differently over time, as illustrated in Figure 4.2.

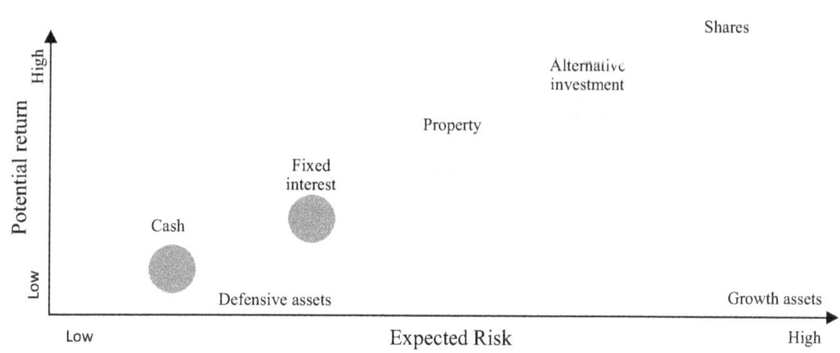

Figure 4.2 Asset Class Risk and Return Characteristics

Source: UniSuper.[28]

Investment management in universities comprises two types—managed either by the investment office in the university itself or by an external asset management firm. Examples of universities applying the first type of investment management include Yale University (i.e. Yale Investments Office) and Emory University (i.e. Emory Investment Management Office). By contrast, examples of universities applying the second type of investment management are Harvard University (i.e. Harvard Management Company [HMC]), the University of Texas and Texas A&M University Systems (i.e. The University of Texas/Texas A&M Investment Company), and Duke University (i.e. Duke Management Company).

Despite two types of investment management, the selection of managers of endowment and *waqf* funds needs to be emphasised to ensure the selection of the right manager. There are three criteria for the selection of investment managers: 1) investment performance, 2) investment philosophy, and 3) professional skills.[29] However, only managers with skills can contribute to the success of university endowments because they can explain the differences in investment performance[30] to generate more returns. Therefore, managerial skill is the key to developing successful portfolios. The importance of this criterion for selecting investment managers was emphasised by Ellis, who contended that managers with professional skills learn through an unpleasant experience, leading to their meticulous investment ('bold, but not too bold' and 'modern, but not too modern') without following the way of the crowd.[31] This criterion was also applied by Yale in selecting their investment managers. In the Malaysian context, the SCM has listed the following criteria for qualifying as an investment manager (especially external):[32]

1) Is duly licensed or authorised by the relevant authority;
2) Has adequate financial resources;
3) Has an adequate track record in the performance of the function; and
4) Has adequate and appropriate human resources, systems, procedures, and processes to perform the function in compliance with applicable requirements and policies, including the procedures on internal controls.

Given that external managers can be appointed for investment management at universities, management fees are another aspect that needs to be considered in the selection besides their skills. The evaluation of management fees by the university is important, especially for universities that implement an active investment strategy to achieve higher returns. Considering the controversy of high payment to internal investment managers at some schools, the payment to external investment managers may be higher.[33] This was illustrated through the survey by Callan Associates, which stated that

> External investment management fees represent the lion's share of total fund expenses at 90%. This figure has grown steadily over time, from 83% in 1998. The increase can largely be attributed to growing allocations to more expensive alternative asset classes, namely hedge funds and private equity.[34]

The top-performing college endowments, such as that of Yale University, offer higher payments to external managers. Although it was criticised, Yale argued in its annual report that a low-cost passive strategy would have 'shortchanged' the Ivy League School students and faculty.[35] Consequent to higher payments to external managers, Yale emerged as the university with the second-largest endowment fund in the world.[36]

Given the difficulty in accessing the information on fees paid by an institution to external managers, this study referred to the analysis by Charles Skorina & Company for the three fiscal years from 2013 to 2015.[37] The analysis, presented in Table 4.3, shows that all universities (only 9 out of 15 universities responded) paid a higher amount of money to external managers compared to internal managers, with an average of 124 basis points, which was $112,573,684. However, the total management cost of universities remained at a satisfactory level if combined with payment to external managers, which averaged 143 basis points, which was $131,686,416. The Commonfund Institute stated that an endowment is considered 'well-diversified' if the total management cost is between 100 and 175 basis points,[38] which is around $17,230,000–$509,407,000.

Table 4.3 Management Costs Incurred by University Endowments

	School	*Internal Costs $*	*Internal Cost %*	*External Costs $*	*External Cost %*	*Total Costs $*	*Total Costs %*
1	Amherst College	2,115,000	0.10	27,500,000	1.31	29,615,000	1.41
2	Boston University	4,102,333	0.26	15,064,403	0.97	19,166,737	1.23
3	Columbia University	41,514,333	0.46	104,401,188	1.17	145,915,521	1.62
4	Grinnell College	2,820,000	0.16	15,444,667	0.90	18,264,667	1.06
5	Harvard University	85,386,400	0.24	426,932,000	1.20	512,318,400	1.44
6	New York University	4,048,000	0.12	42,808,667	1.30	46,856,667	1.43
7	Princeton University	22,000,000	0.11	270,000,000	1.31	292,000,000	1.42
8	Washington University, St Louis	5,583,411	0.09	80,970,295	1.25	86,553,706	1.34
9	Wellesley College	4,445,109	0.24	23,767,602	1.36	28,212,711	1.60
Mean		**19,112,732**	**0.20**	**112,573,684**	**1.24**	**131,686,416**	**1.43**

Source: Skorina & Company.[39]

In recent years, the investment portfolio of endowment funds managed by external parties has become relatively common despite their fairly expensive fees. In this regard, Narv Narvekar, the Chief Executive Officer (CEO) of HMC, reminded us that

> In the past, HMC's unique approach of investing in internally-managed portfolios generated superior returns. In recent years, however, the tremendous flow of capital to external managers has created a great deal of competition for both talent and ideas, therefore making it more difficult to attract and retain the necessary investment expertise while also remaining sufficiently nimble to exploit rapidly changing opportunities.[40]

This can be attributed to endowments with similar characteristics (e.g. Carnegie Classification, location and market value), which tended to choose the same external managers.[41]

Highlighting how the manager is selected at Yale University is important. Yale 'pays particularly close attention to start-up and early stage firms run by seasoned principals, believing that investment talent and entrepreneurial drive outweigh the risks of backing an unproven firm'.[42] Therefore, the performance of an endowment depends on the management not only by established managers or firms but also by those who are still at an initial stage of their establishment. Moreover, the management costs charged by managers of firms in the start-up and early stage may be lower compared to those charged by established firms or managers, thus leading to cost savings for the university.

In Malaysia, if a university attempts to appoint external managers to manage its endowment fund, the selection of the managers is routed through the SCM because of its power to regulate all matters related to unit trust schemes. Universities can appoint fund managers only among the companies registered with the SCM. These companies are listed in Table 4.4 (as of November 2019).

Table 4.4 List of Islamic Fund Management Companies (IFMC) as of November 2019

No.	*IFMC*	*Status*
1	Aberdeen Standard Islamic Investments (M) Sdn Bhd	Foreign
2	AIIMAN Asset Management Sdn Bhd	Local
3	AmIslamic Funds Management Sdn Bhd	Local
4	Amundi Islamic Malaysia Sdn Bhd	Foreign
5	BIMB Investment Management Bhd	Local
6	BNP Paribas Asset Management Najmah Malaysia Sdn Bhd	Foreign
7	Eastspring Al-Wara' Investments Bhd	Foreign
8	Franklin Templeton GSC Asset Management Sdn Bhd	Foreign
9	Guidance Investments Sdn Bhd	Foreign
10	Hong Leong Islamic Asset Management Sdn Bhd	Local
11	i-Vcap Management Sdn Bhd	Local
12	Kenanga Islamic Investors Bhd	Local

(*Continued*)

Table 4.4 (Continued)

No.	*IFMC*	*Status*
13	Maybank Islamic Asset Management Sdn Bhd	Local
14	MIDF Amanah Asset Management Bhd	Local
15	Muamalat Invest Sdn Bhd	Local
16	Navis Management (I) Sdn Bhd	Foreign
17	Nomura Islamic Asset Management Sdn Bhd	Foreign
18	PMB Investment Bhd	Local
19	Principal Islamic Asset Management Sdn Bhd	Joint Venture
20	RHB Islamic International Asset Management Bhd	Local
21	Saturna Sdn Bhd	Foreign
22	Threadneedle Asset Management Malaysia Sdn. Bhd.	Foreign
23	UOB Islamic Asset Management Sdn Bhd	Foreign
24	Wahed Technologies Sdn Bhd	Foreign

Source: SCM.[43]

Although the SCM has listed IFMCs that can be appointed by universities to avail of their service for investment in bonds, equities, and properties, its implementation by the *waqf* fund is challenging because of complex management. To illustrate, all *waqf*-related matters are under the state jurisdiction (except for Wilayah Persekutuan Kuala Lumpur, Labuan, and Putrajaya) as stipulated in List 2, the Ninth Schedule, Federal Constitution.[44] For instance, the enactment of Selangor (Section 4),[45] Melaka (Section 32),[46] Negeri Sembilan (Section 5),[47] and Terengganu (Section 4)[48] highlights that MAIN acts as a *mutawalli* (sole trustee) for all *waqf* assets located within the state. Moreover, MAIN is an eligible party for preserving *waqf* properties, maximising its revenues, and distributing them.

Nevertheless, the existing law does not prohibit any other body or institution, including universities, to manage the *waqf* fund at their institutions. The *waqf* fund can be managed with permission or consent from MAIN. In the context of *waqf* management, universities can appoint a corporate body to assist in the management and monitoring of the *waqf* fund to fulfil the *waqf* donors' intention. However, all management activities of the *waqf* fund at universities remain under the control and monitoring of MAIN because of their function as the sole trustee of *waqf* assets in Malaysia. This indicates that the *mutawalli* status granted to universities by MAIN does not replace its authority as the sole trustee of *waqf* assets. Therefore, the appointment of external managers to manage *waqf* investments in universities requires approval from the MAIN. The agreement is signed between the MAIN and universities to ensure that the implementation of the *waqf* fund at universities can be performed in a controlled and trustworthy manner.

Alumni Networks

Besides the aforementioned elements, alumni networks are another important factor that could determine the success of endowment in select universities.[49] Typically, communication between a university and students stops once they graduate and leave the university, and their knowledge of the university, especially the implementation of the endowment fund in the university, also ends. However, information related to the endowment fund in the university should always be communicated to alumni to ensure continuous involvement and update on the endowment progress at the university. In the context of Malaysia, the alumni networks should be built and preserved to benefit the endowment fund at the university. Thus, relationship development with alumni cannot be ignored by the *waqf* because of its important contributions to education, as revealed by various scholars, including Abdul Razak et al.,[50] Gustina and Ihsan,[51] and Mujani and Yaakub.[52]

A study on alumni relationships in Chinese HEIs found that 'creating and sharing' the values (e.g. equality, tolerance, and love) should be positioned as the starting point and ultimate goal in building a sustainable relationship between a university and its alumni.[53] The authors also added that this idea not only drove the alumni to recognise their relationship with the university as a 'destiny community' but also prompted them to share support, honour or disgrace, growth, happiness, and benefits.[54] This finding is consistent with the study conducted by another scholar who found that alumni who shared at least one marginalised social identity with students profiled in fundraising solicitations induced them to offer higher amounts.[55] This strategy has been adopted by Harvard University through their slogan, 'Sharing the Harvard Experience'.[56]

The readiness of alumni to support their universities is associated with their experience during the study period at their respective universities. If alumni have a positive experience while being students, they are more likely to recognise the value of students' experiences and donate to their university. This was validated by Morse and Brooks, who asserted that satisfaction drives alumni to contribute to their university,[57] and further by Wang[58] and Saraeh et al.,[59] who illustrated that alumni's experience was strongly related to their intention to donate. The experience could be developed through mentorship, work placement offers, or university infrastructure improvement.[60] Therefore, such programmes should be built by universities to enable students to create positive experiences, which could induce them to contribute to their universities after they graduate.

A sustainable relationship between a university and its alumni can be built and maintained with the help of related organisations, platforms, and decent access.[61] Generally, universities have an alumni association that employs staff to network and communicate with their alumni. This association is a mechanism to develop and maintain a sustainable relationship between university and its alumni. In relation to that, the role of the alumni association needs to be emphasised, as it is one of the most important factors that encourage alumni to contribute to their alma mater as found by the previous scholar.[62]

To ensure that alumni remain connected with their university, the importance of campus events after graduation should not be overlooked. Such events provide a boost for alumni to initiate life-long relationships with their universities.[63] Universities can conduct various campus events, such as alumni award and recognition events, homecoming celebrations, reunion programmes, ceremonies, game-day events, game watches and postseason events, and travel. These events should be organised by universities to encourage alumni participation in the alumni events. Meanwhile, a study revealed that reunion programmes could significantly increase the size and number of gifts compared to the estimated long-term trend in life cycle giving.[64] In this regard, the alumni events in the form of that programme need to be given more attention by the universities to increase the contributions of funds from the alumni. Universities should invest to fund the cost involved in organising all the aforementioned events since it can determine the fundraising success at those institutions.[65]

The role of alumni in contributing to higher education is significant—the annual survey by CASE reported that alumni accounted for 22.6 per cent ($11.20 billion) of the total voluntary support ($49.60 billion) to HEIs in the U.S. in 2019.[66] Princeton University received the highest contributions from its alumni in the last two academic years, with 59.1 per cent of the contribution.[67] Notably, this university was one of the ten universities with the largest endowment.[68]

In the Malaysian context, over 100,000 individuals graduate from public universities every year. The number of alumni has increased consistently from 123,548 in 2014 to 123,639 in 2015, 124,223 in 2016, and 135,141 in 2017, after which it decreased marginally to 132,518 in 2018, according to data published by the MoE Malaysia in 2019.[69] The maximum number of graduates in 2018 were from UiTM, accounting for a share of approximately 37 per cent (49,076 graduates). This was a lost opportunity as universities were unable to attract contributions despite the large and increasing number of alumni graduating annually. Furthermore, within a period of five years (2014–2018), the employment rate after graduation increased annually, with the highest rate being 79.3 per cent in 2018.

Correspondingly, the unemployment rate declined every year, with the lowest being 20.7 per cent in 2018,[70] as shown in Figure 4.3. Logically, if the percentage

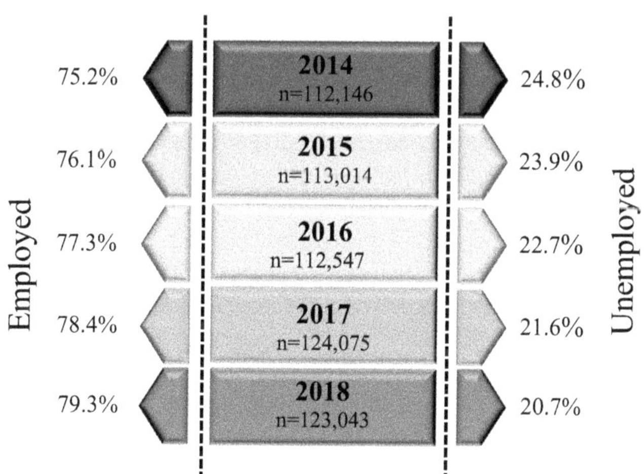

Figure 4.3 Total Graduates and Employment Status (2014–2018)

Source: MoE Malaysia.[71]

of earning graduates increases, more graduates can contribute to their alma mater. For example, in the case of UiTM, with an employment rate of 70 per cent and per head alumni contribution of only RM1 per month to the endowment or *waqf* funds would lead to a total collection of RM34,353.2 per month and RM412,238.4 per year, thus indicating the potential of alumni in enhancing the endowment and *waqf* funds in the university. Therefore, the development of networks should be emphasised in universities to increase alumni's willingness to contribute to the university.

Diversity of Income Sources

The nature of endowment investment in Malaysian universities, especially public universities, is not similar to the top-performing endowment universities where investment is the largest contributor to the growth of universities.[72] The courage of the top-performing universities to expand their endowment size through investments is reflected in the diversification of investment portfolios, including alternative asset investments. Although investment remains the main medium to generate endowment funds in Malaysia, most public universities have a highly passive portfolio, focusing on the local market because the endowment size is too small to take additional risks.[73]

Thus, the generation of endowment funds through other alternatives should be considered to ensure the expansion of endowment funds. Schaffer, Polissar, and Neradilek's study on non-profit success factors demonstrated that the diversity of revenue sources, a component of the business model, was an important variable because of its high correlation with an NPO's success.[74] In this regard, this variable needs to be emphasised since it has a positive correlation with organisational sustainability.[75] This finding is consistent with that of Lee and Shon, who illustrated that the resources obtained from commercial activities were effective for fundraising.[76] Three major types of businesses that can be involved in endowment include (1) services business (e.g. salons, repair shops), (2) merchandising business (buying products at wholesale price and selling them at retail price), and (3) manufacturing business (buy raw materials to produce a new product).

The diversity of income sources is perceived as important for the *waqf*. The significance of this method is reflected in the argument by Mohd Ali, Ahmad, and Ahmad Mahdzan, who reported that the *waqf* has 11,091.82 hectares of land in Malaysia, although 92.8 per cent of it is underdeveloped. This is because of various issues, such as management inefficiencies and lack of funding. The authors added that the development and utilisation of *waqf* lands are not optimised despite their potential to be developed through various instruments. One of the instruments proposed in their study was a business model[77] which was in line with the previously discussed findings on the endowment.

The involvement of NPOs in the business was discussed by Skloot, who contended that the business of NPOs may fail miserably unless certain conditions were fulfilled, such as having a product to sell. NPOs' attempt to engage in business activities indicates that they have a product to sell, a niche market for it, and the ability to fulfil this market demand. Simultaneously, the NPOs should also be cautious of the financial risk and hazards to their organisational mission. Another condition is managerial talent—involvement in business activities requires NPOs to have human resources with skills to perform according to the current market conditions. The third condition is gaining the support of trustees in business, as they can not only contribute money but also provide essential services in various fields (e.g. marketing, law, or accounting). At the same time, they also play a crucial role in analysing whether or not the NPO business is successful. The fourth condition is entrepreneurial spirit. In achieving business success, NPOs need to have employees who possess not only an entrepreneurial spirit but also commercial wisdom as they are expected to perform the job well. The last condition is money or the ability to obtain it. For NPOs with limited financial resources, joint venture has become a highly important mechanism to earn funds. Joint ventures with the private sector are important as the joint venture partner can provide not only funds but also support in terms of marketing and management, which can reduce the business-related risks.[78]

Effective Fundraising

Fundraising is an important activity for many NPOs, including endowment funds—as it is one of the key elements determining an endowment fund's success.[79] Fundraising can help gather voluntary financial contributions from individuals, foundations, corporations, or the government. NPOs can employ various communication channels to attract potential donors to donate money to NPOs through various collection channels available in the market, as depicted in Figure 4.4. The channel diversity leads to fundraising tactics, which can be realised through four segments considered by most fundraising organisations:1) the mass anonymous small gift market, 2) members and their friends' market, 3) affluent citizens' market, and 4) wealthy donors' market,[80] as presented in Table 4.5.

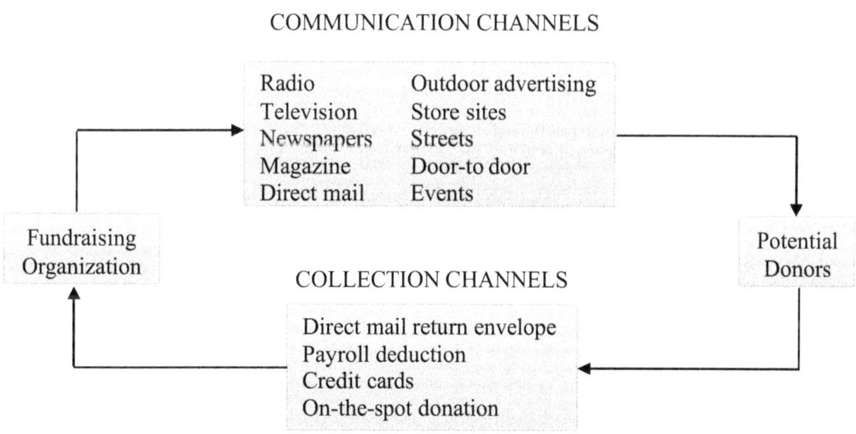

Figure 4.4 Communication and Collection Channels for Fundraising

Source: Kotler and Andreasen.[81]

Table 4.5 Fundraising Methods

Mass Anonymous Small Gift Market	
Charity Cans in Stores, Direct Mail Door-to-Door Solicitation, Street and Sidewalk Solicitation, TV and Radio Marathons Thrift Shops, Plate Passing Cause-Related Marketing	Affinity cards, Raffles, Rummage Sales, Sporting Events, Tours Walkathons, Readathons, Bikeathons, Danceathons, Jogathons, Swimathons Yearbooks
Members and Their Friends' Market	
Affinity Cards, Anniversary Celebrations, Art Shows Auctions Benefits (Theatre, Movies, Sports Events), Bingo Games	Book Sales, Dances Dinners, Suppers, Lunches, Breakfasts Fairs Fashion Shows Parties in Unusual Places Phonathons (Also Called Telethons)
Affluent Citizens' Market	
Convocations Dinners (Invitational and/or Testimonial) Letters From High-Status Individuals	Parlour Meetings Telephone Calls From High-Status Individuals
Wealthy Donors' Market	
Bequests Celebrity Grooming Committee Visit to a Person's Home or Office Memorials	Testimonial Dinner for Wealthy Individuals. A Wealthy Person Invited to Another's Home or Club

Source: Kotler and Andreasen.[82]

The fundraising activities in several NPOs run throughout the year, with most placing their efforts under the umbrella concept of a campaign.[83] Campaign has also become one of the main methods of increasing endowment funds. Kotler and Andreasen defined a campaign as an organised and time-sequenced set of activities and events to raise a given sum of money within a particular time.[84] Typically, a campaign is often designed by fundraisers to induce feelings of guilt, fear, pity, and other negative emotions among potential donors.[85] Campaigns are generally of two types, the annual campaign and capital campaign. Kotler and Andreasen described that an annual campaign is organised to increase the target amount of money every year for various programme operations. The capital campaign comprises a special set of activities designed to raise a large amount of money for a one-time major undertaking or expansion, although it is not conducted annually.[86] The selection of this type of campaign depends on the goals and strategies of the NPOs.

Campaigns entail high investment allocation by the endowment—Chapman, Masser, and Louis revealed that the campaign is the strongest factor determining fundraising success.[87] This was also proven by Harvard University's experience in raising $9.62 billion through its latest campaign.[88] As previously discussed, despite the existence of various communication channels to attract potential donors, all of them need to be paid for and are considered classical trade fairs, as pointed out by Tomczak, Reinecke, and Kuss.[89] Furthermore, each communication channel has a different percentage in inspiring donors to donate based on the 2018 Global Trends in Giving Report.[90]

In recent years, social media has emerged as a strong influencer and has been rapidly gaining popularity in society. This shift has also been leveraged by fundraisers. The use of social media by NPOs for the effective delivery of their marketing messages has been increasing.[91] The significance of social media for fundraising campaigns was revealed by various scholars including Ortiz et al.,[92] Lagazio and Querci,[93] and Lund.[94] The 2018 Global Trends in Giving Report illustrated that social media inspires people the most to offer charity compared to other tools, as depicted in Figure 4.5.

Social media comprises various types, such as social networks, media sharing networks, discussion forums, blogging, and publishing networks. Among these, social networks are viewed as a crucial channel for social fundraising—if an organisation is a part of the social network of an individual, they would actively engage in volunteer service or contribute to the organisation.[95] This was validated in the report by Nonprofits Source, which found that 55 per cent of people in the U.S. who were involved with non-profits on their social networks eventually initiated certain actions.[96] The importance of social networks for the success of fundraising was discussed by various scholars, such as Wang, Osatuyi, and Hou,[97] and Zhou and Ye.[98] The significance of social media was also supported by Milosevic, who contended that strong social networks can contribute to larger fundraising.[99]

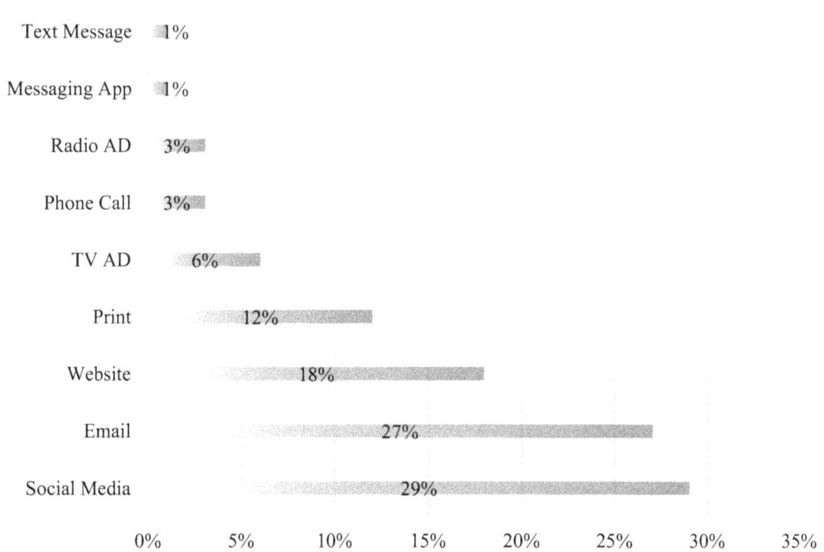

Figure 4.5 Communication Channels That Inspire Giving the Most

Source: 2018 Global Trends in Giving Report.[100]

Various social networking sites, such as Facebook, Instagram, Twitter, and YouTube, currently exist. According to the 2018 Global Trends in Giving Report, 56 per cent of donors worldwide stated that Facebook inspires them to give while 20 percent mentioned Instagram, 13 per cent mentioned Twitter, and 6 per cent stated YouTube, as illustrated in Figure 4.6. In the Asian context, Facebook remained the most important tool, inspiring 63 per cent of donors to donate, followed by Instagram with 13 per cent, and YouTube with 9 per cent. In this context, fundraising campaigns for endowments organised through Facebook, especially in Malaysia, need to be considered as it influences donor contributions. The campaign was also organised to access several potential donors in Malaysia. To illustrate this point, the number of Facebook subscribers in Malaysia is 22 million, as reported by the Internet World Stats.[101] Facebook is also regarded as an effective instrument to reach a greater number of alumni and build an effective relationship more easily and with lower costs. There is a scholar who found that alumni who had 'liked' the university Facebook page had distinctive roles on alumni identity comparable to those who attended a university event.[102] Besides, sharing activities on Facebook influenced campaigns that aimed to supply public goods.[103]

Similar to endowment, a campaign is also important for *waqf* because it can increase the social awareness of contribution to the *waqf*. The awareness campaign on *waqf* is among the factors that should not be overlooked by institutions that implement it as the success and sustainability of this instrument depend on society's awareness. This has been discussed by several scholars, such as Mohamed Nor and Yaakub,[104] Oladapo, Oseni, and Mohammed,[105] and Hasan and Siraj.[106] In

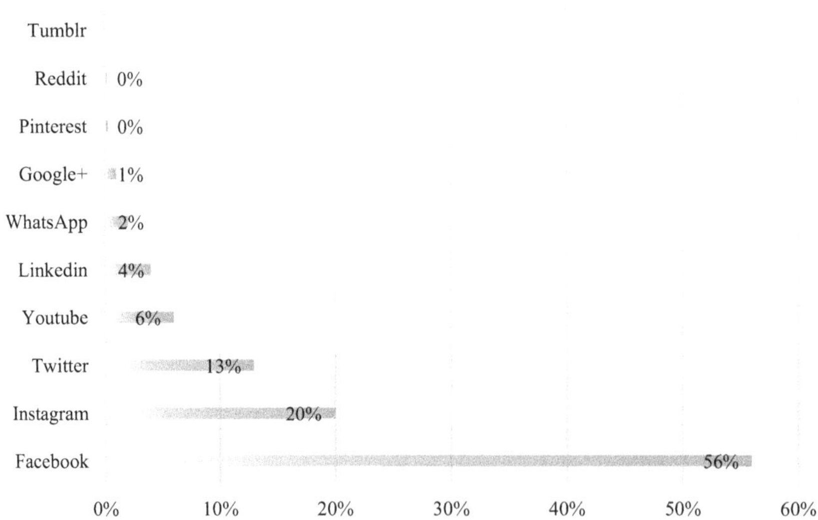

Figure 4.6 Social Networks That Inspire Giving the Most

Source: 2018 Global Trends in Giving Report.[107]

this case, the methods discussed earlier may be considered in the implementation of *waqf* campaigns given ample evidence of their effectiveness.

Religion was one of the vital elements in encouraging an individual's giving behaviour. A study found that religious obligation was strongly associated with donors' intention to repeat the contribution to *waqf* in the future.[108] To ensure that giving becomes a culture for the Muslim community, religious teaching was necessary and added that people will contribute if they have religious consciousness to realise Islamic obligations. Accordingly, Charseatd suggested involving religious beliefs in performing promotional programmes as these could enhance attitudes towards donation and create a positive image.[109] Therefore, religious beliefs should be highlighted when organising *waqf* and endowment campaigns to encourage contributions from more donors.

As highlighted earlier in this subsection, donors can donate money through various collection channels, such as direct mail return envelopes, payroll deduction, credit cards, and on-the-spot donations. Given the rapid development in information technology, NPOs leverage it not only to provide information and persuade potential donors to contribute but also to facilitate the donors to contribute through the implementation of online giving channel. This was in line with the argument by Zhou and Ye,[110] who revealed that social media networking had a positive relationship with online donations. Flannery, Haris, and Rhine also examined online giving within 24 major national NPOs and found that online giving was an increasingly significant source in the acquisition of new donors, and younger generation online donors were more likely to donate a large amount compared to traditional donors.[111]

The 2018 Global Trends in Giving Report recorded that 54 per cent of donors around the world preferred to give online through the use of either credit or debit cards. Meanwhile, 51 per cent of donors in Asia were found to prefer online donations.[112] Various online contribution methods, such as PayPal, mobile app/wallet, and text message, are available in the market. The most popular method among these worldwide, including in Asia, was PayPal, with 9 per cent and 13 per cent usage, respectively.[113] These elements are summarised in Figure 4.7.

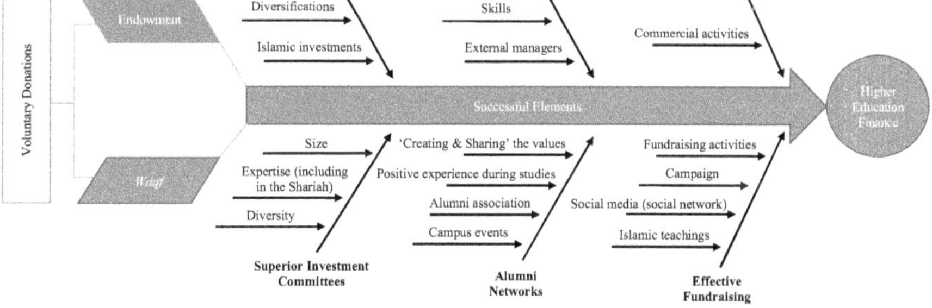

Figure 4.7 Conceptual Framework of the Successful Elements of Endowment and *Waqf*

Source: Developed by the authors.

Conclusion

This chapter presented the elements leading to the success of endowment and *waqf* funds in higher education based on theoretical grounding. One of the studies that discussed this issue was that by Lerner, Schoar, and Wang,[114] who demonstrated that endowment performance in more selective universities was achieved through asset allocation to alternative assets. Several factors led to the success of investments in this asset class, including highly skilled investment managers, superior investment committees, and alumni networks. Given that the risks of investments in alternative assets were higher compared to the traditional assets and the investment diversification strategy recommended by scholars, this chapter adopted the term appropriate investment, which comprised discussions on the investment of endowment funds, including the *waqf* fund, to increase its balance. At the same time, to ensure this chapter's comprehensiveness and suitability in the Malaysian context, other elements (i.e. diversity of income sources and effective fundraising campaign) were reviewed because of their possibility to contribute to the success of endowment and *waqf* funds. The elements discussed in the chapter were used to investigate factors that can help the successful implementation of endowment and *waqf* funds in Malaysian public universities.

Notes

1 J. Lerner, A. Schoar, and J. Wang, "Secrets of the Academy: The Drivers of University Endowment Success," *Journal of Economic Perspectives* 22, no. 3 (2008): 207–22, 214–16
2 D. Swensen, *Pioneering Portfolio Management: An Unconventional Approach to Institutional Investment* (New York: Free Press, 2009).
3 Lerner, Schoar, and Wang, "Secrets of the Academy: The Drivers of University Endowment Success."
4 "Alternative Investments 2020: An Introduction to Alternative Investments," *World Economic Forum* (Cologny/Geneva, 2015), http://www3.weforum.org/docs/WEF_Alternative_Investments_2020_An_Introduction_to_AI.pdf.
5 Lerner, Schoar, and Wang, "Secrets of the Academy: The Drivers of University Endowment Success," 218.
6 A. Taback et al., *Alternative Thinking-Alternative Investments: The Missing Piece in Portfolios?* (New York: Wells Fargo Investment Institute, 2018).
7 Lerner, Schoar, and Wang, "Secrets of the Academy: The Drivers of University Endowment Success," 218.
8 K. Ryder, "The University Endowment Model: Cracked, Not Broken," *CNN Money*, 12 July 2010, accessed on 2 October 2019, https://money.cnn.com/2010/07/06/news/economy/university_endowments.fortune/index.htm
9 S. G. Dimmock, N. Wang, and J. Yang, "The Endowment Model and Modern Portfolio Theory," *NBER Working Paper Series*, no. 25559 (2019): 1–62, 2.
10 M. W. Azlen and I. Zermati, "Investing Like the Harvard and Yale Endowment Funds," *Alternative Investment Analyst Review* 6, no. 3 (2017): 7–13, 7.
11 "Governor's Speech at the 2nd IFSB Summit: The Rise and Effectiveness of Corporate Governance in the Islamic Financial Services Industry," *Bank Negara Malaysia*, 2005, www.bnm.gov.my/index.php?ch=en_speech&pg=en_speech&ac=170&lang=en%0D.
12 *List of Shariah-Compliant Securities by the Shariah Advisory Council of the Securities Commission Malaysia* (Kuala Lumpur: Securities Commission Malaysia, 2019), 2–4.

13 *List of Shariah-Compliant Securities by the Shariah Advisory Council of the Securities Commission Malaysia,* 14.
14 "Statistics for Islamic Capital Market in Malaysia," *Securities Commission Malaysia*, accessed 19 July 2022, www.sc.com.my/analytics/islamic-capital-market.
15 "Sustainable and Responsible Investments," *Capital Markets Malaysia*, accessed 22 November 2019, www.capitalmarketsmalaysia.com/islamic-capital-market/sustainable-and-responsible-investments/.
16 R. Hashim, R. Ramli, N. F. Dahalan, N. Y. Ismon, and S. Romli, "Prospek Penjanaan Dana Wakaf Institusi Pengajian Tinggi," *Paper presented, International Conference on Waqf*, Kuala Terengganu, 2015, 11.
17 Lerner, Schoar, and Wang, "Secrets of the Academy: The Drivers of University Endowment Success," 220.
18 M. Lord, "Smaller University Endowments: Team Characteristics, Portfolio Composition and Performance," *Qualitative Research in Financial Markets* 6, no. 1 (2014): 4–32, 4.
19 P. M. Bosse, D. M. Grim, and F. Chism, "Duty, Opportunity, Mastery: Investment Committee Best Practices," *Vanguard Research* (2017): 1–20, 18.
20 C. D. Ellis, "Best Practice Investment Committees," *The Journal of Portfolio Management* 37, no. 2 (2011): 139–47, 139, https://doi.org/10.3905/jpm.2011.37.2.139.
21 Bosse, Grim, and Chism, "Duty, Opportunity, Mastery: Investment Committee Best Practices," 7.
22 National Association of College and University Business Officers (NACUBO) and Commonfund Institute, *NACUBO—Commonfund Study of Endowments* (Washington, DC: NACUBO, 2017), 67.
23 M. Lord, "University Endowment Committees: How a Learning Orientation and Knowledge Factors Contribute to Portfolio Diversification and Performance," *The European Journal of Finance* (2014): 1–25, 1, https://doi.org/10.1080/1351847X.2013.879536.
24 M. N. Siddiqi, "Shariah, Economics and the Progress of Islamic Finance: The Role of Shariah Experts," *Seventh Harvard Forum on Islamic Finance* (2006): 1–7, 3, www.siddiqi.com/mns/Role_of_Shariah_Experts.htm.
25 Bosse, Grim, and Chism, "Duty, Opportunity, Mastery: Investment Committee Best Practices," 18.
26 M. C. Díaz-Fernández, M. R. González-Rodríguez, and B. Simonetti, "The Role Played by Job and Non-Job-Related TMT Diversity Traits on Firm Performance and Strategic Change," *Management Decision* 54, no. 5 (2016): 1110–39, 1110, https://doi.org/10.1108/MD-10-2015-0464.
27 M. A. Harjoto, I. Laksmana, and Y. Yang, "Board Diversity and Corporate Investment Oversight," *Journal of Business Research* 90 (2018): 40–47, 46, https://doi.org/10.1016/j.jbusres.2018.04.033.
28 "Asset Class Explained," *UniSuper*, accessed on 3 October 2019, www.unisuper.com.au/investments/investment- basics/asset-classes-explained#Asset class characteristics.
29 A. S. Donnelly, *The Three Rs of Investing* (Homewood, IL: Dow Jones-Irwin, 1985), 192 & 193.
30 Lerner, Schoar, and Wang, "Secrets of the Academy: The Drivers of University Endowment Success," 218.
31 Ellis, "Best Practice Investment Committees," 143.
32 Securities Commission Malaysia (SCM), *Guidelines on Unit Trust Funds* (Kuala Lumpur: SC, 2008), 5–2.
33 Lerner, Schoar, and Wang, "Secrets of the Academy: The Drivers of University Endowment Success," 218–19.
34 Callan Associates, *Cost of Doing Business Survey: Executive Summary* (San Francisco: Callan Associates, 2013), 2.
35 Yale University, *The Yale Endowment* (New Haven: Yale University, 2016), 18.

36 E. Kerr, "10 Universities with the Biggest Endowments," *U.S. News & World Report*, 2019, accessed on 25 October 2020, www.usnews.com/education/best-colleges/the-short-list-college/articles/10-universities-with-the-biggest-endowments%0D.
37 "Endowment Costs: The Secret History," *Charles Skorina & Company*, 2017, accessed on 4 February 2020, www.charlesskorina.com/?p=5211%0D.
38 Commonfund Institute, *Counting the Cost: A Commonfund Viewpoint* (Wilton, CT: Commonfund Institute, 2017), 6, www.commonfund.org/wp-content/uploads/2017/03/Viewpoint-Counting-the-Cost.pdf.
39 Skorina, "Endowment Costs: The Secret History."
40 G. Ryan, "Harvard's Endowment Manager Cutting Half Its Staff," *Boston Business Journal* (2017), accessed on 3 February 2020, www.bizjournals.com/boston/news/2017/01/25/harvards-endowment-manager-cutting-half-its-staff.html
41 C. Kaffe, "Peer Effects in Investment Manager Selection: Evidence from University Endowments," *Judge Business School, University of Cambridge* (2019): 1–38, 3.
42 Yale University, *The Yale Endowment* (New Haven: Yale University, 2017), 24.
43 "List of Islamic Fund Management Companies," *Securities Commission Malaysia*, 2019, accessed 18 October 2020, www.sc.com.my/development/icm-v2/statistics/list-of-islamic-fund-management-companies.
44 List 2, the Ninth Schedule, Federal Constitution of Malaysia.
45 Wakaf (Selangor) Enactment 2015, *Enakmen Wakaf (Negeri Selangor) 2015*, accessed 4 December 2019, http://www2.esyariah.gov.my/esyariah/mal/portalv1/enakmen2011/State_Enact_Ori.nsf/f831ccddd195843f48256fc600141e84/b5cf2dc1a89d351848257f6f000e4f0d?OpenDocument.
46 Wakaf (Melaka) Enactment 2005, *Enakmen Wakaf (Melaka) 2005*, accessed 4 December 2019, http://www2.esyariah.gov.my/esyariah/mal/portalv1/enakmen2011/State_Enact_Ori.nsf/100ae747c72508e748256faa00188094/f9beeec5a2228b8c4825715e001612d9?OpenDocument.
47 Wakaf (Negeri Sembilan) Enactment 2005. *Enakmen Wakaf (Negeri Sembilan) 2005*, accessed 4 December 2019, http://www2.esyariah.gov.my/esyariah/mal/portalv1/enakmen/State_Enact_Ori.nsf/100ae747c72508e748256faa00188094/ba87 8ed674ffad6548 2571490015bafd?OpenDocument.
48 Wakaf (Terengganu) Enactment 2016. *Enakmen Wakaf (Terengganu) 2016*, accessed 30 July 2021, www.maidam.gov.my/images/files/enakmen/ENAKMEN%20WAKAF%20 2016-WARTA%20KERAJAAN.pdf.
49 Lerner, Schoar, and Wang, "Secrets of the Academy: The Drivers of University Endowment Success," 208.
50 D. Abdul Razak et al., "A Study on Sources of Waqf Funds for Higher Education in Selected Countries," *Adam Akademi* 6, no. 1 (2016): 113–28, 125.
51 Gustina, and Hidayatul Ihsan. "Financing Higher Education through Waqf Assets." *Paper presented, International Conference of Applied Science on Engineering, Business, Linguistics and Information Technology (ICo-ASCNITech)*, Padang, Indonesia, 2017, 93.
52 W. K. Mujani and N. I. Yaakub, "Waqf for Higher Education in Malaysia: Overview on Challenges," *European Journal of Multidisciplinary Studies* 5, no. 1 (2017): 455–61, 457.
53 L. Zhimin, C. Chunlian, and W. Xian, "Alumni Relations in Chinese HEIs: Case Studies of Three Major Universities," *Frontiers of Education in China* 11, no. 1 (2016): 74–101, 97.
54 Ibid., 91.
55 N. D. Drezner, "Philanthropic Mirroring: Exploring Identity-Based Fundraising in Higher Education," *The Journal of Higher Education* (2017): 1–35, 1.
56 *Sharing the Harvard Experience*, Harvard Alumni (2012), accessed on 22 October 2019, https://alumni.harvard.edu/stories/sharing-harvard-experience.
57 R. Morse and E. Brooks, "Best Colleges Ranking Criteria and Weights," *U.S. News & World Report*, 9 September 2018, accessed on 26 October 2020, www.usnews.com/education/best-colleges/articles/ranking-criteria-and-weights.

58 Y. Wang, "What Influences Alumni Donations?" *Journal of Economics, Business and Management* 6, no. 4 (2018): 160–63, 160.
59 U. N. Saraeh, N. I. Abdul Rahman, N. Noordin, S. N. Ramlan, R. Ahmad, and M. F. Sakdan, "The Influence of Students' Experience on Alumni Giving in Malaysian Public Educational Institution," *Paper presented, MATEC Web of Conferences*, 150, EDP Sciences, 2018, 1–6.
60 M. L. Gallo, "How Are Graduates and Alumni Featured in University Strategic Plans? Lessons from Ireland," *Perspectives: Policy and Practice in Higher Education* 22, no. 3 (2018): 92–97, https://doi.org/10.1080/13603108.2017.1397065.
61 Zhimin, Chunlian, and Xian, "Alumni Relations in Chinese HEIs: Case Studies of Three Major Universities," 97.
62 Wang, "What Influences Alumni Donations?" 160.
63 D. J. Weerts and J. M. Ronca, "Profiles of Supportive Alumni: Donors, Volunteers, and Those Who 'Do It All'," *International Journal of Educational Advancement* 7, no. 1 (2007): 20–34, 32, https://doi.org/10.1057/palgrave.ijea.2150044.
64 J. H. Grant and D. L. Lindauer, "The Economics of Charity Life-Cycle Patterns of Alumnae Contributions," *Eastern Economic Journal* 12, no. 2 (1986): 129–41, 138.
65 W. B. Harrison, "College Relations and Fund-Raising Expenditures: Influencing the Probability of Alumni Giving to Higher Education," *Economics of Education Review* 14, no. 1 (1995): 73–84, 80, https://doi.org/10.1016/0272-7757(94)00035-5.
66 A. E. Kaplan, *Voluntary Support of Education* (London, Mexico City, Singapore and Washington, DC: Council for Advancement and Support of Education, 2020), 4.
67 J. Moody, "10 Schools Where Alumni Donate," *U.S. News & World Report*, December 18, 2018, accessed on 26 October 2020, www.usnews.com/education/best-colleges/the-short-list-college/articles/universities-where-the-most-alumni-donate.
68 Kerr, "10 Universities with the Biggest Endowments."
69 Kementerian Pendidikan Malaysia (KPM), *Laporan Kajian Pengesanan Graduan 2018* (Putrajaya: KPM, 2019).
70 Ibid., 10.
71 Ibid.
72 Lerner, Schoar, and Wang, "Secrets of the Academy: The Drivers of University Endowment Success," 208.
73 B. Abdul Hamid, W. Hassan-Kamarudin, and S. Abdul Syahid Sowell, "The Endowment Fund as a Source of Sustainability for Higher Education in Malaysia: Maximising Investment Returns," *ISRA Research Paper*, no. 103 (2018): 1–32, 26.
74 S. Schaffer, N. Polissar, and M. Neradilek, *Exploratory Analysis of Nonprofit Success Factors* (Seattle, WA: Public Interest Management Group, 2015), 3 & 4.
75 S. I. Ceptureanu et al., "Sustainability Perceptions in Romanian Non-Profit Organizations: An Exploratory Study Using Success Factor Analysis," *Sustainability* 10, no. 297 (2018): 1–23, 16.
76 Y. J. Lee and J. Shon, "What Affects the Strategic Priority of Fundraising? A Longitudinal Study of Art, Culture and Humanity Organizations' Fundraising Expenses in the USA," *Voluntas* (2018), 8, https://doi.org/10.1007/s11266-018-9982-1.
77 N. Mohd Ali, R. Ahmad, and N. S. Ahmad Mahdzan, "The Need of an Effective Business Model for Waqf Land Development in Malaysia," *Paper presented, The 20th International Research Conference on Business, Economics, and Social Sciences*, Istanbul, Turkey, 2015, 1–12, 1.
78 E. Skloot, "Should Not-for-Profits Go into Business?," in *Public & Nonprofit Marketing: Cases & Readings*, ed. C. H. Lovelock and C. B. Weinberg (Canada: The Scientific Press and John Wiley & Sons, 1984), 361–65, 362–64.
79 R. Franz and S. Kranner, *University Endowments: A Primer* (Charlottesville, VA: CFA Institute Research Foundation, 2019).
80 P. Kotler and A. Andreasen, *Strategic Marketing for Nonprofit Organizations*, 4th ed. (New Jersey: Prentice Hall, 1991), 295.

81 Ibid.
82 Ibid.
83 Ibid., 298.
84 Ibid.
85 R. Bennett, *Nonprofit Marketing and Fundraising* (London and New York: Routledge, Taylor & Francis Group, 2019), 5.
86 Kotler and Andreasen, *Strategic Marketing for Nonprofit Organizations*, 298.
87 C. M. Chapman, B. M. Masser, and W. R. Louis, "The Champion Effect in Peer-to-Peer Giving: Successful Campaigns Highlight Fundraisers More than Causes," *Nonprofit and Voluntary Sector Quarterly* (2018), 1–21, https://doi.org/10.1177/0899764018805196.
88 J. S. Rosenberg, "Harvard Campaign Totals $9.62 Billion," *Harvard Magazine*, September 20, 2018, accessed on 4 November 2019, https://harvardmagazine.com/campaigntotal-18%0D.
89 T. Tomczak, S. Reinecke, and A. Kuss, "Planning the Marketing Mix," in *Strategic Marketing* (Wiesbaden: Springer Gabler, 2018), 171–221, 193.
90 Nonprofit Tech for Good, *2018 Global Trends in Giving Report* (n.p.: Nonprofit Tech for Good, 2018), 23.
91 J. Weerawardena, "Non-Profit Marketing Strategy," in *Transformational Leadership and Not for Profits and Social Enterprises*, ed. K. Wiltshire, A. Malhotra, and M. Axelsen, 1st ed. (New York: Routledge, 2018), 332.
92 R. A. Ortiz et al., "Engaging a Community for Rare Genetic Disease: Best Practices and Education from Individual Crowdfunding Campaigns," *Interactive Journal of Medical Research* 7, no. 1 (2018): 1–11, 1.
93 C. Lagazio and F. Querci, "Exploring the Multi-Sided Nature of Crowdfunding Campaign Success," *Journal of Business Research* 90 (2018): 318–24, 323.
94 B. Lund, "Universities Engaging Social Media Users: An Investigation of Quantitative Relationships between Universities' Facebook Followers/Interactions and University Attributes," *Journal of Marketing for Higher Education* (2019): 1–17, 14, https://doi.org/10.1080/08841241.2019.1641875.
95 H. E. Brady, K. L. Schlozman, and S. Verba, "Prospecting for Participants: Rational Expectations and the Recruitment of Political Activists," *American Political Science Review* 93, no. 1 (1999): 153–68, 153.
96 "Social Media Giving Statistics," *Nonprofits Source* (2018), accessed on 4 November 2019, https://nonprofitssource.com/online-giving-statistics/#Social.
97 B. Wang, B. Osatuyi, and W. Hou, "Effects of Donor- and Supporter-Based Campaign Networks on Crowdfunding Campaign Success," in *Proceedings of the 50th Hawaii International Conference on System Sciences*, ed. T. X. Bui and R. Sprague (2017), IEEE Computer Society, 5589–98, 5596.
98 H. Zhou and S. Ye, "Fundraising in the Digital Era: Legitimacy, Social Network, and Political Ties Matter in China," *Voluntas: International Journal of Voluntary and Nonprofit Organizations* (2019): 9.
99 M. Milosevic, "Skills or Networks? Success and Fundraising Determinants in a Low Performing Venture Capital Market," *Research Policy* 47, no. 1 (2018): 49–60, 49.
100 Nonprofit Tech for Good, *2018 Global Trends in Giving Report*, 9.
101 "Asia Marketing Research, Internet Usage, Population Statistics and Facebook Subscribers," *Internet World Stats* (2019), accessed on 19 November 2019, www.internetworldstats.com/asia.htm.
102 J. L. R. Dillon, "Factors and Characteristics of Alumni Role Identity: Implications for Practice in Higher Education Fundraising and Alumni Relations," Ph.D. thesis, The Faculty of the Schools of Education, the University of San Francisco, 2017, ii.
103 Y. Hong, Y. Hu, and G. Burtch, "How Does Social Media Affect Contribution to Public versus Private Goods in Crowdfunding Campaigns?," in *Thirty Sixth International Conference on Information Systems*, Fort Worth, 2015, 1–15, 1.

104 S. Mohamed Nor and N. I. Yaakub, "Educational Endowments Governance for Institutions of Higher Education in Malaysia: A Preliminary Study," *Advanced Science Letters* X, no. XXX–XXX (2015): 1–4, 4.
105 H. B. Oladapo, R. A. Oseni, and M. O. Mohammed, "A Comparative Analysis of Waqf Institution and Endowment Foundation: Determinants of Sustainability," *International Journal of Novel Research in Humanity and Social Sciences* 3, no. 4 (2016): 151–62, 158.
106 R. Hasan and S. A. Siraj, "Toward Developing a Model of Stakeholder Trust in Waqf Institutions," *Islamic Economic Studies* 25, no. Special Issue (2017): 85–109, https://doi.org/10.12816/0036187.
107 Nonprofit Tech for Good, *2018 Global Trends in Giving Report*, 9.
108 F. Johari et al., "Factors That Influence Repeat Contribution of Cash Waqf in Islamic Philanthropy," *Malaysian Accounting Review* 14, no. 2 (2015): 55–78.
109 P. Charseatd, "Role of Religious Beliefs in Blood Donation Behavior among the Youngster in Iran: A Theory of Planned Behavior Perspective," *Journal of Islamic Marketing* 7, no. 3 (2016): 1–20, 14.
110 Zhou and Ye, "Fundraising in the Digital Era: Legitimacy, Social Network, and Political Ties Matter in China," 1.
111 H. Flannery, R. Harris, and C. Rhine, *2008 DonorCentrics Internet Giving Benchmarking Analysis* (Charleston, SC: Target Analytics, 2009), 1.
112 Nonprofit Tech for Good, *2018 Global Trends in Giving Report*, 6 & 18.
113 Ibid.
114 Lerner, Schoar, and Wang, "Secrets of the Academy: The Drivers of University Endowment Success," 8. *Journal of Economic Perspectives* 22, no. 3 (2008): 207–22.

5 Application of Endowment and *Waqf* at Malaysian Public Universities

Introduction

Malaysia is among the countries adopting the cost-sharing concept between public and private sources to provide the higher education finance, especially from the public sector. In reducing the burden of the public and private sectors, the role of philanthropy as one of the sources of higher education finance is being increasingly accepted in Malaysia. All 20 public universities in the country employ endowment funds while 17 of the universities employ *waqf* funds. Notably, the highest total collections for the endowment fund in 2019 were recorded from Universiti Malaya (UM), followed by Universiti Kebangsaan Malaysia (UKM), and Universiti Teknologi Malaysia (UTM) with total collections of RM1.37 billion, RM84 million, and RM74 million, respectively. The university with the highest collections of *waqf* funds was Universiti Putra Malaysia (UPM), followed by Universiti Sains Islam Malaysia (USIM), and Universiti Sultan Zainal Abidin (UniSZA) with total collections of RM10.8 million, RM6.73 million, and RM6.21 million, respectively. Given that these universities were among the top three in the total collection of endowment and *waqf* funds, they were selected for this study.

This chapter discusses further the application of endowment and *waqf* at the selected universities. The chapter begins with the introduction of public universities in Malaysia in the second section, followed by a discussion on the application of endowment and *waqf* at Malaysian public universities from a general perspective in the third section. The fourth section discusses the application of endowment and *waqf* at the selected Malaysian public universities. Finally, the fifth section concludes this chapter.

Malaysian Public Universities

Malaysian HEIs comprise public universities, private universities, polytechnics, and community colleges. As the scope of this chapter involves public universities, the discussions focus more on this sector. Based on the latest statistics provided by the MoHE, 20 public universities[1] in the country were established under the Universities and University Colleges Act 1971 (popularly known as AUKU 1971). These public universities fall under three categories—research university, comprehensive university, and focused university. Malaysia has five research universities,

DOI: 10.4324/9781003435976-5

Table 5.1 Listing and Categorising of Malaysian Public Universities

No.	*Name of Institution*	*Category*
1	Universiti Malaya	Research University
2	Universiti Sains Malaysia	
3	Universiti Kebangsaan Malaysia	
4	Universiti Putra Malaysia	
5	Universiti Teknologi Malaysia	
6	Universiti Islam Antarabangsa Malaysia	Comprehensive University
7	Universiti Malaysia Sarawak	
8	Universiti Malaysia Sabah	
9	Universiti Teknologi Mara	
10	Universiti Utara Malaysia	Focused University
11	Universiti Pendidikan Sultan Idris	
12	Universiti Sains Islam Malaysia	
13	Universiti Malaysia Terengganu	
14	Universiti Tun Hussein Onn Malaysia	
15	Universiti Teknikal Malaysia Melaka	
16	Universiti Malaysia Pahang	
17	Universiti Malaysia Perlis	
18	Universiti Sultan Zainal Abidin	
19	Universiti Malaysia Kelantan	
20	Universiti Pertahanan Nasional Malaysia	

Source: MoHE (directory)[2] and (category).[3]

four comprehensive universities, and 11 focused universities. The lists of universities and their categories are presented in Table 5.1.

Research universities focus on the research field while comprehensive universities offer a wide range of courses and fields of study. Meanwhile, focused universities offer courses in specific areas related to the technical, educational, management, or defence establishment. As these universities are public, the government as the main stakeholder of the national higher education sector funds their expenses. Based on the 'Purple Book' published by the MoHE, the dependence of public universities on government funding exceeded 90 per cent of their expenses.[4] The remaining expenses were covered by tuition fees imposed on students and contributions from the public.

The overall budget allocated to the higher education sector reached RM13.30 billion in 2018, higher than RM12.55 billion allocated in the previous year,[5] with public universities being the main recipients. Although this allocation was likely to be high, its sustainability raised questions given the current higher education system scenario of higher student admissions and increasing costs to fund university operations. In this context, MoHE initiated granting of autonomous power to public universities for income generation. This autonomy entailed universities generating 30 per cent of their income.[6]

The aforementioned initiative was consistent with the Ministry's plan under the Malaysia Education Blueprint 2015–2025 (Higher Education) to reduce the dependence of HEIs on the government. Shift 5 on the Blueprint, which is Financial Sustainability, has highlighted that HEIs in Malaysia should strive to gain additional income sources as an alternative to being financially more flexible, stronger, and sustainable.[7] However, on the flip side, the granted autonomous power may lead to increasing job scopes instead of simply teaching and researching in a place where the expertise of universities is built, trained, groomed, and created to be well-known. The faculty and administration need to be actively involved in income generation for the university to fulfil the recent requirements. In meeting this requirement, training on and exposure to commercialisation and understanding of different funding models are important to develop new sources of income.[8]

The success of leading global universities, such as Harvard University and Yale University, in income generation through the endowment fund has led the Malaysian government to also encourage its implementation in public universities in the country. At the same time, the government also encourages public universities to empower the long-standing *waqf* instrument at the aforementioned institutions. The serious encouragement from the government to public universities to implement endowment and *waqf* instruments is evident in the publication of the 'Purple Book' and 'Panduan Pengurusan Wakaf: Institusi Pendidikan'. These books contain guidance for public universities on enhancing their income generation through endowment and *waqf* funds. The source of endowment and *waqf* funds originating from public contributions (e.g. individuals, companies, and foundations) indicates that the implementation of the cost-sharing concept between the public and private sources to provide funding to public universities has been expanding. The discussion on the endowment and *waqf* instruments in Malaysian education, especially higher education, is presented in the next section.

General Overview of Endowment and *Waqf* at Malaysian Public Universities

As pointed out by various scholars including McElhaney,[9] Dimmock,[10] Madanchi, Shahverdiani, and Hamidifar,[11] and Kaffe,[12] managing the endowment fund at HEIs involves two types of legal structures: 1) a part of the university itself and 2) a separate legal entity, such as foundations or investment management companies. However, in the context of Malaysia, particularly in public universities, the endowment fund is managed by a university's financial division, specifically the Bursar's Office of the university. This was highlighted by Abdul Hamid, Hassan–Kamarudin, and Abdul Syahid Sowell, who stated that the endowment fund in Malaysian public universities is managed by the bursar, where a small investment or endowment unit is set up.[13] Although the Bursar's Office has the power to receive and manage the endowment fund, a report of all the endowment activities and finance should be submitted to the university's Board of Directors (BoD).

As an endowment is regarded as a trust fund, the legislation governing this fund, including for higher education, in Malaysia is subject to local legislation, specifically the Trustee Act 1949 (Act 208). This act consists of 69 provisions that focus on the matters of trust, executorships, and administratorships, as stated in Section 2 of this Act.[14] Despite the function of this Act as the main source of the trust law, the judiciary in Malaysia still refers to English law in deciding a case. An example is the case of *Liew Choy Hung v. Fork Kian Seng*, where the judge referred to the case of *Springgette v. Defoe*, *Pettit v. Pettit*, and *Halsbury's Laws of England*.[15] This practice is in line with the stipulations in the Civil Law Act 1956 (Section 3), which clarifies that Malaysia's judiciary can apply the UK Common Law. Such law can be applied in appropriate circumstances and subject to the qualifications required by local conditions.[16]

In 2017, Fong reported in the *New Straits Times* that all public universities in Malaysia employed an endowment fund.[17] This was supported by the data provided by the Public HEI Governance Division, Department of Higher Education (Malaysia) to the author through email. The data reveal that within a period of three years (2017–2019), Universiti Malaya collected the highest total endowment, amounting to RM1.6 billion, RM1.4 billion, and RM1.4 billion, respectively. It was followed by Universiti Kebangsaan Malaysia with endowment collections of RM71 million (2017), RM80 million (2018), and RM84 million (2019), and Universiti Teknologi Malaysia with RM 59 million (2017), RM 69 million (2018), and RM 74 million (2019). The endowment fund collection by these three and other universities is presented in Figure 5.1.

Apart from the endowment fund, the *waqf* fund is also implemented at public universities in Malaysia. However, as indicated by Mahamood, Ab. Rahman, and Che Seman,[18] despite its long history in Sekolah Agama Rakyat (SAR), Sekolah Agama Negeri, madrasah, and *pondok*, its implementation at Malaysian public universities is still relatively new. The first university that implemented the *waqf* fund was Kolej Islam Malaya. The establishment of *waqf* at this institution inspired other universities within the country to implement the *waqf* fund. The first public university in Malaysia to implement the *waqf* was the Universiti Islam Antarabangsa Malaysia (UIAM), which established the *waqf* known as IIUM Endowment Fund in 1999.[19]

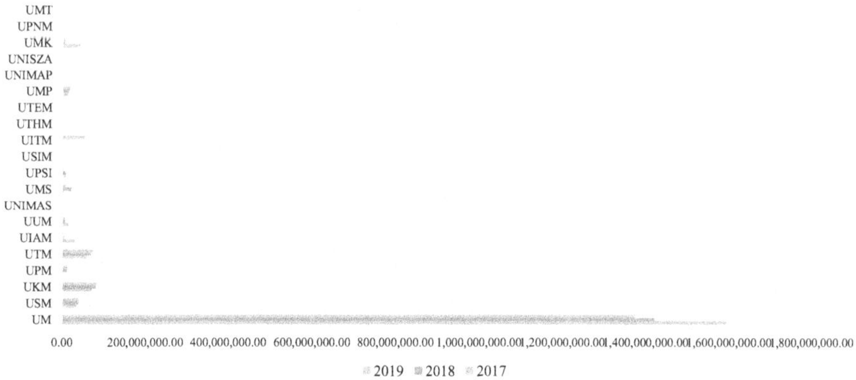

Figure 5.1 Collection of Endowment at Malaysian Public Universities (2017–2019)

Source: The Public HEI Governance Division, Department of Higher Education (Malaysia). See Mohamad Afizal Mehat. (Senior Assistant Director, Public HEI Governance Division, Department of Higher Education (Malaysia)), data obtained through email, 9 February 2020.

Endowment implementation by Malaysian universities does not face any legal problems because of the specific regulation that allows universities to receive and manage investments for endowment funds, as stipulated in the Universities and University Colleges Act 1971, specifically Item 4 (1) of the First Schedule.[20] Based on this provision, a university acts as a trustee of the properties that have been endowed. However, the implementation of *waqf* in Malaysian universities is relatively complex because it is under the state jurisdiction (except Wilayah Persekutuan Kuala Lumpur, Labuan, and Putrajaya), as stipulated in List 2, the Ninth Schedule, Federal Constitution.[21] For example, the enactment of Selangor (Section 4),[22] Melaka (Section 32),[23] Negeri Sembilan (Section 5),[24] and Terengganu (Section 4)[25] mentioned that MAIN acts as the sole trustee for all *waqf* assets that are located within the state. If a university attempts to implement the *waqf* fund in its institution, permission from their respective MAINs needs to be obtained. If permission is provided, the university would hold the status of *mutawalli*, which is the *waqf* manager. Therefore, they are entitled to accept and manage the *waqf* fund. Mahamood, Ab. Rahman, and Che Seman explained that the *mutawalli* is located at the second stage in the hierarchy of the *waqf* management in Malaysia.[26]

Public universities in the country could adopt any *waqf* governance models suggested by the MoE Malaysia in the 'Purple Book'. These models consist of Model 1, Model 2, and Model 3, as illustrated in Figures 5.2, 5.3, and 5.4, respectively.

In the first model, a unit or department is established under a university's management itself. The *waqf* committee falls under the university BoD as it is one of the Board committees, indicating that all resolutions about the *waqf* activities, all accounts, and financial management are under the university management authority. This model is similar to the model applied by endowments at most public universities, as discussed earlier.

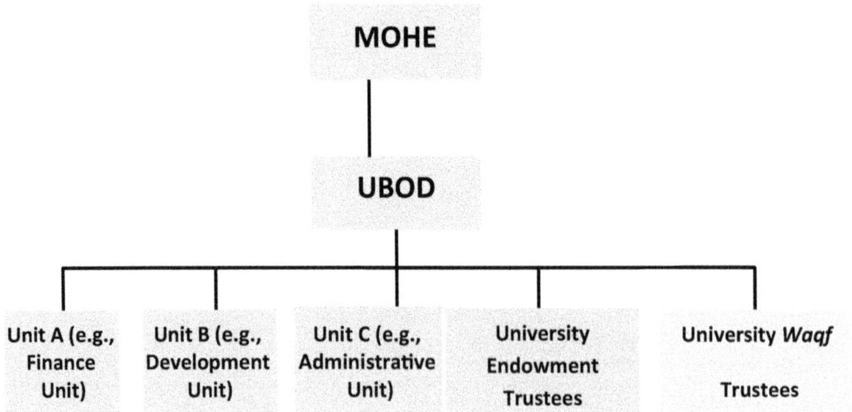

Figure 5.2 Model 1 of *Waqf* Governance at Public Universities

Source: Modified from MoE, Putrajaya, 2016.[27]

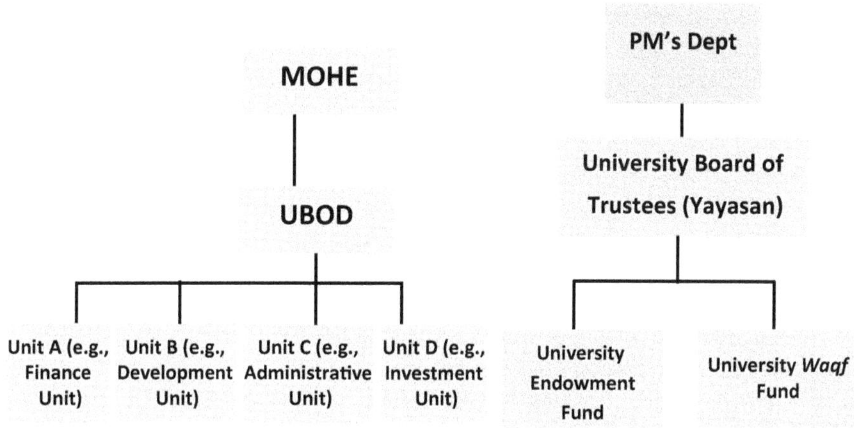

Figure 5.3 Model 2 of *Waqf* Governance at Public Universities

Source: Modified from MoE, Putrajaya, 2016.[28]

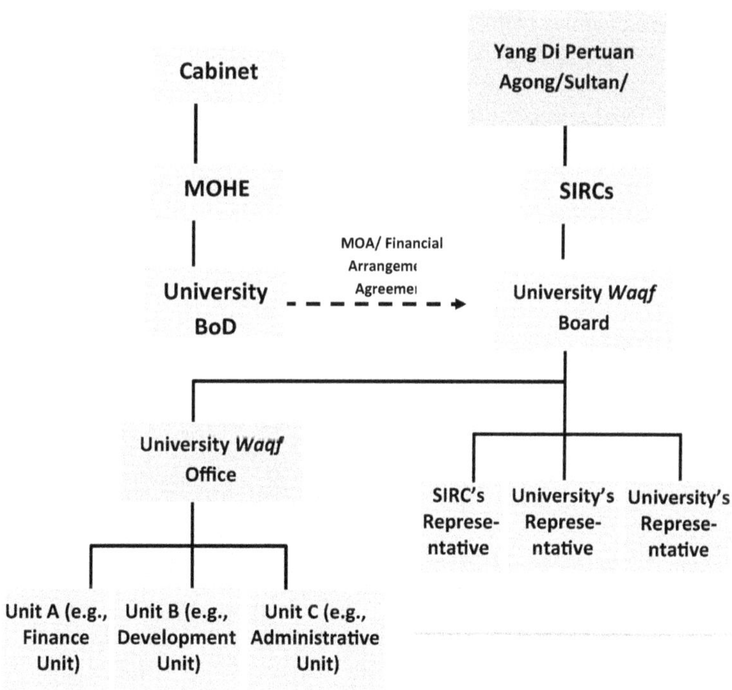

Figure 5.4 Model 3 of *Waqf* Governance at Public Universities

Source: Modified from MoE, Putrajaya, 2016.[29]

In the second model, the *waqf* office is established under a university's Board of Trustees (BoT). The *waqf* fund at the university is under the BoT as a project, which is managed by the university foundation (*Yayasan*). This fund allows universities to create their account and manage their finances. In the third model, a university inaugurates a separate and self-governing body of the University *Waqf* Board (UWB) from the university. The cooperation, organisation, roles, and accountabilities of the UWB are stipulated in a written agreement or *waqf* deeds. The UWB members comprise representatives from the MAIN and university.

In 2017, only 12 public universities received permission from their respective MAINs to implement the *waqf* fund at their institution. This increased to 17 universities in 2019, following positive feedback to the government's encouragement to enhance the *waqf* fund at their institutions. The UKM, UM, UPM, USM, UTM, UMP, UniMAP, UTeM, UTHM, UiTM, UNIMAS, UMT, UniSZA, UPNM, UPSI, USIM, and UMS were among these institutions, as notified by the Public HEI Governance Division, Department of Higher Education (Malaysia) through email. The five public universities included in the list of 2019 were UM, UNIMAS, UPNM, UPSI, and UMS while some universities (e.g. UM, UNIMAS, UPNM, and UMS) did not receive the status of *mutawalli* in 2017. Another university (i.e. UPSI) did not establish the fund in the same year. Among the universities on the list for 2019, the UPM had the highest collection of *waqf* funds, which amounted to RM9.2 million, RM9.7, and RM10.8 million in 2017, 2018, and 2019, respectively. The UPM was followed by the USIM, with funds amounting to RM5.6 million (2017), RM6.2 million (2018), and RM6.7 million (2019), and the UniSZA with RM6.5 million (2017), RM5.1 million (2018), and RM6.2 million (2019). The trend in the collection of *waqf* funds by the aforementioned universities is presented in Figure 5.5.

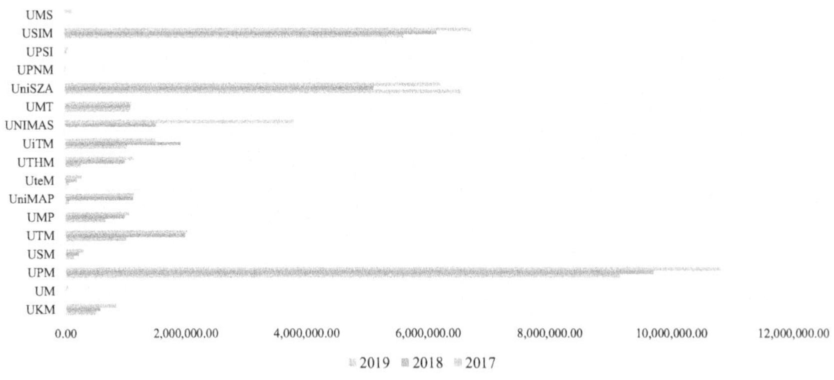

Figure 5.5 Collection of *Waqf* at Malaysian Public Universities (2017–2019)

Source: The Public HEI Governance Division, Department of Higher Education (Malaysia). See Mohamad Afizal Mehat. (Senior Assistant Director, Public HEI Governance Division, Department of Higher Education (Malaysia)), data obtained through email, 9 February 2020.

The other three Malaysian public universities that did not achieve the status of *mutawalli* from their respective MAINs until 2019 were the UIAM, UMK, and UUM. The *waqf* fund of UIAM has been discussed in several studies, such as those by Mokthar,[30] Abdul Razak et al.,[31] Ali Hamdan and Mahamood,[32] Mahamood and Ab Rahman,[33] and Mustaffa and Muda.[34] However, these studies did not include the data provided by the Public HEI Governance Division, Department of Higher Education (Malaysia) as the UIAM did not register their fund as *waqf* but as IIUM Endowment Fund. Out of the total contributions to Malaysian public universities, the *waqf* funds received only 2 per cent (RM37,249,484.72) in 2019. By contrast, 98 per cent of contributions were to the endowment fund (RM1,685,936,236.64), as illustrated in Figure 5.6. Overall, this was consistent with the argument of scholars that the *waqf* implementation at the higher education level in Malaysia is relatively new.

Although *waqf* implementation at public universities is relatively new, its collection by certain public universities including UPM, USIM, and UniSZA is significant as the fund was implemented in 2011, 2013, and 2016, respectively. A study reported that the implementation of endowment funds at public universities in Malaysia is low compared to that in Western universities, such as Harvard University, Yale University, and the University of Texas System.[35] However, all the aforementioned Western universities are private, suggesting that they cannot be compared with Malaysian public universities, which are funded by the government and employ endowment funds (including the *waqf* fund) only as an alternative funding source. The achievement of certain universities, such as UM, UKM, and UTM in the implementation of endowment fund indicates the ability of the

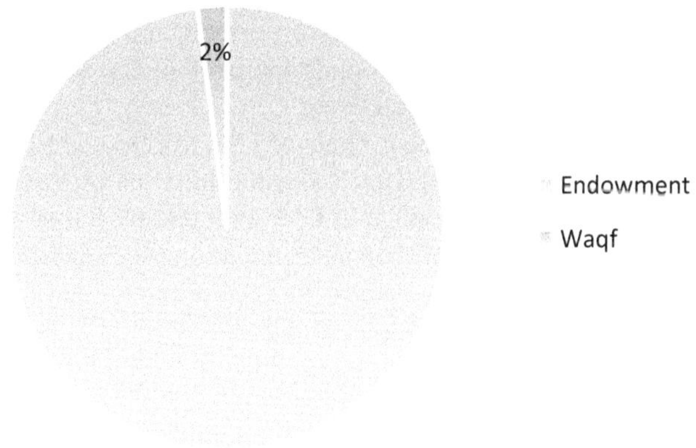

Figure 5.6 Total Collection of Endowment and *Waqf* Funds by Malaysian Public Universities in 2019

Source: Public HEI Governance Division, Department of Higher Education (Malaysia).[36]

national public universities to respond to government challenges by generating income themselves. To explain the application of endowment and *waqf* at Malaysian public universities, several universities (viz. UM, UKM, UTM, UPM, USIM, and UniSZA) were selected as their collection was among the highest. The related discussion is presented in the subsequent section.

Application of Endowment and *Waqf* at the Selected Malaysian Public Universities

Snapshot of Endowment Application

Universiti Malaya

UM is the oldest public university in Malaysia and officially established on 1 January 1962. According to Rabiatun Adauyah Ishak, Head of Fund Management and Credit Division, Bursar's Office of UM, the endowment at the university has been long-standing and was present even before it separated from the National University of Singapore on 15 January 1959. However, in mid-2019 (6 July 2019), the endowment fund at UM was relaunched and named UM Endowment Fund (UMEF), to defray the costs related to students' welfare, research and innovation, creation of teaching and learning infrastructure facilities, and publications, as well as funding unexpected needs.

As mentioned by Maizatul Yusliana Ab Sofi, Financial Officer of Fund Management and Credit Division, Bursar's Office of UM, the university's endowment is based on the applications submitted from the faculty, or student affairs section, or other endorsed parties for academic/research activities to the Deputy Vice-Chancellor (VC) (for student activities). The approval of the application by the Deputy VC (Research and Innovation) leads to the setting up of a chair. Every established chair comprises its committee, which is set by the members. The university has three types of endowment applications—true, term, and quasi-endowment. The use of endowment funds at this institution is approved by the committee of each chair, based on the aforementioned objectives.

The funds for the endowment chair of UM can be contributed through cash and shares. Notably, the university is flexible in terms of ownership of the contributed funds, although it belongs to UM, as stated by Rabiatun Adauyah Ishak. Nine endowment chairs established since the university's inception are still active as listed in Table 5.3.

Universiti Kebangsaan Malaysia

Similar to UM, UKM does not directly employ an endowment fund—the endowment is made based on the chair applied by the faculty, institute, or other departments. One of the earliest endowment chairs set up in the UKM was Kursi Pok Rafeah in 1996, with the chair sponsored by the Yayasan Pok Rafeah. Although the establishment of chairs at the UKM is based on its objective, most chairs are set up to fund students and research activities, as indicated by Muhammad Faris Zaharudin, Officer at Yayasan Canselor UKM. The establishment of each chair is under the Chancellor's Foundation of UKM. Nevertheless, the governance and management of the chair are under the jurisdiction of the Trust Council of each chair.

Two types of endowment applied at UKM are term and true endowment with the latter endowment type being mostly applied at this institution. As mentioned by the informant, true endowment entails the acquired funds to be invested first to generate income and cover all costs incurred. The usage of endowment funds at this institution is based on decisions made by the committee of each chair. Meanwhile, the contribution to the endowment chair of UKM can be made through monetary or non-monetary approaches. Specifically, the non-monetary contribution should be equal to the value of money, where it means that the donated item has a high value at the present time. Meanwhile, the ownership of the funds contributed to this university is flexible. According to Muhammad Faris, the fund ownership depends on the decision made by either the Trust Council under the university or donors if the specific project or time stipulations are met. UKM has 14 endowment chairs that are active since its inception: Kursi Tan Sri Noah, Kursi Pok Rafeah, Kursi Kecemerlangan Rashid Hussain (RHB), Dana Endowmen Kaneka Corporation, Kursi Tun Ismail Mohamed Ali, Dana Endowmen Tengku Ampuan Afzan, Kursi Ulung Tun Abdul Razak, Kursi Syeikh Abdullah Fahim, Kursi Ekonomi Tengku Razaleigh, Kursi Perubahan Iklim UKM-YSD, Kursi Pembangunan Lestari UKM-YSD, Kursi Kepimpinan Wanita, Kursi Endowmen MPOB-UKM, and Dana Endowmen Nippon Foundation.

Universiti Teknologi Malaysia

UTM is another public university in Malaysia with an endowment fund, known as UTM Endowment Fund established in 2009.[37] The establishment of the UTM Endowment Fund is based on vice-chancellor's allocations and is used for investment purposes.[38] According to Associate Prof Dr Yusof Boon, Director of UTM Endowment, the endowment fund at the UTM was established to fund student welfare through scholarship provision. The financial assistance for students in the form of scholarships is sourced from four types of funds: Tabung Endowment Merdeka, Tabung Endowment Azman Hashim, Tabung Endowment Alumni, and Tabung Endowment Ainuddin Wahid. The first three endowment funds focus on assisting undergraduate students while Tabung Endowment Ainuddin Wahid focuses on assisting postgraduate students.

All endowment funds at UTM are managed by the UTM Endowment Unit, which is under the Development Division, Deputy Vice-Chancellor's Office. The endowment application at this university is of three types—true, term, and quasi-endowment—and can be contributed in the form of cash or non-cash, as highlighted by the informant. Financial contributions from donors are generally owned by the university. UTM has established three committees under the UTM Endowment Unit to manage the endowment fund, namely Endowment Trustee Committee,

Endowment Management Committee, and University Endowment Committee. The functions of each committee are listed in Table 5.2.

The application of the endowment fund at the selected universities (i.e. UM, UKM, and UTM) discussed here are summarised in Table 5.3. The establishment of an endowment fund at UM and UKM is based on a chair upon application from certain Responsibility Centres (PTJ). Meanwhile, the endowment at UTM is established under the UTM Endowment Fund managed by the UTM Endowment unit for student welfare. UM was the first university to establish an endowment (e.g. chair) in Malaysia. In terms of legal structure, the endowment chairs and funds at UM and UTM are established under the Deputy Vice-Chancellor while those at UKM are under the Chancellor (i.e. Chancellor's Foundation). This indicates that endowment funds in the Malaysian public universities are managed by respective universities as one of the legal structures in the management of the endowment fund at HEIs.

Table 5.2 Functions of Committees Under the Endowment Unit of UTM

Committee	*Functions*
Endowment Trustee Committee	1) Assisting the University Trustee Board in achieving UTM Endowment goals; 2) Identifying the effective strategy for the growth of the university endowment and monitoring the implementation of the endowment strategy; 3) Managing the university endowment funds and ensuring the capability of the endowment income to maintain and improve academic, research, and knowledgeable activities at UTM; and 4) Approving the endowment proposal that is already presented at the university level.
Endowment Management Committee	1) Assisting the University Trustee Committee in achieving the UTM Endowment goals; 2) Planning the strategy for the growth of the university endowment and monitoring the implementation of the endowment strategy; 3) Planning the use of the university endowment funds and ensuring the capability of the endowment income to maintain and improve the academic, research, and knowledgeable activities at UTM; and 4) Viewing and certifying the endowment proposal to be presented to the University Trustee Committee.
University Endowment Committee	1) Reporting the planning and implementation of endowment activities at the faculty level; 2) Reporting the total Faculty Endowment Fund collections; and 3) Discussing and coordinating the activity and programme of the faculty endowment fund generation.

Source: Endowment Unit.[39]

Table 5.3 Application of Endowment at UM, UKM, and UTM

Item		*UM*	*UKM*	*UTM*
Name of Fund		• Based on the chair established • Universiti Malaya Endowment Fund (relaunched)	Based on the chair established	UTM Endowment Fund
Year of Establishment		Before 1959	1996 (based on the earliest chair established)	2009
Purpose of Establishment		Based on the chair established	Based on the chair established	Student welfare
Manager		Responsibility Centre (PTJ)	Responsibility Centre (PTJ)	UTM Endowment Unit
Legal Structure		Deputy Vice-Chancellor (Research and Innovation)	Chancellor (Chancellor's Foundation)	Deputy Vice-Chancellor (Development)
Donation	**Cash**	/	/	/
	Non-cash	/	/	/
Types	**True**	/	/	/
	Term	/	/	/
	Quasi	/		/
Ownership	**University**	/	/	/
	Donor	/	/	
Schemes/Chairs Established		1) Kursi Dr. Siti Hasmah Mohd Ali 2) Kursi Khazanah Nasional 3) Kursi Pelindungan Kewangan Warga Tua 4) Kursi Perakaunan Maybank 5) Kursi Perkhidmatan Kewangan AmBank 6) Kursi Petronas 7) Kursi Profesor Diraja Ungku Aziz 8) Kursi Tun Ismail Ali 9) Kursi Tunku Abdul Rahman	1) Kursi Tan Sri Noah 2) Kursi Pok Rafeah 3) Kursi Kecemerlangan Rashid Hussain (RHB) 4) Dana Endowmen Kaneka Corp. 5) Kursi Tun Ismail Mohamed Ali 6) Dana Endowmen Tengku Ampuan Afzan 7) Kursi Ulung Tun Abdul Razak 8) Kursi Syeikh Abdullah Fahim 9) Kursi Ekonomi Tengku Razaleigh	1) Tabung Endowment Merdeka 2) Tabung Endowment Azman Hashim 3) Tabung Endowment Alumni

(*Continued*)

Table 5.3 (Continued)

Item	*UM*	*UKM*	*UTM*
		10) Kursi Perubahan Iklim UKM-YSD 11) Kursi Pembangunan Lestari UKM-YSD 12) Kursi Kepimpinan Wanita 13) Kursi Endowmen MPOB-UKM 14) Dana Endowmen Nippon Foundation	4) Tabung Endowment Ainuddin Wahid
Committee	Trustee Committee based on every chair established	Trust Council based on every chair established	1) Endowment Trustee Committee 2) Endowment Management Committee 3) University Endowment Committee

Source: Developed by the authors.

The contribution to the endowment chairs and funds at these universities can be in either cash or non-cash form, although cash contributions are crucial for this fund. To illustrate this point, the fund's investment would generate returns for permanent use, which is in line with the concept of endowment. As discussed in Chapter 3, endowment funds are of three types, true endowment, term endowment, and quasi-endowment. These types of endowments have been implemented in UM and UTM while UKM has only true and term endowments.

Moreover, the ownership of the fund at UM and UKM is flexible based on the chair's agreement on whether it belongs to the university or needs to be returned to donors. By contrast, UTM has full ownership of the contributed fund, which becomes one of the elements to be differentiated from the *waqf* fund (which solely belongs to Allah). The flexible ownership of endowment funds practised by these universities is in line with the explanation by Kazemi and Wilkens,[40] Getz,[41] Sherlock et al.,[42] and Monti.[43] The three universities have various chairs and endowment and their details are presented in Table 5.3. Every chair at UM and UKM has its trustee while at UTM, all the endowment funds are under the Endowment Trustee Committee, Endowment Management Committee, and University Endowment Committee. As previously mentioned, this practice is in line with the specific regulation stipulated in the Universities and University Colleges Act 1971, specifically Item 4 (1) of the First Schedule, which allows the university to receive and manage investments for endowment funds.[44]

Snapshot of Waqf *Application*

Universiti Putra Malaysia

Apart from the endowment fund, UPM is one of the public universities in Malaysia that employ the *waqf* fund, known as Dana Wakaf Ilmu UPM. The fund's inception initiative began on 16 August 2011, to provide a financial instrument to fund UPM operations in terms of creating infrastructure facilities for scientific activities including teaching and learning programmes, da'wah activities and gathering, research and innovation, services,[45] and student welfare (e.g. scholarship and donation).[46] As all matters related to *waqf* in Malaysia are under the jurisdiction of MAIN (Majlis Agama Islam Selangor (MAIS) in the context of UPM), MAIS and UPM agreed on 2 February 2012, which allows the UPM to act as *mutawalli* in collecting and managing the UPM *waqf* fund.

However, the status of *mutawalli* granted to UPM by MAIS is applicable within a specific time only.[47] This indicates that UPM should renew their *mutawalli* status after this period expires to enable continuous collection and management of the *waqf* fund at the UPM. Based on the information obtained from the Public HEI Governance Division, Department of Higher Education (Malaysia), the current agreement period between the MAIS and UPM is five years from 24 March 2017 to 23 March 2022.[48] In this current agreement, the MAIS introduced a new position of the *waqf* collector in the state. This position would involve an agent of Perbadanan Wakaf Selangor (PWS) to collect the *waqf* funds as the PWS was established by MAIS as its representative.

After undergoing several processes of enhancement in *waqf* management at the UPM, the Centre for Management of *Waqf*, *Zakat*, and Endowment (WAZAN) was established on 1 October 2016 under the administration of the Deputy Vice-Chancellor.[49] The *waqf* at the UPM adopted Model 3 proposed by the MoHE Malaysia in the 'Purple Book', which was discussed in the previous chapter, as its governance model.

Donations to this fund can be in either cash or non-cash form. Donors are provided various cash *waqf* schemes such as General *Waqf*, *Waqf* Kitab, *Waqf* Facility, and *Waqf* Special Vehicle. The *Waqf* Kitab, *Waqf* Facility, and *Waqf* Special Vehicle are categorised as special *waqf* used for specific purposes according to the type of the scheme. The use of the General *Waqf* is general and aims for a sustainable long-term infrastructure to be used in the form of savings and investment returns or permanent assets (e.g. building) as a part of the revenue-generating activities.[50]

The sections are divided according to the types of financial instruments under the WAZAN. The *waqf* instrument is under the jurisdiction of the Dana Wakaf Ilmu Management Section, whose function is to manage the project, generate investment income, and distribute the benefits of the *waqf* funds. Two committees have been formed to manage the *waqf* funds of this institution, the Trustees Committee and the *Waqf* Distribution Committee. The functions of each committee are presented in Table 5.4.

Universiti Sains Islam Malaysia

The *waqf* fund is also implemented in USIM as Dana Wakaf al-Abrar. According to the Public HEI Governance Division, Department of Higher Education (Malaysia), the *waqf* fund at this institution was established on 26 March 2013.[51] Dana Wakaf al-Abrar aims to provide funding for various activities at USIM, such as da'wah, education, research, publication, health, educational development, and health facilities.[52] It also provides welfare to students in terms of scholarship, as mentioned by Ustaz Razman

Table 5.4 Functions of the Trustees Committee and *Waqf* Distribution Committee in the Dana Wakaf Ilmu UPM

Committee	*Functions*
Trustees Committee	1) Determine how the Dana Wakaf Ilmu UPM should be administrated and managed; and 2) Determine how the Dana Wakaf Ilmu UPM should be spent.
Waqf Distribution Committee	1) Fully responsible for the Trustees Committee of the Dana Wakaf Ilmu UPM; 2) To devise and plan any profitable and potential distribution projects to be implemented, which comply with the Shariah standards and fulfil the trust of the *waqf* donors. 3) Coordinate any procedures, guidelines, and agreements related to distribution projects; and 4) Monitor the implementation and ensure the efficiency of distribution projects to guarantee their success.

Source: Trustees of UPM *Waqf* Fund[53] and *Waqf* Distribution.[54]

Ibrahim, Assistant Registrar at the Pusat Wakaf dan Zakat, USIM. The Dana Wakaf al-Abrar is managed by the PTJ, which is Pusat Pembangunan Pembiayaan Wakaf (PPPW) and currently known as Pusat Wakaf dan Zakat (PWZ). The PTJ is under the administration of the Deputy Vice-Chancellor (Student and Alumni Affairs). According to the informant, unlike UPM, USIM adopted Model 1 as the *waqf* governance model.

The establishment of Dana Wakaf al-Abrar was approved and registered with MAINS. On 22 July 2013, USIM was appointed as *mutawalli* by the MAINS to develop, manage, and distribute the benefits of the *waqf* fund in this state, specifically at USIM.[55] In contrast to UPM, granting *mutawalli* status to the USIM implies full autonomy by the MAINS to manage the *waqf* assets.[56] However, the Dana Wakaf al-Abrar is still required to submit management and financial report periodically to the MAINS through Perbadanan Wakaf Negeri Sembilan (PWNS), a subsidiary of the MAINS, which possesses the power to manage *waqf* and any matter related to it in Negeri Sembilan.[57]

The contributions to this fund can only be in cash form, known as Cash *Waqf* al-Abrar. Although USIM has only one type of *waqf*, according to the informant, it can still be used to fund any *waqf* project (e.g. *waqf* site) as it is regarded as a general *waqf*. Previously, two committees were involved in managing the *waqf* fund at USIM—USIM-MAINS *Waqf* Council Committee and *Waqf* Management Committee. Both committees were later merged and named *Waqf* Management Committee, as revealed by the informant. All *waqf* matters (e.g. making policies and investing) at USIM are decided only by this committee.

Universiti Sultan Zainal Abidin

UniSZA is another public university in Malaysia with a *waqf* fund, known as Dana Wakaf UniSZA. According to the Public HEI Governance Division, Department of Higher Education (Malaysia), the *waqf* fund at this institution was established on 1 August 2016 to fund the university infrastructure facilities (e.g. gym, graduate lounge, and studio al-Quran) and student welfare (e.g. scholarship, donation, financing, and initial business aid), as informed by Noor Mizan Arifin, Assistant Registrar, Office of *Waqf* and Endowment, UniSZA.

UniSZA obtained approval from the Majlis Agama Islam dan Adat Istiadat Melayu (MAIDAM) for the establishment of the *waqf* fund on 20 October 2016.[58] This approval allows UniSZA to collect and manage the *waqf* fund. In contrast to the approval obtained by UPM and USIM, although the approval by MAIDAM to UniSZA is not based on the status of *mutawalli*, it is a joint venture (JV) between the two parties, as disclosed by the informant. A memorandum of understanding (MoU) was signed to bind the agreement between the MAIDAM and UniSZA. According to the informant, each party has the right to terminate the agreement by providing a six-month notice, as stipulated in the agreement.

The Dana Wakaf UniSZA is managed by the Pejabat Wakaf dan Infaq (WAQIAH) under the Chancellery structure (i.e. vice-chancellor). In January 2019, the name of the office was changed to Pejabat Wakaf and Endowment as it was more suitable given its role in managing the funds of *waqf*, *infaq*, *zakat*, and endowment at the UniSZA,[59] although it is commonly known as Wakaf UniSZA. As conveyed by the informant, UniSZA adopted Model 3 as the *waqf* governance model.

According to the informant, the contribution to the Dana Wakaf UniSZA can be in either cash or non-cash form, although only cash *waqf* is available at UniSZA. Despite the availability of only one type of fund, it can still be used to fund any *waqf* project because of its categorisation as *waqf am*. UniSZA has three committees to manage the *waqf* fund: UniSZA *Waqf* Fund Committee, *Waqf* and *Zakat* Distribution Committee, and Financial and Investment Committee. The function of the UniSZA *Waqf* Fund Committee is to set the policies while *Waqf* and *Zakat* Distribution Committee distributes the *waqf* fund, and the Financial and Investment Committee makes investments and manages the financial matters of *waqf*. As for the UniSZA *Waqf* Fund Committee, half of its members are representatives from MAIDAM.[60]

The application of *waqf* funds at the selected universities (i.e. UPM, USIM, and UniSZA) is summarised in Table 5.5. As evident, *waqf* funds at these

Table 5.5 Application of *Waqf* at UPM, USIM, and UniSZA

Item		*UPM*	*USIM*	*UniSZA*
Name of Fund		Dana Wakaf Ilmu	Dana Wakaf al-Abrar	Dana Wakaf UniSZA
Date of Establishment		16 August 2011	26 March 2013	1 August 2016
Purpose of Establishment		• University infrastructure facilities • Student welfare	• University infrastructure facilities • Student welfare	• University infrastructure facilities • Student welfare
Manager		WAZAN	PWZ	Wakaf UniSZA
Legal Structure		Deputy Vice-Chancellor	Deputy Vice-Chancellor	Vice-Chancellor
Model		Model 3	Model 1	Model 3
MAIN		MAIS	MAINS	MAIDAM
Approval		*Mutawalli* status	*Mutawalli* status	Joint venture (JV)
Status Period		Contract (five years)	Full autonomy	Contract (six months)
Date of Status Given		24 March 2017	22 July 2013	20 October 2016
Donation	**Cash**	/	/	/
	Non-Cash	/		/
Types	**General**	• General *Waqf*	• Cash *Waqf* al- Abrar	• Cash *waqf*
	Special	• *Waqf* Kitab • *Waqf* facility • *Waqf* special vehicle	• Based on project	• Based on project
Committee		• Trustee committee • *Waqf* distribution committee	• *Waqf* management committee	• UniSZA *waqf* fund committee • *Waqf* and *zakat* distribution committee • Financial and investment committee

Source: Developed by the authors.

universities, namely Dana Wakaf Ilmu (UPM), Dana Wakaf al-Abrar (USIM), and Dana Wakaf UniSZA (UniSZA), are managed by the WAZAN, PWZ, and Wakaf UniSZA, respectively. Notably, UPM was the first university to establish a *waqf* fund among all public universities in Malaysia, including the two selected in this study. The establishment of the *waqf* fund at the selected universities aims to fund the university's infrastructure facilities and student welfare. As for the legal structure, the *waqf* fund managed by the WAZAN and PWZ is under the Deputy Vice-Chancellor, while that in UniSZA is under the Vice-Chancellor. The *waqf* funds at UPM and UniSZA have adopted Model 3 while that at USIM has adopted Model 1 for governance. Both these *waqf* governance models have been suggested by the MoHE in the 'Purple Book'.[61] The application of these models by these universities offers specific advantages—Model 1 allows a university to make a decision related to *waqf* governance while Model 3 allows the university to gather views from two parties, which originate from the MAIN and the university itself as this model involves a combination of members from these parties. The government prefers Model 3 to Model 1 to govern the *waqf* fund at public universities.[62]

The implementation of *waqf* funds at these universities has also been permitted by their respective MAINs, MAIS for UPM, MAINS for USIM, and MAIDAM for UniSZA. The permission is required because the MAIN acts as the sole trustee for all the *waqf* assets in the states, as stipulated in the enactment of Selangor (Section 4),[63] Negeri Sembilan (Section 5),[64] and Terengganu (Section 4).[65] The status of permission gained by UniSZA is under the JV agreement while the UPM and USIM act as *mutawallis*. They are located at the second stage in the hierarchy of the *waqf* management in Malaysia, as highlighted by Mahamood, Ab. Rahman, and Che Seman.[66] The status period of the fund varies by the university—UPM has a five-year contract, USIM receives full autonomy, and UniSZA has a six-month leeway to terminate its contract.

Currently, the UPM and UniSZA receive *waqf* contributions in both cash and non-cash forms while USIM receives them only in the form of cash. The *waqf* contribution in the form of cash practised by the universities has established the development of *waqf* in Malaysia.[67] At the same time, this contribution facilitates the involvement of universities in investment activities to generate *waqf* funds. Therefore, the *waqf* contribution in the form of cash should be emphasised by universities as it was also one of the success factors of the Ottoman Empire.[68] As discussed in Chapter 3, *waqf* funds are of two types, *waqf am* and *waqf khas*. All the three selected universities have implemented these types of waqf funds at their institutions, which also comprise the respective committees for fund management.

Conclusion

The endowment and *waqf* funds have been implemented at public universities in Malaysia. Given the encouragement from the government for these institutions to enhance income generation through endowment and *waqf* funds, all Malaysian public universities implemented the endowment fund in 2019, with 17 universities implementing the *waqf* fund after obtaining permission from the respective MAINs. Some universities, namely UM, UKM, and UTM, achieved considerable collection through endowment funds while other universities such as UPM, USIM, and UniSZA collected substantial funds through the *waqf* fund. The application of funds at these universities varied from one another. For example, endowment funds at UM and UKM were created based on chairs while at UTM through Endowment Unit. For waqf, UPM and USIM are allowed to manage waqf funds with *mutawalli* status granted while at UniSZA it is based on a JV agreement.

Notes

1 "Direktori Universiti Awam," *Kementerian Pendidikan Malaysia* (Jabatan Pendidikan Tinggi) (2017), accessed on 27 September 2018, http://jpt.mohe.gov.my/index.php/ipta/institusi-pendidikan-tinggi-awam/direktori-universiti-awam.
2 Ibid.
3 "Kategori UA," *Ministry of Higher Education*, accessed 19 October 2018, www.mohe.gov.my/institusi/universiti-awam/kategori-ua.
4 Ministry of Higher Education Malaysia, *University Transformation Programme, Purple Book: Enhancing University Income Generation, Endowment & Waqf* (Putrajaya: Kementerian Pendidikan Tinggi Malaysia, 2016), 6.
5 Kewangan Malaysia, *Anggaran Perbelanjaan Persekutuan* (Kuala Lumpur: Percetakan Nasional Malaysia Berhad, 2020), 25.
6 A. Amran and J. Muhammad, "Changes and Challenges in Financial Autonomy," in *Governance Reforms in Public Universities of Malaysia*, ed. F. Md. Taib and M. N. L. Y. Abdullah (Pulau Pinang: Penerbit Universiti Sains Malaysia, 2015), 59–77, 66.
7 Ministry of Education Malaysia, *Malaysia Education Blueprint 2015–2025 (Higher Education).* (Putrajaya: Ministry of Education Malaysia, 2015), E-14.
8 J. Fielden, "Global Trends in University Governance," *Education Working Paper Series*, no. 9 (2008): 1–65, 18.
9 R. L. S. McElhaney, "The Effects of Higher Education Endowment Management Practices on Endowment Performance," Ph.D. thesis, The University of Southern Mississippi, 2010, 38–39.
10 S. G. Dimmock, "Background Risk and University Endowment Funds," *The Review of Economics and Statistics* 94, no. 3 (2012): 789–99, 790.
11 M. Madanchi, S. Shahverdiani, and F. Hamidifar, "Endowment and Charity Financing Model to Develop Science and Technology," *International Journal of Finance and Managerial Accounting* 1, no. 4 (2016): 55–70, 65
12 C. Kaffe, "Peer Effects in Investment Manager Selection: Evidence from University Endowments," *Judge Business School, University of Cambridge* (2019): 1–38, 2.
13 B. Abdul Hamid, W. Hassan-Kamarudin, and S. Abdul Syahid Sowell, "The Endowment Fund as a Source of Sustainability for Higher Education in Malaysia: Maximising Investment Returns," *ISRA Research Paper*, no. 103 (2018): 1–32, 21.
14 'Trustee Act 1949 (Act 208)', 7.
15 G. Dhillon, N. Mohammed, and N. Y. Min, "Equity & Trust's Law Applications in Malaysia, UK and US—In Tandem or Apart?" *Current Law Journal* 1, no. IXXIV (2011), 6.
16 'Civil Law Act 1956 (Act 67)', 7–9.
17 F. Fong, "RM23m for 'Wakaf' Collected by 13 Public Universities," *New Straits Times*, August 7, 2017, accessed on 19 October 2019, www.nst.com.my/news/nation/2017/08/264977/rm23m-wakaf-collected-13-public-universities-date.
18 S. M. Mahamood, A. Ab. Rahman, and A. Che Seman, "Cabaran Pelaksanaan Wakaf Universiti Awam Di Malaysia: Analisis Menurut Perundangan Di Malaysia," *Kanun* 30, no. 2 (2018): 383–409, 387.
19 "IIUM Endowment Fund," accessed 7 June 2018, www.iium.edu.my/division/ief.
20 "Universities and University Colleges Act 1971 (Act 30)," 36.

21 List 2, the Ninth Schedule, Federal Constitution of Malaysia.
22 *Wakaf* (Selangor) Enactment 2015.
23 *Wakaf* (Melaka) Enactment 2005.
24 *Wakaf* (Negeri Sembilan) Enactment 2005.
25 *Wakaf* (Terengganu) Enactment 2016.
26 Mahamood, Ab. Rahman, and Che Seman, "Cabaran Pelaksanaan Wakaf Universiti Awam di Malaysia: Analisis Menurut Perundangan di Malaysia," 396.
27 Ministry of Higher Education Malaysia, *The University Transformation Programme (UniTP) Purple Book: Enhancing University Income Generation, Endowment & Waqf*, 25–26.
28 Ibid., 25.
29 Ibid., 26.
30 M. Z. Mokthar, "Perceptions of Universiti Sains Malaysia Muslim Staff on Factors Influencing Their Intention to Perform Cash Waqf," *Journal of Islamic Studies and Culture* 4, no. 2 (2016): 101–09, 101, https://doi.org/10.15640/jisc.v4n2a11.
31 D. Abdul Razak et al., "A Study on Sources of Waqf Funds for Higher Education in Selected Countries," *Adam Akademi* 6, no. 1 (2016): 113–28, 117–25.
32 S. U. Ali Hamdan and S. M. Mahamood, "Aplikasi Prinsip Berkekalan Wakaf di Institusi Pengajian Tinggi Terpilih: Perspektif Perundangan," *Journal of Shariah Law Research* 1, no. 2 (2016): 229–50, 241.
33 S. M. Mahamood and A. Ab Rahman, "Financing Universities through Waqf, Pious Endowment: Is It Possible?" *Humanomics* 31, no. 4 (2015): 430–53, 432.
34 N. Mustaffa and M. Z. Muda, "Pengurusan Wakaf Pendidikan Di Institusi Pengajian Tinggi Malaysia: Satu Sorotan Literatur," *International Journal of Management Studies* 21, no. 2 (2014): 63–81, 64, https://doi.org/10.11113/umran2014.1n1.5.
35 A. Abu Hasan, N. A. Hamzah, and A. I. Ismail, "Dana Endowmen: Malaysia Jauh Ketinggalan," *Sinar Harian Online*, August 13, 2019, accessed on 24 October 2020, www.sinarharian.com.my/article/42648/BERITA/Nasional/Dana-endowmen-Malaysia-jauh-ketinggalan%0D.
36 Mohamad Afizal Mehat. *Senior Assistant Director, Public HEI Governance Division*, Department of Higher Education (Malaysia).
37 S. Ahmad, "Tabung Endowment UTM Terima Sumbangan RM5 Juta," *Universiti Teknologi Malaysia*, 2013, accessed on 24 October 2020, https://news.utm.my/2013/03/tabung-endowmen-utm-terima-sumbangan-rm-5-juta/.
38 Amran and Muhammad, "Changes and Challenges in Financial Autonomy," 64.
39 "Peranan Unit Endowmen," *UTM Endowment*, n.d., accessed on 25 October 2020, https://endowmen.utm.my/fungsi/.
40 H. Kazemi and K. Wilkens, "A Simple Approach to the Management of Endowments," *All About Alpha*, 2017, accessed on 19 October 2018, www.allaboutalpha.com/blog/2017/08/07/a simple-approach-to-the- management-of-endowments/.
41 Malcolm Getz, "Endowment," *The Bottom Line* 4, no. 2 (2007): 37–41, 37, https://doi.org/10.1108/eb025286.
42 M. F. Sherlock et al., "College and University Endowments: Overview and Tax Policy Options," *Congressional Research Service* (2015): 1–27, 2.
43 F. A. Monti, "The Surprisingly Complex ABCs of Endowment Funds," *Inside Philanthropy*, 2015, accessed on 24 February 2020, www.insidephilanthropy.com/the-gift-adviser/2015/3/4/the-surprisingly- complex-abcs-of-endowment-funds.html.
44 Universities and University Colleges Act 1971 (Act 30).
45 "Introduction," *Centre for Management of Waqf*, Zakat and Endowment (WAZAN), 2018, accessed on 23 October 2018, www.wazan.upm.edu.my/waqf/upm_trust_fund_for_knowledge/introduction-38931.
46 Nuruliman Ibrahim Head, Waqf Management Section, Centre for Management of Waqf, Zakat & Endowment (WAZAN), Universiti Putra Malaysia (UPM), in an interview with the authors, 31 March 2020.

47 R. Hussin et al., "The Approaches Adopted by the Selected States in Appointing Universities as Waqf Managers," in *Islamic Development Management: Recent Advancements and Issues*, ed. N. Z. Mohd Sidek, R. Said, and W. N. Wan Hasan (Singapore: Springer, 2019), 239–48, 244, https://doi.org/10.1007/978-981-13-7584-2.
48 Mohamad Afizal Mehat (Senior Assistant Director, Department of Higher Education (Malaysia), Public HEI Governance Division), data obtained through email on 9 February 2020.
49 Z. Bahari and A. S. A. Ahmad Shukor, "Pemerkasaan Tadbir Urus Wakaf Pendidikan Tinggi Malaysia," in *Proceeding Strengthening Local Communities Facing the Global Era* 1 (2017): 28–44, 34, http://jurnal.unmuhjember.ac.id/index.php/pslcf/article/view/886.
50 "Cash Waqf Scheme," *Centre for Management of Waqf*, Zakat and Endowment (WAZAN), 2018, accessed 23 October 2018, www.wazan.upm.edu.my/waqf/upm_trust_fund_for_knowledge/cash_waqf_scheme-38933.
51 Mohamad Afizal Mehat (Senior Assistant Director, Department of Higher Education (Malaysia), Public HEI Governance Division), Data obtained through email on 9 February 2020.
52 M. Alias, F. Johari, and A. Abdul Rahman, "Waqf Financing for Islamic Higher Education: USIM's Perspectives," in *Waqf Financing for Higher Education: Issues, Challenges and the Way Forward*, ed. M. R. Ab. Aziz et al. (Bandar Baru Nilai: USIM Publisher, 2014), 27–42, 38.
53 "Trustees of UPM Waqf Fund," *Centre for Management of Waqf*, Zakat and Endowment (WAZAN), 2018, accessed on 25 October 2020, https://wazan.upm.edu.my/about_us/trustees_committees/trustees_of_upm_waqf_fund-38935
54 "Waqf Distribution," *Centre for Management of Waqf*, Zakat and Endowment (WAZAN), 2018, accessed on 25 October 2020, https://wazan.upm.edu.my/about_us/trustees_committees/waqf_disbursement-44095?L=en
55 "Pusat Wakaf Dan Zakat (PWZ)," *Pusat Wakaf dan Zakat (PWZ)*, accessed 27 November 2019, http://pwz.usim.edu.my/.
56 R. Hussin et al., "The Approaches Adopted by the Selected States in Appointing Universities as Waqf Managers."
57 K. A. Kamarudin et al., "Konsep Dan Pembangunan Wakaf Di Negeri Sembilan Daripada Perspektif Majlis Agama Islam Negeri Sembilan," in *Waqf Financing for Higher Education: Issues, Challenges and the Way Forward* (Bandar Baru Nilai: USIM Publisher, 2014), 55–72, 58.
58 Mohamad Afizal Mehat (Senior Assistant Director, Department of Higher Education (Malaysia), Public HEI Governance Division), data obtained through email on 9 February 2020.
59 "Pengenalan," *Wakaf UniSZA*, accessed 27 February 2020, https://wakaf.unisza.edu.my/pengenalan/%0D.
60 "UniSZA Waqf Fund Committee," *UniSZA Waqf*, accessed 28 February 2020, https://wakaf.unisza.edu.my/jawatankuasa-dana-wakaf-unisza/.
61 Ministry of Higher Education Malaysia, *The University Transformation Programme (UniTP) Purple Book: Enhancing University Income Generation, Endowment & Waqf*, 25–26.
62 Ibid., 25.
63 *Wakaf* (Selangor) Enactment 2015.
64 *Wakaf* (Negeri Sembilan) Enactment 2005.
65 *Wakaf* (Terengganu) Enactment 2016.
66 Mahamood, Ab. Rahman, and Che Seman, "Cabaran Pelaksanaan Wakaf Universiti Awam Di Malaysia: Analisis Menurut Perundangan Di Malaysia," 396.
67 A. R. Ahmad et al., "Transformation of Waqf Implementation at Malaysian Public Universities," *Advanced Science Letters* 22, no. 9 (2016): 2184–86, 2184.
68 M. Bulut and C. Korkut, "Cash Waqfs (CWs) and Financing of Education at Ottoman Experience," *Paper presented, International Symposium on Waqf and Higher Education (ISWHE 2016)*, Istanbul, Turkey, 2016, 16–19, 19.

6 Elements of Successful Implementation of Endowment and *Waqf* at the Selected Malaysian Public Universities

Introduction

The successful elements in the implementation of endowment and *waqf* at Malaysian universities are evident from the experiences of UM, UKM, and UTM for the endowment fund and UPM, USIM, and UniSZA for the *waqf* fund.

Successful Elements of Endowment and *Waqf*

The successful elements of endowment and *Waqf* are discussed in the following subsections.

Appropriate Investment Planning

As discussed in Chapter 3, funds that are classified as endowments are invested to generate income. Given that the income earned is used to fund the operation of HEIs, including Malaysian public universities, the principal value of the fund can be maintained. Based on the cases examined in this study (i.e. UM, UKM, and UTM), all universities are responsible for investing in endowment funds under the Bursar's Office at their respective universities. This is corroborated by Abdul Hamid, Hassan–Kamarudin, and Abdul Syahid Sowell, who mentioned that the majority of public universities in Malaysia are managed by the Bursar.[1] As for the universities that employ the *waqf* fund and are involved in investment activities to generate *waqf* income, such as UPM, the investment dealings are managed by the Bursar's Office. However, this is not the case in UniSZA, in which the *waqf* unit comprises a special investment committee to manage the investment of the *waqf* fund and submits only reports to the Bursar's Office.

The universities abroad have been actively investing the endowment fund in alternative assets (e.g. hedge funds and private equity), as discussed by Lerner, Schoar, and Wang.[2] However, endowment funds at Malaysian universities have not actively invested in this asset class—all the universities examined in this book (i.e. UM, UKM, and UTM) invested in only traditional assets, with fixed deposits being the main option for these universities. The investment in fixed deposits is managed directly by the Bursar's Office at the respective universities while other

DOI: 10.4324/9781003435976-6

investments (e.g. bonds, equity, and properties) are managed by the appointed fund managers. Notably, traditional investments are preferred to alternative investments by these universities as they carry low risk and are liquid, which are in line with the Investment Guidelines issued by the MoE Malaysia. The investment rationale explained by some of the informants was as follows:

> No, the university does not have this type of investment (alternative). Approval from the investment committee and board is needed for any new investment and the investment committee does not allow investment activities that have very high risk. As I said, it is through fixed deposits and fund managers only. For the fund manager, the discretion is on their side. So, we do not tell them whether we must invest in this industry or not. It is not like that. They have their own agreement and conditions. However, they will invest as long as it does not . . . it is much more to look at their ethics. For those who are against Shariah, we will not appoint them. It is based on the conventional ethic. The Shariah has been followed and the conventional one is in accordance with the ethical base. So, they will invest in the industry like . . . we have bonds, we have equities. So, for the equities, they will invest in the companies. There are also properties, although a very small percentage. But not exactly. But they are more into shares. Shares in various industries. The construction also exists. They provide a report to us that states where they have invested. So, during the quarterly meeting, they will submit a report to us.[3]
>
> At the UKM, we have two types of investments that are available now. The first is the fixed deposit, and the second includes investments by fund managers. Any fund that has no specification is invested in fixed deposits. For example, if the donor has not specified the areas where the funds need to be invested, then we just invest in the fixed deposits. This is because we assume that the funds may be needed anytime, and therefore, should be liquid. In case of unanticipated fund requirements, we should not face any problems to liquidate that fund. The second type includes funds that are managed by fund managers. For this type of funds at the UKM, we have investments in Amanah Raya Berhad (ARB), Permodalan Nasional Berhad (PNB), RHB, and KAF investment. So, aside from ARB, for the other three investments (i.e. PNB, RHB, and KAF), we invest according to what has been specified by the donors. Then, we give money to the fund managers to decide the type of investments. However, from what I have seen, most of their investments are in the form of equity. They do not reveal the equity breakup, but we generally know that it primarily includes shares.[4]
>
> The investment must be low risk.[5]
>
> As I said just now, we can only invest in fixed deposits because the UTM has not yet received the approval to invest beyond fixed deposits. So now, all the endowment money is invested in the fixed deposits. No hedge funds, no bonds.[6]
>
> In fact, most of our investments, our money, we put in fixed deposits. They are important because we do not want to invest as the concept of the investment itself is risky. Although its returns are high, the risks are also

high. At the same time, our endowment is still not ready to absorb the risk as it is oriented more towards executing the responsibilities of the donors. When the risk is high, we are apprehensive that the money will be lost and so on. As a result, we cannot execute the responsibilities of the donors. Trust is important. The endowment uses the income. As long as the moon, stars, and sun exist, the endowment will continue to function.[7]

In the case of *waqf*, although its principles do not include the investment of the *waqf* fund, it should be preserved. However, this study found that universities including UPM and UniSZA were involved in investment activities as they are the mechanisms to generate income from the *waqf* fund, particularly in the form of cash. This was accomplished through fixed deposits before the project began. The following are the statements of the informants from these two universities:

The approved investment that can be implemented by the UPM for all funds, including the *waqf* fund, is fixed deposits. This is subject to the policies or guidelines issued by the government.[8]

The bursar invests in fixed deposits. Their investment is only in fixed deposits, not any other instrument.[9]

Since the *waqf* currently is cash *waqf*, the principal value of cash *waqf* cannot be used unless income is generated. How to earn income if no investment has been made? The fixed deposit is a medium which has very low risk and its returns are also guaranteed by the bank.[10]

Based on the earlier discussions, Table 6.1 summarises the types of investments and assets preferred by universities for investing their endowment and *waqf* funds. Three universities invested their funds in a single asset (i.e. fixed deposit) only,

Table 6.1 Investment Selection

Question 6.1: Which types of investments (i.e. traditional or alternative) the endowment/*waqf* fund of this institution is likely to invest in?
Apakah jenis-jenis pelaburan (i.e. tradisional atau alternatif) tabung endowmen/wakaf di institusi ini yang cenderung untuk melabur?

Fund	*Informant*	*Traditional Investments*	*Alternative Investments*
Endowment	UM3	Fixed deposit, equity, bond, and properties	–
	UKM2, UKM3	Fixed deposit and equity	–
	UTM1, UTM2	Fixed deposit	–
Waqf	UPM1, UPM3	Fixed deposit	–
	UniSZA	Fixed deposit	–
	USIM	–	–

Note: (–) not related.

Source: Developed by the authors.

except for UKM and UM, which invested in assets other than a fixed deposit. The UKM invested in equity while UM invested in equity, bond, and properties. The investment in these assets (besides fixed deposits) was undertaken by the fund managers at these universities. Furthermore, the selection of these assets was subject to the discretion of the fund managers when the donor did not provide any instruction. The endowment fund at UM and UKM complied with the investment portfolio diversification strategy, whose importance has been highlighted by various scholars such as Leković,[11] Jayeola, Ismail, and Sufihani,[12] and Gurrib and Alshahrani.[13] In USIM, the symbol (-) was set to indicate that investment activities were yet to be implemented, although the process of implementation was underway.

However, the investment portfolio in UM and UKM was not diversified enough as the numbers of fund managers were only ten and five, respectively. One of the reasons for this was the small size of endowments compared to endowment sizes at universities abroad, such as Harvard University and Yale University, which normally have 100 or more fund managers to diversify their investment portfolio, as explained by Tuttle.[14]

In the context of *waqf*, despite the returns gained from investing the *waqf* fund (e.g. cash *waqf*) in fixed deposits, one of the informants criticised the practice of the *waqf* institution. He argued that this practice empowers the capitalists instead of the *ummah*. Subsequently, cash *waqf* was recommended to be converted or treated as a purchased property (e.g. shop lot) as greater benefits could be reaped while the value of this type of asset would increase rapidly. The following is the argument of the informant:

> I do not agree with the management methods of cash *waqf* in most *waqf* institutions. This is because, the existing method is actually to empower capitalists, not for empowering the *ummah*. We want to empower the *ummah*, not the capitalists. In this instance, in the current situation, for example, WAZAN has RM 11.4 million. What can the WAZAN do with that amount? Give to the bursar to transfer into fixed deposits. How much funds does Yayasan Wakaf Malaysia have? Approximately RM 140 million. Another example is MAIS—how much cash assets do they have? It is approximately RM80 million. This does not include other MAINs. My question is, what do these *waqf* institutions do with the cash? Frankly speaking, just ask any *waqf* institution, most of them invest the money in fixed deposits. Right? If you interview a *waqf* manager, they would respond that they invest only in fixed deposits. When we invest in fixed deposits, who will gain from it? For me, capitalists. What is the reason? The banking institutions that manage the fixed deposits want to profiteer. So, how they can profit is by giving a loan to anyone who wants to borrow. Most of the borrowers are big capitalists like manufacturers. So, most of them are non-Muslims. Although the bank is an Islamic bank, the big borrowers are usually manufacturers and housing developers. Right? And the bank will charge approximately 15–20 per cent. Afterwards, the bank will give us approximately 3–4 per cent. So, do we feel comfortable with this 3–4 per cent? For me, this is wrong because we do not empower

> the *ummah*. Instead, we empower the capitalists, that is, we provide capital injections to the capitalists. Supposedly, what we should do is, this—anyone who manages the cash *waqf* must think quickly to change the cash *waqf* to the asset. This is the best. For example, buy properties such as shop lots as much as possible. Buy these assets. This is the right way. So, this is for me. If any new town is growing, buy the properties there. This is because the value of properties rises quickly and never falls. The second is when *waqf* properties in new towns and the big cities are increased; then our holdings at these locations become stronger. This is important so that we can control the ownership. This is what we call empowering the *ummah*. Recently, who conducts the business in most towns and cities? Indeed, non-Muslim people because they are conquering these places. So, how do empower Muslims? That is why the Maqasid Shariah exists in the *waqf*. When I talk about this, it will be controversial. But, for me, I do not agree with the culture of the cash *waqf* management in the existing *waqf* institutions. I also disagree even with the WAZAN itself. Why do we need to keep cash up to RM 11 million with the return only around 3 or 3.7 per cent? The people who donated their properties as *waqf* want to see results. If we buy properties, it is fine for me. When we buy properties even with the amount of RM 2 million, the value of RM 2 million is still there, not including the rental payment that we will earn. Definitely, the shop lots can be rented out to Muslims. Although non-Muslims can also rent, we must prioritise Muslims. So, indirectly, when we conquer several properties in towns, we can control the rental payment although non-Muslims are likely to increase it. So, we can act as a counterbalance, the counterbalance to market pressures.[15]

This argument by the informant corresponded with the *waqf* practice of one of the universities discussed in this study, USIM. Based on the interview conducted with the representative, he explained that the fund contributed to the university was used to purchase the building to establish health clinics and haemodialysis centres for the benefit of the community. The following is the informant's explanation:

> There is a project that we have succeeded in, for example, specialist clinic, dental clinic, and haemodialysis centre that were developed separately at three shop lots located near the Nilai Square. Our haemodialysis centre has received funds from Permodalan Nasional Berhad (PNB). They gave approximately RM700,000. So, we used RM 500,000 to buy the building from Majlis Perbandaran Nilai (MPN) and the balance to buy the equipment. That is why we call it MAINS—PNB Haemodialysis Centre.[16]

Based on the explanation by the informant from UPM and the practice of the *waqf* fund at the USIM, the income generation for the *waqf* fund should not be concentrated on investments in fixed deposits. Converting funds in the form of money to property should be considered by the institutions that implement *waqf* fund in Malaysia.

While investing either the endowment or the *waqf* fund, the Malaysian context should be considered, as discussed in Chapter 4. All the universities examined in this study prioritised investing their endowment and *waqf* funds in the Shariah-compliant investment instruments in the form of either fixed deposits or investments managed by fund managers, such as in *Sukuk* and I-REIT. Although some universities previously invested in instruments that did not comply with the Shariah, they strove to convert it to an Islamic investment to ensure that (related to halal and haram) the investments were not doubted. The evidence that universities prioritised investment in Shariah-compliant instruments is reflected in the following statements:

> Our investment in fixed deposits is a mixture of Islamic and conventional. For fund management, we mainly have shariah-compliant fund managers who handle equity and bond (*Sukuk*). There is not much investment in REIT, or Islamic or conventional instruments.[17]
>
> The first one is we need to refer back to our agreement with them. This is because most agreements are old. For example, the agreement with RHB was signed in 1996, while PNB was in 2000. These agreements are old and were signed long back and we have received the entire money. But, when we started managing the investment more aggressively, we established a committee that we called the investment committee, which has existed since then. So, through that committee, we have provided a guideline or the Statement of Philosophy. In that guideline, the first thing that must be accomplished is selecting Islamic investments. That means Shariah-compliant investments. So, Alhamdulillah, all our investments in fixed deposits now have been invested in Islamic products such as mudharabah and murabahah. The funds with the fund managers have also applied the Shariah principles after our review. Alhamdulillah, that means Shariah-compliant except RHB. However, we have just conducted a meeting with the RHB and the board and have agreed to transfer the fund to Shariah-compliant instruments. So, as I know, in the last two months, the process of converting the investments to Shariah-compliant has been completed.[18]
>
> All the investment activities in the UKM must comply with the Shariah as decided by the University Management Board (LPU). The Shariah-compliant investments are implemented by the UKM Bursar.[19]
>
> Generally speaking, UTM has rules where every investment must comply with Islamic principles, especially for the latest products. Previously, before Islamic banking in Malaysia expanded, UTM had subscribed to conventional products. But I can say that in the new millennium, for all current accounts as well as fixed deposits, we used Islamic banking products.[20]
>
> Because most of the donors are Muslims, investments must be made Shariah-compliant.[21]
>
> The *waqf* fund in UPM is invested in Shariah-compliant fixed deposits.[22]
>
> Yes, of course (Shariah-compliant). This is because, in our investment committee, we appoint persons who are *fakih* in this area. We have the

Faculty of Islamic Contemporary here, who know the matters related to fatwa and other relevant aspects.[23]

The information presented here is summarised in Table 6.2. UM was the only university employing Islamic and conventional investments for the fixed deposit and other assets managed by fund managers. However, this was not an issue as the endowment fund involved not only Muslim donors but also non-Muslim donors. For investments at other universities, Shariah-compliant investments became a choice in the investment of endowment and *waqf* funds. This practice increases the confidence of Muslim donors about income generation using the money they had contributed to the funds.

The tax on the earned investment dividend is not payable by universities (for either endowment or *waqf* fund) if the investment is managed by the bursar (e.g. fixed deposit), as explained by the informants in the interviews. For universities, such as UM and UKM, with other investments (e.g. bond and equity) managed by fund managers, specific taxes should be paid. Fund managers normally deduct the tax before the net dividend is transferred to the bursar. Therefore, no other taxes need to be paid by the bursar after the dividend of the investment is received. The following are the explanations by the informant:

> Basically, we do not have to pay taxes. But once we receive the dividend transferred by the fund managers, there are maps. So, the companies who need to pay the taxes deduct their dividend before transferring them to us. So, the dividend that we receive has maps. The maps mean tax. So, we do not

Table 6.2 Shariah-Compliant Investments

Question 6.2: How does this institution ensure that its endowment/*waqf* fund* investment activities are Shariah-compliant?
Bagaimanakah institusi ini memastikan bahawa aktiviti pelaburan tabung endowmen/wakaf adalah patuh Syariah?

Fund	*Informant*		*Type of Investment*	
			Conventional	*Islamic*
Endowment	UM3	Fixed deposit	✓	✓
		Fund manager (equity, bond, and properties)	✓	✓
	UKM2, UKM3	Fixed deposit	–	✓
		Fund manager (equity)	–	✓
	UTM1, UTM2	Fixed deposit		✓
Waqf	UPM1	Fixed deposit	–	✓
	UniSZA	Fixed deposit	–	✓

Note: (✓) yes; (–) not related.

Source: Developed by the authors.

> have to pay the taxes. Basically, UM is not taxable. But for the dividends, we usually receive net of tax.[24]
>
> For the fixed deposit, we are exempted from paying the tax as we are under the institution. But fund managers like ARB, RHB, PNB, and KAF have to pay service tax based on the profits that we earn. They are also based on the withdrawal charge. For example, like ARB, we have a withdrawal charge, an annual charge, and then their tax is based on how much they charge.[25]

The universities and types of funds that need to pay tax on investment returns are summarised in Table 6.3.

Each endowment or *waqf* fund has a model for the distribution of dividends or income/*hibah*. The distribution model varies for each university selected for this study. As the endowment fund in UM and UKM was established based on the chair that was created according to the request of certain Responsibility Centre (PTJ), the distribution model at these universities cannot be provided as it differed between one chair to another depending on their agreement. The models at other universities, such as UTM (for the endowment fund), UPM, and UniSZA (for the *waqf* fund) are summarised in Table 6.4.

For UTM, the informant explained that each endowment fund donor at this institution employed the university's model. However, the return from the investment was generally divided into two portions, 90 per cent and 10 per cent—90 per cent was used for the benefit of the beneficiaries (e.g. scholarships) while 10 per cent was used for the management of the endowment fund at UTM. As for 10 per cent, the remaining money after covering all the expenditure was reinvested to generate more revenue. The explanation of the model is as follows:

> It depends on the donors. For Azman Hashim, out of 100 earnings, RM 22 million is a huge amount. You imagine that for RM 1 million, returns amount to RM 40,000 a month. It means around RM 400,000 a year. So, 10 per cent for the endowment management (RM 80,000), 15 per cent for academic development, and 75 per cent for scholarships. For others, 10 per cent for the management, and 90 per cent for scholarships. It does not include academic development because it depends on the donor's wishes. For academic development, we incur expenses for conducting seminars, courses, and others. For Azman Hashim, he has specified these things.[26]

The dividend distribution model of the endowment fund at UTM is illustrated in Figure 6.1.

In the case of *waqf*, every university employed the respective income/*hibah* distribution model. As for UPM, 50 per cent of the *waqf* income from investments was used for the beneficiaries, 20 per cent was used for the management of WAZAN, 15 per cent was transferred to Perbadanan Wakaf Selangor (PWS) as an agent of MAIS to collect the *waqf* fund, and 15 per cent was used for reinvestment. For UniSZA, although MAIDAM was the sole trustee of the *waqf* fund in Terengganu, MAIDAM had no share in the *waqf* income collected by the UniSZA. To illustrate,

Table 6.3 Tax on Dividend/Income Earned

Question 6.3: Does this institution need to pay tax from the investment dividend/ income earned?
Adakah institusi ini perlu membayar cukai daripada dividen/ pendapatan pelaburan yang diperolehi?

Fund	*Informant*	*Fixed Deposit*	*Fund Manager*
Endowment	UM3	X	✓
	UKM2	X	✓
	UTM1	X	–
Waqf	UPM1	X	–
	UniSZA	X	–

Note: (✓) yes; (X) no; (-) not related.
Source: Developed by the authors.

Table 6.4 Dividend/Income Distribution Model

Question 6.4 How are the dividends/income distributed in this institution?
Bagaimana dividen/pendapatan diagihkan di institusi ini?

Fund	*Informant*	*Model*
Endowment	UM	Based on the chair agreement
	UKM	Based on the chair agreement
	UTM2	General: 90%—Beneficiaries 10%—Management
Waqf	UPM3	50%—Beneficiaries 35%—Management (20% WAZAN, 15% PWS) 15%—Reinvestment
	UniSZA	60%—Beneficiaries 20%—Management 20%—Reinvestment

Source: Developed by the authors.

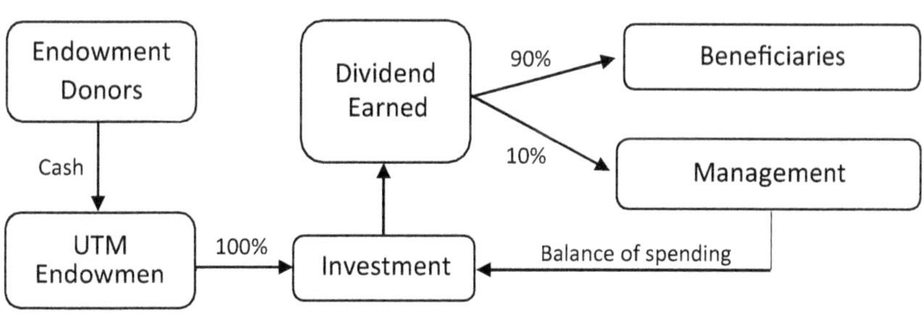

Figure 6.1 Dividend Distribution Model at UTM Endowment
Source: Developed by the authors.

the *waqf* income was distributed only to the beneficiaries (60%), the management of *waqf* at the UniSZA (20%), and reinvestment (20%). The explanation of the informants from both universities related to the *waqf* income distribution model is as follows:

> For the principal, an income exists. For example, from RM 7 million, we earned more than RM 400,000 (income). From the amount of RM 400,000, 50 per cent is distributed as per the donor's wishes, which is *al-mawqūf 'alayh*, 15 per cent is for the Perbadanan Wakaf Selangor (PWS), 20 per cent for the management of WAZAN, and 15 per cent for reinvestment.[27]
>
> The income earned, mainly from fixed deposits, is known as the generated income. It depends on the term of deposit—either for 6 months or 12 months. Once it matures, we divide it based on the ratio of 60:20:20. 60 for the welfare, which is transferred to students in any form based on what has been determined by the committee. We have three committees actually. So, 20 per cent for reinvestment and the other 20 per cent for the maintenance. The maintenance is in terms of, for example, promoting the *waqf*. No portion is allocated to MAIDAM.[28]

The income distribution model of the *waqf* fund at the UPM is illustrated in Figure 6.2.

Meanwhile, Figure 6.3 illustrates the income distribution model of the *waqf* fund at the UniSZA.

Figures 6.2 and 6.3 suggest that the income distribution models at UPM and UniSZA differ, specifically in terms of the portion that should be distributed by the WAZAN to their MAIN (e.g. PWS), which was 15 per cent according to their mutual agreement. As for UniSZA, no allocation was made for their MAIN (e.g. MAIDAM). As the status of *mutawalli* is granted to the university by the MAIN in managing the *waqf* fund at the institution, the share of income distribution to the MAIN can affect the operations of *waqf*. To illustrate, if the university can fully utilise the income without allocating any portions to the MAIN, the income can benefit more beneficiaries or a greater amount can be used for the management and reinvestment.

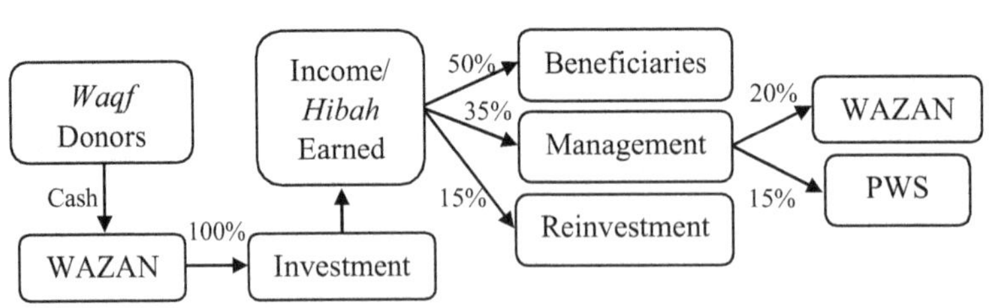

Figure 6.2 Income Distribution Model at WAZAN, UPM

Source: Developed by the authors.

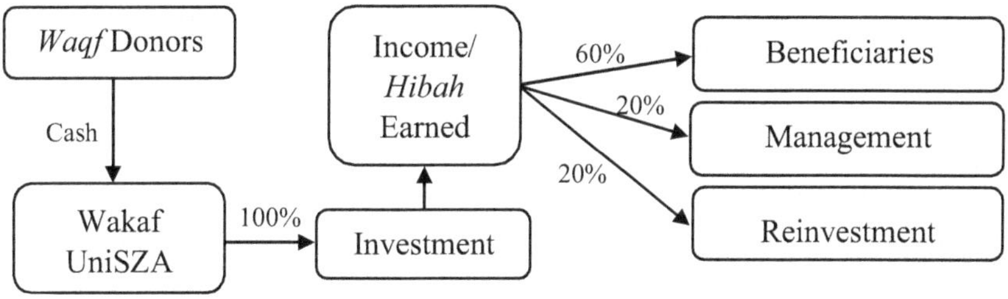

Figure 6.3 Income Distribution Model at Wakaf UniSZA

Source: Developed by the authors.

The discussion of this element (e.g. appropriate investment planning) leads to the conclusion that all universities examined in this study have invested in traditional assets with fixed deposits being the preferred option. Given that most universities have been investing only in fixed deposits, the investment portfolio is not diversified although most of the investments comply with the Shariah. While UM and UKM invest in assets other than fixed deposits, such as equity, bond, and properties, the diversification in the investment portfolio has not reached a satisfactory level, with the number of funds managed being ten for UM and five for UKM. The number of funds required for the fund managers to reflect the best diversification of the investment portfolio is 100 or higher. Therefore, this element does not lead to a successful implementation of the endowment and *waqf* in funding Malaysian public universities.

Superior Investment Committees

Generally, the investment committee of endowment and *waqf* funds at Malaysian public universities refers to the university investment committee located at the Bursar's Office. Besides managing other funds, such as gifts and general contributions, this committee is also responsible for managing the investment of endowment and *waqf* funds in the form of fixed deposits, as discussed in the previous section. To ensure that the committee applies the best practice in managing the investment in the university, three basic elements should be evaluated—size, expertise, and diversity—as suggested by Boose, Grim, and Chism.[29] Based on these basic elements, the investment committees for the endowment and *waqf* funds at the selected universities are investigated, and the findings are discussed here.

In terms of size, the investment committee at UM, UTM, and UPM had six members each, while UniSZA and UKM had seven and nine members, respectively. This data was derived based on the following statements by the informants:

We are indeed the investment committee at the university level. Only one. It is a central university. But its members include the board of directors,

VC, and Finance Committee (FC). Board normally has four people. Therefore, overall, the committee has four board members, one VC and one FC.[30]

As I see, now it is nine. First of all is our LPU (which consists of four persons), VC, and we have two experts in investment/finance, an economist, a director of Khazanah, and a bursar.[31]

At the UTM, the investment committee at the university level has only one committee. Its members consist of the chairman, a representative of LPU, a bursar, VC, Deputy VC (Development), and a representative of the ministry. The number is thus six including the chairman.[32]

Six (subject to the LPU's decisions).[33]

Our investment committee has seven members. We follow what is outlined by the MoHE. VC usually chairs every committee. However, as we have adopted Model 3, the chairman of our master committee is the chairman of the MAIDAM itself. Thus, the co-chairman is our VC. Both our committees, i.e. investment and distribution are monitored by VC. For our FC, we have one Islamic advisor.[34]

The size of the investment committee at the universities discussed here is summarised in Table 6.5. All the universities achieved the minimum number of six investment committee members set by the government in the Investment Guidelines. Notably, the members of the investment committee in endowment and *waqf* funds were under the university investment committee, except for UniSZA, which employed their investment committee at the Office of *Waqf* and Endowment to manage the investment of *waqf* fund. However, all the investment activities of *waqf* fund need to be reported to the bursar.

For the selection of the members of the investment committee, each university presented its justification of the basis on which the members have been selected. According to the informants, the members were selected based on interviews, Investment Guidelines, and other qualifying aspects such as

Table 6.5 Number of Investment Committee Members

Question 6.5: How many members are present in the endowment/*waqf* investment committee?
Berapakah bilangan ahli yang wujud dalam jawatankuasa pelaburan endowmen/wakaf?

Fund	*Informant*	*No. of Members*
Endowment	UM3	6
	UKM2	9
	UTM1	6
Waqf	UPM2	6
	UniSZA	7

Source: Developed by the authors.

knowledge, experience, and expertise. The justification provided by each informant is as follows:

> This is because of the board decision. Indeed, we have a predetermined term. So, according to that term, its members are appointed by the Board and consist of Board members, top management, and representatives from the MoF and MoE. Recently, we have also appointed independent members who have knowledge and experience in accounting and investment.[35]
>
> They are appointed based on their expertise. Like the LPU members, they are appointed because of the quota for them. So, they should be involved with any decision concerning the university. So, we cannot challenge it. For others, we only choose one, based on their expertise. The second one is about the position. The position here implies an important position such as Khazanah where their representative is a person who oversees our revenue. So, we must include them in our list.[36]
>
> Our rules of governance indicate that we must have an LPU representative and the chairman must be the representative of the university board. So, individuals who are on the university board and whom the university thinks is a decent person to chair our meeting. Afterwards, we must have another representative from the LPU as an ordinary member. VC of course for their position. Then Deputy VC (Development) because basically, the person is our boss who monitors finance. So, of course, they need to be engaged in financial matters. Next is the bursar because they are a Chief Financial Officer (CFO). That is the justification. In all of this, we follow the governance that has been established by the Registrar Office.[37]
>
> GP investment of MoHE and LPU.[38]
>
> Basically, for the investment committee, we find experienced people. Like Dato' Wan Ismail who has held the position for more than 30 years in the bank. The last one is an advisor at Bank Islam. So, now the person was appointed as a member of the Board of Directors at MAIDAM based on their expertise.[39]

As the investment of endowment and *waqf* funds at the selected universities examined in this study was under the authority of the university investment committee, individuals who were determined to become committee members should be accepted. Furthermore, the individuals' knowledge, experience, and expertise were proven as they were selected by the top management of the university. Similar to UniSZA, the presence of experienced and expert members in the investment field in the Financial and Investment Committee led to their willingness to invest on their own. Overall, the results are summarised in Table 6.6.

The previous chapter (i.e. Chapter 4) discussed the requirement to appoint members who had expertise in the Shariah field. Although the informants from UPM could not answer the related question in this study, some other universities

Table 6.6 Selection Basis of the Investment Committee Members

Question 6.6: On what basis are the members appointed?
Atas dasar apakah ahli-ahli tersebut dilantik?

Fund	*Informant*	*Basis of Selection*
Endowment	UM3	Board decision, knowledge, experience
	UKM2	Expertise, position
	UTM1	Governance
Waqf	UPM2	Investment Guidelines
	UniSZA	Expertise, experience

Source: Developed by the authors.

employed expert members in the Shariah field, which was in line with the following statement from the informants interviewed for this study:

> We recently appointed a member who was in an investment bank and she probably is very knowledgeable in both shariah and non-shariah investment.[40]
>
> In Shariah, I am not very sure. But we have an economic expert, including on the Islamic economy.[41]
>
> Whether we have an expert or not, I am not very sure. But we have an accountant on the committee. I mean our LPU member is a person who is from a banking institution and he is also an accountant. But, if you want to know whether he is a Shariah expert or not, I think I do not know the answer. Maybe yes and maybe not. As he knew about the procedure in accounting and was also an entrepreneur, it could be the reason he was appointed to the committee. This is because we want to use the expertise that he has.[42]
>
> Yes, we have. A lecturer from the Faculty of Islamic Contemporary like Ustaz Ahmad Tirmizi and Dr Nadhirah. They are indeed experts.[43]

This case proved the earning of dividends or income from the investment of the endowment and *waqf* funds at the selected universities in this study. This situation was attributed to the existence of expert and knowledgeable members in the Shariah field in the investment committee.

All cases examined in this study involved investment committee members with varied backgrounds in terms of gender, race, age, education, tenure, expertise, and experience, as summarised in Table 6.7. Although the informants from the UPM did not provide any specific answer, their response was adequate to demonstrate the diversity of their investment committee members. The involvement of members with various backgrounds could help limit the issues related to group dynamics (e.g. groupthink, confirmation bias, group polarisation) in decision-making. All

Table 6.7 Diversity of Investment Committee Members

Question 6.7: How do you ensure that the issues related to group dynamics (e.g. groupthink, confirmation bias, group polarisation) can be limited in the investment committee?

Bagaimana untuk memastikan isu-isu yang berkaitan dengan kumpulan dinamik (seperti kumpulan berfikir, pengesahan berat sebelah, polarisasi kumpulan dll.) dapat dihadkan dalam jawatankuasa pelaburan?

Fund	*Informant*	*Factor*						
		Gender	*Race*	*Age*	*Education*	*Tenure*	*Expertise*	*Experience*
Endowment	UM3	✓	✓	✓	✓	✓	✓	✓
	UKM2	✓	–	✓	✓	✓	✓	✓
	UTM1	–	✓	✓	✓	✓	✓	✓
Waqf	UPM1, UPM2	In general						
	UniSZA	✓	-	✓	✓	✓	✓	✓

Note: (✓) yes; (-) not related.

Source: Developed by the authors.

informants agreed that experience and expertise were the most important factors for the best decision-making on investments, as proven in the following statement:

> All members have wide knowledge in terms of accounting, management and finance and they are from various fields. Thus, the board of UM has already chosen those whom they believe can monitor and evaluate the investment on their behalf. What was their specific factor that the board deemed to be important, I am not sure but my guess would be their expertise and experience in various fields.[44]
>
> The most important is their expertise and experience. Gender or age does not indicate a role. For the Management Committee (JKP), they must have the expertise to make decisions in matters related to the financial or investment aspects. For instance, market analysis, instrument selection, and performance evaluation.[45]
>
> Definitely, it is about their expertise and experience. If not, there is no benefit that we can gain if the people who are appointed are unable to give us any input. If they provide inputs that we do not need, then it is meaningless. We want people who can give us the input, this is what we can do.[46]
>
> Expertise.[47]
>
> In my opinion, it must have a combination actually. The experience must be there, especially the people who have been involved with the bank dealings before. So, they know where are we supposed to invest to generate more profit. And expertise also is needed here. So, when there is a combination of these two factors, it can contribute to the success of an investment.[48]

This statement indicates that the presence of diversified committee members in terms of experience and expertise is the most significant factor compared to other factors (e.g. gender, race, age, education, and tenure) for gaining the best investment results.

In discussing this element (e.g. superior investment committee), the investment committee at the selected universities in this study could be considered superior. Although the committee members have been selected by the university's top management, all the members meet the minimum criteria in terms of size, as specified in the guidelines. Besides the expertise in investing, they also have the expertise in the Shariah field, as determined by the top management of the university. The diversity of members is also present, especially in terms of experience and expertise, as found in the interview session with the representatives from those universities. Although UniSZA employs its investment committee at the *waqf* unit level, the indicators discussed earlier could also be observed in the investment committee.

Highly Skilled Investment Managers

Malaysian public universities do not have internal investment managers to manage their endowment and *waqf* funds. The entire endowment and *waqf* funds-related investment is solely under the jurisdiction of the University Investment Committee, which is located at the Bursar's Office, as discussed previously. However, two universities, examined in this study, UM and UKM, used fund management services to manage investments besides fixed deposits, such as bonds, equities, and properties. This was validated by the informants from the selected universities, for example, from the UM, who provided the following explanation:

> Currently, most are under fixed deposits or equities and bonds only. Equity and bond investments are handled by the appointed fund managers. Investment in properties also exist, but are not significant.[49]

For managing the endowment investments in bonds, equities, and properties, the informants from the universities stated that the selection criteria of the fund managers were based on performance, expertise, resources, registration with the SCM, and the banks partnering the fund managers. This result is summarised in Table 6.8. The explanation offered by the informant is as follows:

> Many of our fund managers have long been appointed. Recently, we have had no newly appointed fund managers. Indeed, all of them have long existed. Usually, they are chosen based on their performance or something like that. This is because we do not have any structured product. So their discretion is according to our requirements. However, they assess and decide themselves the best investment options. So their expertise and resources, which we lack, become one of the reasons why we have appointed the fund managers to invest on our behalf.[50]
>
> For the past one, I am not sure. However recently, we have conducted an exercise to choose the fund managers. Among the features to select them

are, first: must meet investment needs. For example, we want the investment in the form of equity and people who manage such funds must also invest in equity. Second, they must be registered with SCM and bank back, which implies that banks are partnering with the fund managers. In simple words, we do not select a fund manager who manages the investment privately. Only people who work in a bank and are not agents but officers.[51]

This justification is summarised in Table 6.8, which illustrates that fund managers' expertise is required by the funds involved in investment activities, especially for the endowment, given their ability to invest in other assets, such as bonds, equities, and properties. The advantages offered by fund managers were also perceived as factors contributing to the success of a fund, which was in line with Lerner, Schoar, and Wang's argument that managers with skills and experience could contribute to the success of endowment investments at a university.[52] This argument was further reinforced by UM accounting for the highest endowment fund collection among public universities in Malaysia. This element can be clarified as being the most important in contributing to the successful implementation of endowment in funding Malaysian public universities.

Fund managers were further clarified as being external parties, which is reflected in the following statements:

Outsiders. They are from banks and financial institutions. But, we appointed them. The Board appoints them.[53]

The fund managers here are external parties.[54]

Given that fund managers are external parties, the aspect of their management fees needs to be highlighted. The informants from the UM and UKM stated that the payment to the fund managers was based on the signed agreement. When the dividends are received by the bursar, nothing is required to be paid for the service of the fund manager as the receipts are net dividends. Besides, the payment amount is deducted before being submitted to the respective bursar, although the exact percentage paid to the fund managers was not provided by the informants. This is summarised in Table 6.9.

Table 6.8 Basis of Investment Manager Selection

Question 6.8: On what basis is the investment manager appointed?
Atas dasar apakah pengurus pelaburan tersebut dilantik?

Fund	*Informant*	*Basis of Selection*
Endowment	UM3	Performance, expertise, resources
	UKM2	Has investment, managed investment, registered, bank back (fund managers are partnering with the banks)

Source: Developed by the authors.

Table 6.9 Investment Manager's Fee

Question 6.9:	How much does this institution spend every month to pay the fund manager? *Berapa banyakkah institusi ini membelanjakan setiap bulan untuk membayar pengurus dana?*

Fund	*Informant*	*Manager Fee*
Endowment	UM3	Based on agreement and net dividend received
	UKM2	Based on agreement and net dividend received

Source: Developed by the authors.

The informants from the selected universities opined that the fees paid to fund managers were worth it, although a few fund managers did not demonstrate positive performance. This is evident from the following statements of the informants:

> Yes, because we do not have the resources that fund managers have to trade in equities and bonds in terms of expertise, cost, and manpower.[55]
>
> To be frank, a few of them are okay and a few of them are not. Some of them have recorded the market value under the principal value. So, it is like that. However, we cannot eliminate them since the deal with the donors has been made. So, they want to manage it on their own.[56]

Based on the responses provided by the informants, the authors further asked about the specific area where the fund managers performed well. The informants provided the following responses:

> Ours are more on the capital appreciation and income generation. Not on high returns as it would require assuming a higher risk. Our criterion is that they must be able to achieve the benchmark as per the agreement.[57]
>
> For the external managers, they are only doing the investment. But, for the fund management (e.g. expenditure) and other matters are managed or decided by the chairs. So, based on your question just now, they perform in what area, my answer is on the return earned by them. We have an investment manager with whom we agreed a long time ago, since 1996. He has helped earn a four-fold return on the original principal fund value.[58]

Other than fixed deposits, the appointment of fund managers in universities to manage endowment investments in assets is important. With their skills, the managers can generate higher returns on the invested funds.

The investment managers appointed at the UM and UKM are known as fund managers. In other universities, these fund managers are not present as a fixed deposit is the only investment asset. The appointment of the fund managers at UM and UKM benefits these universities because of the capability of fund managers to invest in other traditional forms of assets, such as bonds, equities, and properties.

In the case of the endowment fund, fund managers are highly important in ensuring the success of the fund as they can help diversify the investment portfolio as one of the investment strategies. The skills of fund managers at Malaysian public universities (e.g. UM and UKM) have been established as they are among the best financial institutions in this country. The fund managers appointed at the universities should also be considered professional fund managers as they are registered with the SCM.

Alumni Networks

The element of alumni network is discussed in this section. However, the alumni information at the UM and UKM cannot be provided as the endowment funds established at these universities are based on the chair. In other words, the donors for each endowment chair are established. Besides the implementation of the endowment at the UTM, including *waqf* at the UPM, USIM, and UniSZA, new contributions were required to allow a project to run. One of the methods of obtaining this contribution continuously is through the alumni, given the consistent increase in their number every year.

Among the selected universities in this study (i.e. UTM, UPM, USIM, and UniSZA), the alumni of USIM and UniSZA were not highly active in contributing to the *waqf* funds. This was in contrast to the endowment fund at UTM, where their alumni were considered highly active in contributing to the endowment fund (e.g. Tabung Endowmen Alumni) and recording a collection of approximately RM4.6 million at the end of 2019. This finding corresponds to the following statement by the UTM informant:

> Alhamdulillah, although in general, we are still low, for our alumni, we have a specific fund called Tabung Endowmen Alumni, in which the financial sources are contributed by the alumni either in small or large amounts. For your information, until the end of 2019, the total amount of money in that fund was approximately RM 4.6 million. That is why we mentioned that funds for scholarships are contributed by the alumni. We give 75 per cent of investment return in the Tabung Endowment Alumni to students in the form of scholarships.[59]

As for UPM, the informant stated that he could not specify whether or not the alumni at the university actively contributed. However, the collaboration between the Centre for Management of WAZAN, the alumni centre, and the alumni association has yielded good results, being rated nine on a scale of one to ten. This is captured in the following explanation:

> I cannot give the measurement in the form of a percentage. However, in terms of activities, I can say that almost all activities in the alumni centre and alumni association have the involvement of the WAZAN. For me, the cooperation from them is very good. On a scale of 10, I think I can rate them

> 9, or excellent. This rating also includes the parameter of developing the *waqf* projects and the distribution of *waqf* income. In the context of alumni, it also includes the pensioners. The cooperation from the UPM pensioners is also very good.[60]

To the query on how the institutions ensure that their alumni contribute continuously to the endowment or *waqf* funds, the informants responded that they had set up a network with the alumni. Therefore, the alumni networks were indicated as highly important in encouraging alumni contribution to the funds. This finding was supported by Wang, who revealed that network building with the alumni was one of the most vital elements in persuading the alumni to contribute to their universities.[61] The only approach in this study was to build a network through the role of the alumni association, which is reflected in the following statements by the informants:

> UTM itself has over 180,000 alumni. If we assume that the total number of alumni who are still alive is approximately 150,000 and each alumni contributes only RM 1 per month, then we can collect RM 150,000 from the alumni alone. So, this means that the endowment in the university should move together with their alumni unit. This is because we hope and expect more from our alumni. Therefore, we provide various channels to contribute. We have online banking, we have Jom Pay so that all channels can be used to contribute.[62]
>
> So far, I think the consistent one is during the convocation ceremony. All graduates are declared alumni on that day and each of them will contribute RM 10.00. That is what we call consistency because it happens every year. However, before the establishment of Waqaf Ilmu, we did not have a method to attract alumni support. What is interesting in the case of WAZAN is that the number of staff is minimal, only three. We created a method that we called a satellite project. I mean, we did a project with the colleges, faculties, and institutions, for example, through their alumni cluster. So, they created their own programme, the alumni dinner for example. All the programmes held are initiatives taken by colleges or faculties with their respective alumni. That is what I mean when I say that the cooperation from the alumni is good, really good.[63]

The cooperation from the alumni association could assist the university to convey the information about the endowment or *waqf* funds to their alumni. A good collaboration between the endowment or *waqf* unit with their alumni association could be created when each endowment or *waqf* activity involves both parties. The endowment or *waqf* unit involvement is highly important as the information about these funds can be delivered more rapidly and widely while the implementation of the activities can be more efficient with the involvement of greater manpower.

Closer cooperation with the alumni association can benefit the university from another angle—when some activities such as dinner are organised by the alumni association, the involvement of endowment or *waqf* unit is required. This was experienced by several universities examined in this study, such as UTM, UPM, and USIM, which could create an opportunity to promote their funds to the alumni. This was also emphasised in the explanation of the UniSZA informant, where campus events involving the alumni, such as dinner, should be implemented to encourage contribution. This is evidenced in the following explanation by the informant:

> The alumni give their commitment to contribute at the beginning of the fund establishment. However, their contributions are not very active. We may have to set up a programme such as a dinner to attract and unite the alumni.[64]

Internal aspects also play a crucial role in influencing alumni giving. One of the aspects includes positive experience during learning, as demonstrated by the UTM informant that the donors from alumni previously received scholarships from the endowment fund. This suggests that the experience during the period of studies fostered the alumni's contribution, which was in line with the findings by Wang,[65] Saraeh et al.,[66] and Vidal and Pittz,[67] who revealed that the alumni's experience was a significant determinant of their contribution. Therefore, universities through the endowment or *waqf* fund should provide a good experience to their students in terms of facilities and welfare to strengthen the alumni network and encourage contribution after they have graduated. In line with this, a UTM informant stated the following:

> Those who have received the benefits from the alumni endowment fund contribute even to us. Some of them are already working, then they contribute back to the fund.[68]

Awareness is another internal aspect that could influence the alumni to contribute to endowment or *waqf* fund at their university, as mentioned by the respondents in this study. The awareness among the alumni could provide support to the funds even with minor efforts. This was acknowledged by the informants of USIM and UniSZA, who mentioned that the lack of awareness among the alumni led to challenges in mobilising alumni contributions. To illustrate this point, the implementation of the *waqf* fund at HEIs was still considered new, particularly at public universities, as discussed by Mahamood, Ab. Rahman and Che Seman.[69] Therefore, the alumni should be sensitised about the endowment or *waqf* fund, especially from universities where the implementation of these funds is relatively recent. The alumni would then be able to contribute. This awareness could be achieved through marketing efforts before and after their graduation.

This awareness is also present in a close relationship with a sense of belonging. Even if the alumni are aware of the funds in their universities, contributing to the funds without a sense of belonging towards their universities may not be possible. This was supported by a UniSZA informant who mentioned that no sense of belonging among alumni might lead to challenges in eliciting contribution from them, captured by the following statement:

> Actually, we have several alumni. One of the contributions that we can collect is from the alumni. However, realising it, in reality, is difficult. Even attracting our existing staff is also difficult. Maybe, the alumni have no sense of belonging. Therefore, to me, this problem needs to have a solution, which is an effort to attract the alumni to contribute.[70]

The significance of alumni in the university endowment or *waqf* fund should not be overlooked. A large number of alumni led to an increase in these funds through their contribution and the ability to deliver information related to endowment or *waqf* fund to the public. Their involvement in attracting the public to contribute to these funds was also acknowledged by the informants of UTM, UPM, and USIM, with the following statements:

> Yes, of course, because our relationship with the alumni is very close. That is why we have the UTM Alumni Association on Instagram. They can partner with us by informing the public about the endowment. During our convocation also, based on UTM's experience, we encourage the alumni to contribute. University students usually have board, and the local students must pay around RM 200. When they are about to graduate, when wearing the robe, we tell them about the endowment and seek their consent on not returning the board's money and channelling 50 per cent each to the alumni association and the endowment accounts. Recently, Alhamdulillah, almost 4,000 alumni agreed, which means that we can receive approximately RM 800,000–900,000. We can then divide it into two, where 50 per cent is allocated to the alumni association to run the activities as they have no financial sources, and 50 per cent to the endowment fund. This means cooperation from the alumni association exists as they are the ones who create the promotion campaigns, manage the form, then submit it to Bursar's office and so on. Therefore, our cooperation with the alumni is very close. Besides promoting, they also help us in terms of activities.[71]
>
> Yes, we have. For example, our alumni have their own companies. What do we need to do so that their staff contribute their *zakat* and *waqf* at WAZAN? We introduced a monthly deduction method by the company itself. Actually, no method exists for salary deduction. However, when we collaborate with the human resources team in that company (owned by our alumni), it issues a cheque every month to WAZAN. The cheque includes how many people would like to contribute. For example, if 20 staff members want a salary deduction for *zakat* in a month, then the company issues the cheque by listing the names of the contributors. For me, this is a very good method that must be expanded by WAZAN to all companies that are owned by our alumni. The collection through this method is indeed enormous. I think other universities have not adopted this method yet as it is quite technical. For example, Ismail owns an alumni

company located at Shah Alam and has a large staff of 200. Normally, all his staff members make a deduction for *zakat* directly to Lembaga Zakat Selangor (LZS) because his company is a private company. Then how do we receive the *zakat* payment from his 200 staff members? It is easy. What we need to do is just sensitise his human resources team and the chief executive officer. We create awareness among the staff. When they agree, the same payment to WAZAN can be made just like before (to LZS). The receipts issued are receipts from the LZS also. Their *zakat* will be sent to LZS also. The same thing happens in the context of *waqf*. The receipts issued are from LZS. The difference is only in terms of 50 per cent of *zakat* obtained will be transferred to WAZAN which will be used for the benefit of UPM students. If *waqf*, 100 per cent is received by the UPM. If they paid *zakat* directly to LZS, the total amount of *zakat* can only be obtained by the and not by WAZAN. Thus, if they understand this, they will say that paying *zakat* to WAZAN is better. The rebate tax and receipt remain the same as well. This is also for *waqf*. Therefore, creating the *waqf* fund at the UPM is better as 100 per cent can be obtained by the university.[72]

Like Hariri. Our management appointed him as a PWZ ambassador based on his capacity to garner alumni contributions. He acts accordingly and his actions have borne fruit given that many people want to contribute either as a *waqf* or as a *zakat*.[73]

Despite the approaches used by the universities selected in this study, they were adequate to demonstrate that the alumni play a vital role in encouraging contribution from the public to the endowment or *waqf* fund. Alumni involvement in encouraging the public to contribute is summarised in Table 6.10. At UniSZA, the alumni involvement was not implemented as the university was still in the strengthening phase of the *waqf* fund, which was established in 2016. This was in contrast to other universities that were in the advanced phase as the funds had been long established.

Table 6.10 Alumni Involvement in Attracting Contribution From the Public

Question 6.10: Does this institution use its alumni to attract contributions to endowment/waqf fund from the public?
Adakah institusi ini menggunakan alumni untuk menarik sumbangan kepada tabung endowmen/wakaf daripada orang awam?

Fund	*Informant*	*Approach*
Endowment	UTM2	Promotions and activities
Waqf	UPM3	Building a relationship with alumni-owned companies
	USIM	Appointment of an influential icon among the alumni
	UniSZA	X

Note: (X) not yet implemented.

Source: Developed by the authors.

The discussion of this element (i.e. alumni networks) leads to the conclusion that UTM and UPM employed significantly strong networks with their alumni, as reflected in their participation in every activity of endowment and the *waqf* fund. These strong networks encouraged the alumni to contribute to the endowment and *waqf* funds at these universities, in contrast to the experience of USIM and UniSZA. The alumni association played an important role in encouraging the alumni to contribute to the funds. According to the UTM informant, other internal factors such as the positive experience during the period of their studies also influence alumni contributions. Similarly, awareness had a role in increasing alumni contribution to the funds as the informants of USIM and UniSZA stated that the lack of awareness might lead to challenges in mobilising alumni contributions.

Diversity of Income Sources

For endowment, the return from investments should be regenerated to provide additional income from diversified sources. Besides reinvestment, other income sources should be considered and applied in universities such as UKM and UTM. In the case of UKM, the car number plates were sold among others[74] while UTM sold mineral water, books (Eco-Shift: Holistic Transformation towards Environmental Sustainability), the Little Genius Therapy and Learning Centre for children with special needs, and others.[75] All the income-generation activities at UTM, such as Warta Endowmen UTM 2019, can be referred to in its annual bulletin.[76] Given that UTM implemented various activities to generate endowment fund, Munadi, in his empirical study, found that the activities implemented at UTM were the largest contributors to the endowment collection at this university, even greater than the investment return.[77] Therefore, the diversification of income sources other than investments for endowment funds should be emphasised by universities. Furthermore, the studies by Schaffer, Polissar, and Neradilek[78] and Ceptureanu et al.[79] revealed that the diversity of income sources is significant in determining the success and sustainability of NPOs.

The informant of these two universities mentioned that besides the monetary profit, other benefits can be gained from the activities undertaken. In the case of UKM, the informants stated that the value of the sense of belonging to the university among alumni could be instilled and the branding of UTM Endowment for the public could be commercialised. This was reflected in the following statements:

> Like the number plate of UKM, we can indeed observe this thing. Mostly, alumni buy more than the UKM staff. We do not see that they (staff) buy the number plate. It is more significant to the alumni because they feel a sense of belonging to the university.[80]
>
> This one is important to show to the donors that actually, UTM Endowment and UTM itself are trying to help their students through the products. At the same time, we continue to approach people to contribute. During the fasting month, the endowment sold dates and Alhamdulillah received a positive response because it was a charity sale. This one I like because

> our strategy is to brand the endowment. Thus, people will know and talk about the UTM Endowment. Although at that time they are unable to contribute, they know that the UTM has an endowment. If they are capable to contribute, later on, they will contribute to the UTM Endowment. This is our strategy.[81]

As for *waqf*, investment returns should be regenerated to provide additional income. Similarly, other activities should be explored. The diversification of income sources is important for *waqf* as the fund can be invested only in fixed deposits, which is in line with its principle to preserve the *waqf* property. One of the instruments proposed in the study by Mohd Ali, Ahmad, and Ahmad Mahdzan was to design a suitable business model.[82] The importance of diversity of income sources for the *waqf* fund was also emphasised by Sulaiman and Zakari, who highlighted activities such as rental, fees, agriculture, and sales that could be implemented to generate *waqf* income.[83] Given that the *waqf* fund was recently established in the universities selected in this study, few activities were implemented to generate *waqf* income while ongoing projects continued. Products such as mineral water, dates, and books were sold at UPM while USIM conducted health projects, such as specialist clinics, dental clinics, and a haemodialysis centre at Nilai Square, Bandar Baru Nilai. The conversion of cash *waqf* to those health centres carried out by USIM offered high value for the *waqf* fund, which was in line with the following statement by the informant:

> Actually, the salary deduction is still low. Perhaps they (MoHE) see a value in building specialist clinics.[84]

The initiative taken by the USIM was in parallel with the opinion of the UPM informant that the cash *waqf* should be transferred in the form of properties to further expand its monetary value and provide benefit to the community by owning a property in certain places. The informant's opinion was discussed earlier in the section on appropriate investment planning. He further explained that the projects such as selling products were important to generate *waqf* income as the public felt more comfortable contributing if they were provided something in return. This is reflected in the following statement:

> Probably due to increasing costs, the value of people's spending is getting less. Based on my analysis, the total contribution was reduced but the number of people who contributed increased. This means that the awareness to contribute increased given the increasing number of donors. However, the value of the contribution was generally not significant. This is likely due to their capabilities. We need to implement methods such as selling water, selling dates, and selling books. This is because people who contribute want something in return. He got something, but at the same time, he had contributed. The mindset of people nowadays is like that—focusing too much on counting money to contribute.[85]

All projects that were implemented to provide sources of income either for endowment or for *waqf* funds at universities are summarised in Table 6.11. UniSZA was still planning this implementation as it was still in the strengthening phase.

One of the informants stated that all income-generation activities were profitable. Through these projects, they could promote their fund and improve familiarity among the community besides gaining monetary profit.

> Yes, correct. In fact, all the projects are profitable. This is because it is profitable to us in monetary terms, as I have mentioned. We create such projects as our platform to promote our endowment. Therefore, by purchasing our products, people will know and talk about them. Alhamdulillah, the effects from it are large. Very large actually.[86]

Although the projects (e.g. selling of mineral water and dates) organised by the universities selected in this study appeared small, their impact on society was highly significant. Apart from buying while donating, the buyers would also familiarise themselves with the existence of endowment or *waqf* funds at the university. Consequently, this created a possibility for them to contribute to these funds in the future.

The discussion of this element (i.e. diversity of income sources) suggests that UTM is highly active in regenerating the investment returns of its endowment fund. The regeneration activities were conducted through the involvement of various income-generation sources besides reinvestment. Notably, the involvement in various activities was important as it was believed to expand and promote the funds.

Table 6.11 Other Sources of Income

Question 6.11: Besides returns on investments, are there any other sources of income for this institution's endowment/*waqf* fund?
Selain daripada pulangan pelaburan, adakah terdapat sumber-sumber pendapatan lain bagi tabung endowmen/wakaf di institusi ini?

Fund	*Informant*	*Activities*
Endowment	UKM3	Selling car number plates
	UTM2	Selling products (e.g. mineral water, dates, books), car number plates, aeroplane models (JV with Air Asia), supplying bio materials (single use), rental of buildings and profit-sharing (JV between Endowment Therapy Centre and Hospital Penawar)
Waqf	UPM3	Selling products (e.g. mineral water, dates, books)
	USIM	Health project (i.e. specialist clinic, dental clinic, and haemodialysis centre)
	UniSZA	In planning

Source: Developed by the authors.

People would become indirectly aware of the existence of their funds. At UKM, they were also involved in income-regeneration activities, although the endowment chairs had obtained the donors. This was also applied by the *waqf* funds at other universities such as UPM and USIM. For *waqf*, the income regeneration from various sources was highly important as *waqf* funds can be invested only in fixed deposits.

Effective Fundraising

To ensure the increase in endowment and *waqf* funds, the contribution from the public (e.g. individuals, corporate) is essential. The informants provided various responses on the best mechanisms to encourage the public to contribute. These included raising awareness, branding the fund, tax exemption to donors, increasing the number of *waqf* institutions that offer *waqf* collection (easy access for the public to contribute), and asking for the contribution based on the project. The explanation of each informant is captured here:

> First of all, from the donor's perspective, they will know that by giving, they can avail of tax exemptions. A double tax exemption can be obtained if their contribution is for research. This needs to be informed to the companies to entice them to contribute. Second is creating an awareness of the importance of research activities and comparing with the top five universities in the world.[87]
>
> I can say that when I took over two years ago, one of the important things was branding. In this regard, we have adopted various methods to approach donors.[88]
>
> The first point is that compared to earlier times, I think more people now are aware of the importance of contributions. The second is that more institutions are managing the contribution collection, perhaps because the Malaysian population has increased. My conclusion is that the awareness to contribute has increased and the number of institutions that offer contribution collection has also increased.[89]
>
> One is the project, depending on the project need of the university. If the project is too large, attracting contributions from donors will be difficult. Although we approach corporate companies, receiving contributions is quite hard. However, it is based on the *waqf* project.[90]
>
> Awareness is the most important thing for me. To create awareness about *waqf*, we have conducted many roadshows where the details of this fund are shared in several sessions. The first thing we do is to explain the meaning of *waqf* because some people do not know what *waqf* is. They cannot differentiate between the *waqf* and *infaq, sadaqah* and so on. Thus, when awareness already exists, they will prefer *waqf* to *ṣadaqah* because of its perpetual characteristic. Therefore, for me, the best method is to create the awareness first.[91]

Awareness and branding are possibly correlated. The public would be aware of a certain fund when they are familiar with it. This awareness would encourage contributions to the fund in the future. Bekkers and Wiepking[92] and Sargeant and Woodliffe[93] identified awareness as one of the factors of charitable giving in traditional contexts. The informants also stated that the public would be encouraged to contribute through tax exemptions, as Chua and Wong found that charitable giving by individuals was based on tax incentives.[94] The tax incentives is not an impossible thing to be implemented in Malaysia since the Inland Revenue Board of Malaysia has issued guidelines under Subsection 44(11D) of the Income Tax Act 1967 (ITA) where the tax incentives are provided to donors who contribute monetary gifts in the form of *waqf* and endowment to the public universities. The allowable deduction is subject to the following conditions:[95]

1) *Wakaf* or endowment is made for the purpose of achieving the objective of establishment of the appropriate religious authority, body, or public university;
2) The appropriate religious authority, body, or public university is approved by the Director General of Inland Revenue (DGIR) for the purpose of Subsection 44(11D) of the ITA on the application of the appropriate religious authority, body, or public university concerned; and
3) The amount to be deducted shall not exceed the difference between the amount of 10 per cent of the aggregate income and the total amount that has been deducted pursuant to the proviso to Subsections 44(6), 44(11B), and 44(11C) of the ITA.

Based on this discussion, the best methods to entice the public to contribute according to the informants are summarised in Table 6.12.

Most of the informants (from UTM, UPM, USIM, and UniSZA) agreed that promotion activities of endowment and *waqf* fund under the umbrella concept of a campaign were important for encouraging people to contribute to the fund. The same method also applied to the encouragement of contribution from the staff and alumni of the university, which was in line with Weinstein and Barden's argument that a campaign is one of the main mechanisms to raise funds.[96] The campaign mechanism was also applied by the endowment chair (e.g. UKM), although it was only for specific projects (e.g. number plate) as the chair was established with a

Table 6.12 Methods to Attract the Public's Contribution

Question 6.12: What are the best methods to attract the public to contribute to the endowment/*waqf* fund?

Apakah cara-cara terbaik untuk menarik orang awam untuk menyumbang kepada tabung endowmen/wakaf?

Fund	*Informant*	*Methods to Attract Public*
Endowment	UKM3	Tax exemption and awareness
	UTM2	Branding
Waqf	UPM3	Awareness and increasing number of *waqf* institutions
	USIM	Project
	UniSZA	Awareness

Source: Developed by the authors.

larger fund and included corporate contributions. This is reflected in the following explanations by the informants:

> One of the methods is campaigning and is the key success factor of our funds. When we do not create a campaign, people do not know about it. For example, when it is *ṣadaqah*, people will say *ṣadaqah*. Usually, *ṣadaqah* to *surau* and *masjid*. They do not know that actually, at the university, many parties need financial assistance, especially the underprivileged students. We have tried to change it now so that people will know that several people at the university need assistance. This is why I said that a campaign is important. We organise it regularly in various forms. Like endowment, Alhamdulillah . . . It receives support from the Corporate Affairs Office, which also helps in sharing information related to the endowment with the public. Thus, information related to the endowment can be spread widely. Alhamdulillah. When people know about the endowment, their contributions can be gained easily, which means that they know. When talking about the endowment, they know that the Endowment UTM seeks to help students; they will then contribute depending on their capability. They will contribute based on several reasons, one of which is because of the campaign. We can inform them that they can contribute through various methods. If we do not create a campaign, people do not know about it. Therefore, it is very important.[97]
>
> That one is called an integrated marketing method in marketing. I think considerable marketing mixed formations exist in terms of advertising, promotions, events, experience, public relations, publicity, direct marketing, direct selling etc. We have implemented all those things. For example, advertising includes several types of methods, either online or offline. In summary, most people who have managed the *waqf*, do not manage it like corporates, that is, they do not manage it like business institutions—this is what I mean. Supposedly, people who managed the Islamic, *waqf*, or *zakat* institutions, need to manage them like business organisations. However, when we talk about *waqf* or *zakat*, and what are our products . . . When people sell books, we can observe that their product is indeed a book. What would we want to sell to people who offer others to practice *waqf*? Reward? Do we sell to them God's blessing? Definitely, the reward and God's blessing cannot be seen. This was a real challenge for us. *Waqf* is a product that we cannot observe. When we attract people to practice *waqf* for masjid for example, yes we can observe the masjid. However, what we want to sell is actually about the blessing, God's blessing. The things like that (i.e. reward) which we want, although performing it is not easy. That is the challenge.[98]
>
> Campaign. Along the way, we manage the fund, and people want to observe it. Even for the corporate, when we organise a Mock Cheque ceremony for *zakat*, we conduct it during the convocation ceremony. Tuanku came and it becomes a recognition for us. Therefore, they want to contribute again. The same thing applies to the staff. We have created some ideas that we want to include. One of them is the campaign. The campaign was also held to provide awards to staff who have contributed the highest *waqf* for the faculty as well as PTJ, or individuals in the APC awards. We want to raise

> these people who practice *waqf* so that they can be icons who can be followed by others. Specific prizes are earmarked for them.[99]
>
> We have *Hari Ramah Mesra bersama Pewakaf* three or four times in a year. It is organised internally only. For the external stage, we have conducted a collaboration with JAWHAR, which we planned to organise with MAIDAM. Basically, in the roadshows, we explain aspects such as how much *waqf* funds we have collected and how much funds have been distributed. Usually, people want to view what we have done with their contribution. This is because some people will ask if they contribute, how would their money be used? Therefore, when we inform in the form of distribution, it will motivate them to contribute again.[100]
>
> Chairs or endowment fund is a big value. The endowment fund amounts to RM 1 million. For chairs, the value is RM 5 million. Thus, the campaign that we have conducted is not for the public as contributing this amount is not easy for people. However, if it is in the form of specific projects, such as *waqf*, contributions for COVID-19, and food for the students of UKM, then our answer is yes.[101]

All the universities selected in this study applied or utilised almost all existing communication channels discussed in this study. Given that the target donors at UKM are corporates, the communication channels do not focus on attracting public contributions.

However, they are used to announce the chair establishment, such as scholarships. Nevertheless, the announcement of the contributions to the public depends on the donors' permission. In the implementation of a certain project (e.g. selling number plates), which requires the participation of the public, other communication channels are available including social media, website, printed materials (e.g. newspaper), and messaging (e.g. WhatsApp) to encourage participation. In the case of other universities, all communication channels are used to encourage contribution from the public, including their staff and alumni. The application of communication channels used for each university is summarised in Table 6.13.

Table 6.13 Selection of Communication Channels

Question 6.13: What are the communication channels (e.g. radio, television, newspapers) used to inform potential donors in executing such a method?

Apakah saluran-saluran komunikasi (iaitu, radio, televisyen, surat khabar dll.) yang digunakan untuk memaklumkan kepada bakal penderma dalam melaksanakan kaedah tersebut?

Fund	*Informant*	*Communication Channels*							
		Social Media	*Email*	*Website*	*Print*	*TV*	*Call*	*Radio*	*Messaging (WhatsApp)*
Endowment	UKM3	✓	-	✓*	✓*	*	-	*	✓
	UTM2	✓	✓	✓	✓	✓	✓	✓	✓
Waqf	UPM3	✓	✓	✓	✓	–	✓	-	✓
	USIM	–	✓	✓	✓	✓	✓	-	✓
	UniSZA	✓	✓	✓	✓	✓	✓	-	✓

Note: (✓) applied for public contribution; (*) announcement; (-) not related.

Source: Developed by the authors.

Regarding the most effective communication channel, all informants, either from the endowment or from the *waqf* fund, agreed that social media was the most effective communication channel to attract participation or contribution from the public, or staff, or alumni. This finding was in line with the assertion by Weerawardena, who stated that the usage of social media by NPOs can convey the marketing message effectively.[102] Alignment with the current time, ability to reach more people, cost-effectiveness, efficiency to reach potential donors, and convenience in communicating with people even at home were the main reasons cited by the informants to use this communication channel. This channel is also powerful for communication with the staff. The observations of the informants are presented here:

> In line with the current time, people nowadays spend more time on social media. If Radio Television Malaysia (RTM), there are targeted groups, but we cannot reach other target groups. If using social media, maybe we can reach other target groups.[103]
>
> Actually, the campaign that we are conducting right now is simple. The money required is not substantial, but it is active. It means that we do the campaigns through social media platforms such as Facebook and Instagram. This method does not need huge money to implement the campaign. We have reoriented our methods in this direction because reaching the target group is easy. The second reason is low cost, unlike earlier where a campaign required opening a canopy and the need to speak within one day. Thus, as mentioned earlier we organised the campaign continuously, involving several activities.[104]
>
> In the current context, I view Facebook ads because they are effective. Although it costs relatively more, it is an effective platform as almost every individual has a Facebook and Instagram account. Thus, it can attract their attention as they always have their handphone and like to engage with social media. Thus, it became an effective method, especially during the COVID-19 period when Movement Control Order (MCO) was enforced. What other methods can we apply if everyone is just with their handphone?[105]
>
> Nowadays, people tend to look through their handphones. Most social media platforms such as Facebook, Twitter, and Instagram can be accessed via the handphone. It is a new medium in the current time as we face difficulty meeting people, especially in the current time of MCO. Therefore, we collaborate with the Students' Representative Council (SRC) to run our contribution and others through Facebook. We display information on the activities that we have performed, such as the contribution to the students. So it can be a fact where the people can see the initiatives of the PWZ. It is one of the good initiatives because all people use the Facebook, Instagram and so on.[106]
>
> For me, the most effective one is social media. Social media is the most frequently used medium in this 21st century. This technological change is one of the main reasons why this medium becomes the most effective one.[107]

Religious teachings are the factors that encourage Muslims to contribute, as indicated in Quranic verses and prophetic tradition (*ḥadīth*). These elements were found to be applied by the selected universities in their campaigns to provide the public with religious consciousness. This practice was acknowledged by Charseatd, who argued that it could enhance attitudes towards donation through the development of a positive image.[108] The explanation offered by the informants is stated here:

> *Waqf* has evidence. In contrast to the number plate of a car, there is no *ḥadīth* or Quranic verse. If chairs or endowment fund, it depends. For the faculty, it depends on the PTJ. If faculty of Islamic studies, it exists. If corporate like Chinese, I think it does not have. Based on the need.[109]
>
> Insert the verses of the al-Quran and the *ḥadīth* to convince because sometimes people do not understand the *ṣadaqah*. The concept of *ṣadaqah* becomes one of our strengths to share. Islam says that the *ṣadaqah* is an honourable practice which can gain rewards. Therefore, it is always used and reminded us that in Islam, the *ṣadaqah jāriyah* is important. In engaging with anyone, I always remind them that when we die, three things will continue and one of them *is ṣadaqah jāriyah*. We do not bring our wealth, we do not bring our big home, we do not bring our beautiful wife, we do not bring our handsome husband, what is sure that we can bring is our *ṣadaqah jāriyah*. That is why we say that no particular amount is specified for *ṣadaqah*. The important point is sincerity, which must exist.[110]
>
> Inserts the Islamic elements (e.g. Quranic and *ḥadīth* verses) in organising the campaign. However, in the current context, for me, we need to attract those who are less and do not understand about Islamic teaching. Those who are knowledgeable with Islamic teaching, are certainly targeted by the waqf institutions to collect the contributions. If we access Facebook, we can find many advertisements that seek contribution. So, I think we need to attract the contribution from those who are not becoming the target group. The method that can be used in attracting them is through Tickketoyou.com as I mentioned earlier. After that, for example also, what are other approaches that we can use instead of verses from *ḥadīth*. What we can quote is the wisdom, the words from the specific figures. The verses of the al-Quran and the *hadīth* are indeed used, but we can introduce other quotes as well. After all, there is a challenge for us to make it in English or Chinese language. Thus, we do not see that it is da'wah-oriented solely. The non-Muslims or Muslims far away from Islam will feel uncomfortable with words such as *waqf*, *zakat*, and *hibah*. Therefore, using other terms becomes an important strategy in marketing, so that they can contribute.[111]
>
> Insert the Islamic elements in campaign.[112]

Usually on Facebook, we will find the verses of al-Quran and *ḥadīth* so that, as I said earlier, to inform people that the awareness is the most important thing. When a person is aware, I think they will practice the *waqf*.[113]

In terms of collection, various channels were applied by the universities examined in this study. For internal collection (e.g. staff), the common channels applied by the universities included salary deduction and e-claim. Meanwhile, the channels used for external collection (e.g. public) were commonly online, cash/cheque, bank/wire transfer, and mobile app/wallet. Various collection channels were used to facilitate the donors in their contribution, which is reflected in the following statements:

> We are human beings and realise the existence of significant human diversity. For example, if we say that we will organise the collection only through bank transactions, they will argue that why not collect through electronic fund transfer. Or they will contend that I like to contribute through Jom Pay because it is easy. It means that people want to contribute through Jom Pay. Another example, at the UTM, we have UTM Smart. Later on, some of them will argue that using UTM Smart is difficult. That is why we provide various collection channels. In this regard, people no longer have a reason not to contribute because of a lack of payment channels. They can choose the channel according to their interests. If some of them prefer to use Jom Pay, they can use Jom Pay to contribute. If some of them like to contribute at the counter, they can go and queue there. If some of them like to do aqad to convey their intentions, then they can come to the office. If some of them are quite lazy (just want to contribute RM 2 only for example), then they can contribute electronically. This implies that even when they are ready to sleep, they can still contribute by just clicking. What is important is they succeed in doing *ṣadaqah*. That is why we need to diversify the collection channels because the human desire varies based on their interest. When we do not provide some of the collection channels, they will ask about it. Therefore, the simplest solution is that we provide all the collection channels. Then, they can select the channel they tend to use.[114]
>
> For me, the facilities must be diversified. We must provide variation, which is fundamental for the facilities as each donor is different in terms of their background or ability. Their environment is also different. Sometimes, even when we provide this type of channel, they will ask for another one. Therefore, we try our best to provide all forms of facilities. For example, we create a moving counter where they come and bring their credit card. But we do not provide the device for that card. We only provide it at our fixed counter. At this moving counter, we only accept the contribution in the form of cash or cheque, this also becomes an issue. In this regard, we had to set up the facility (device) even though we think that this is not worth providing. Thus, we need to provide various facilities.[115]

> The reason is many people are using Internet banking nowadays. Therefore, we have included it in the *waqf* guidelines where we specify several mechanisms that donors can use to contribute to *waqf*, including through cash counter by coming to USIM, as well as Internet banking applications that are Shariah-compliant. For example, we have a deal with Maybank to use QR codes because it does not have a limitation. Thus we open up opportunities for the public to contribute easily. Besides, we have an internal system. That is why I mentioned the boost. Although the amount of boost is not substantial, its use has been increasing because common people use it. Therefore, we have QR codes for boost in our name tags and name cards. Thus, they can snap directly there. Now, we are leveraging technology to facilitate the donors to contribute. Using the conventional methods has a limitation on the number of people who can contribute. That's why the study shows that by using the website, it becomes slow to reach to the page that we want to visit due to many pages must be over through. We do not have our applications yet; it is still being planned. We just harness the boost, Maybank right now. We still visit corporates and it is still running because it is more of a networking channel. However, for the public, as I said just now, we simplify and widen the channels for contribution.[116]
>
> Various collection channels are provided so that all levels of donors can contribute according to their priorities.[117]

The collection channels used at the universities examined in this study are summarised in Table 6.14.

The conclusion based on the discussion of this element (i.e. effective fundraising) is that all universities, especially the UTM, UPM, USIM, and UniSZA, are

Table 6.14 Collection Channels Available

Question 6.14: What are the collection channels provided to facilitate people's contribution?

Apakah saluran-saluran kutipan yang disediakan bagi memudahkan orang ramai untuk menyumbang?

Fund	*Informant*	*Collection Channels*							
		Salary Deduction	*e-Claim*	*Online (Credit /Debit Card)*	*Cash/ Cheque*	*Bank/ Wire Transfer*	*PayPal*	*JomPay*	*Mobile App/ Wallet*
Endowment	UTM2	✓	–	✓	✓	✓	–	✓	✓
Waqf	UPM3	✓	✓	✓	✓	✓	–	–	✓
	USIM	✓	–	✓	✓	✓	–	✓	✓
	UniSZA	✓	✓	✓	✓	✓	✓	–	✓

Note: (✓) yes; (–) not related.

Source: Developed by the authors.

highly active in promoting endowment and *waqf* funds under the umbrella concept of a campaign to increase the funds. The universities almost leveraged all the available communication channels to promote their funds. The funds were also actively promoted on social media (e.g. social networking sites) as this is an easy, cheap, and effective tool to reach the target community on a wider scale. Islamic teaching is included in the promotion activities to further motivate Muslims to contribute to the funds.

Volunteers

Apart from the contribution in the form of money, another form of contribution encouraged by the universities selected in this study for the public and students is the contribution in the form of energy, known as volunteering. The involvement of volunteers in the management of endowment and *waqf* funds at these universities is important to assist them in promoting the funds and safeguarding the endowed and *waqf* property. Although volunteers are not paid, Muslims believe in the great reward granted by Allah through voluntary practice. The evidence that universities use volunteers in their management of endowment and *waqf* funds is captured in the following statements:

> Actually, for endowment, we appoint anyone interested in helping our endowment. We call them *Sahabat Endowment*. They contribute in the form of energy. For example, during the fasting month, which is Ramadhan, we have conducted charitable sales projects such as selling dates. Our *Sahabat* then promotes our sales and helps in collecting the orders from the buyers. During Hari Raya, we made *angpau* in large quantities and promote and sell it to people who are interested in buying it. Our *Sahabat* helps in promoting our products. Many have been sold. It means that buyers want to buy our products. This is what I have said that they contribute in the form of energy.[118]
>
> We have many volunteers in the form of energy. Free shop, Rakan WAZAN, Sahabat Masjid exist. The most active is Sahabat Masjid UPM. They have collected many contributions of *waqf* from the public. People understood that *waqf* can be practised not only in the form of the property but also in the form of energy. Al-Quran has a verse, *li amwalikum wa anfusikum*, either property or ourselves. Not only martyred in the way of Allah (i.e. to uphold the religion), *anfusikum* also can be in the form of ideas, energy etc.[119]
>
> Volunteers are present among the students. Recently, our SRC has been formed. We network with them so that they can assist us.[120]
>
> We are about to establish one with our SRC which we call *Sahabat Wakaf*. Basically, we have assets that we provide to students, such as a water filter (Cuckoo) at the library, and ask them to safeguard it. Therefore, we have students to take care of the asset. We have established Sahabat Wakaf. The student will monitor that asset, whether it needs to be cleaned, whether it is damaged, etc. At end of the day, these students are given a certificate for their contribution.[121]

Table 6.15 Comparison of the Successful Elements of Endowment and *Waqf* at the Selected Malaysian Public Universities

University *Element*	*Endowment*			*Waqf*		
	UM	*UKM*	*UTM*	*UPM*	*USIM*	*UniSZA*
Appropriate Investment Planning	X	X	X	X	X	X
Superior Investment Committees	✓	✓	✓	✓	✓	✓
Highly Skilled Investment Managers	✓	✓	–	–	–	–
Alumni Networks	–	–	✓	✓	X	X
Diversity of Income Sources	–	✓*	✓	✓	✓	X
Effective Fundraising	–	–	✓	✓	✓	✓
Volunteer	–	–	✓	✓	✓	✓

Note: (✓) yes; (X) no; (*) on certain activity; (-) not related.

Source: Developed by the authors.

The involvement of volunteers in the management of endowment and *waqf* funds was indicated as another element to be considered by universities that implemented these funds. The volunteers could assist the university in promoting the funds. Lysakowski stressed that the use of volunteers in a capital campaign is crucial for its success.[122] However, as the volunteers used by universities selected in this study were unpaid, as highlighted by the informants, costs can be reduced. This was in line with the argument of Bales, who mentioned that cost savings could be achieved by using volunteers instead of paid services providers.[123] In this regard, Malaysian public universities should endeavour to involve volunteers in their fund management.

The conclusion from the discussion on this element (i.e. volunteers) is that the universities selected in this study involved volunteers in the management of endowment and *waqf* funds. This element was important for assisting universities in various activities, such as promotion, and for safeguarding the properties that were contributed by the donors through endowment and *waqf*.

The discussion in this section about the elements that can contribute to the successful implementation of endowment and *waqf* at the selected Malaysian public universities is summarised in Table 6.15. Based on this table, the elements that can drive the successful implementation either for the endowment or *waqf* funds in certain public universities can be clearly captured.

Link Between the Elements

Among the analysed elements, appropriate investment planning and highly skilled investment managers were linked, which indicated the existence of fund managers and thus, diversified investment portfolios. This result was in line with the following statement made by the informants of UM and UKM:

> Fund managers will invest in the industry like . . . We have bonds, we have equities. For equities, they will invest in companies. There are also properties. But not exactly, just a very small percentage.[124]
>
> For fund managers, what I have seen, most of their investments are in the form of equity.[125]

The link between the two elements was supported by Turtle's statement on diversification being the key to investing.[126] What was applied at UM and UKM should be an example, where the presence of fund managers allowed investment in assets other than fixed deposits, such as bonds, equities, and properties. Notably, the investment in these assets is highly important given their ability to generate higher returns compared to fixed deposits when the market condition is amenable, as informed by the UM's informant.

Other elements that were linked were alumni networks and effective fundraising. The link between these two elements could be evidenced when the promotion activities under the campaign concept were applied to encourage the alumni to contribute. Their action of giving was caused by the awareness obtained through the campaign, as highlighted by the informants based on the following:

> We have many campaigns, engagements and other activities, especially with the UTM alumni so that they continue to contribute to the Tabung Endowment Alumni.[127]
>
> Actually, on the awareness—how do we want to deliver the message to the alumni so that awareness can be increased? For me, the WAZAN's advantage lies in marketing compared to other *waqf* institutions. Its strength is marketing.[128]
>
> For alumni, it is difficult to instil. Except for we conducting the campaign before their graduation. They contributed their convocation fees as *waqf*.[129]

The promotion activities were also found to be related to the alumni association. To illustrate, a few universities examined in this study, such as UTM, were involved in the alumni association to promote the endowment fund to their alumni.

> It means that our alumni association implements the promotion activities, manages the form, then submits it to Bursar's office and so on. Thus, our cooperation with the alumni is very close. Besides promotion, they also help us in terms of other activities.[130]
>
> In terms of activities, I can say that almost all activities in the alumni centre and alumni association have the involvement from the WAZAN. For me, the cooperation from them is very good. On a scale of 10, I think I can rate them at 9, which is excellent. This rating also includes the parameter of developing the *waqf* projects and the distribution of *waqf* income.[131]

> The alumni event is conducted by the alumni centre, not us. We were invited to join. Therefore, we participated and sponsored one table, and also explained about *waqf*.[132]

The involvement of the alumni association in the promotion of the funds either through endowment or through *waqf* is important to encourage the alumni to contribute, as illustrated by Wang.[133] Social media (e.g. Facebook) is important for the institution to build a network with the alumni as it could link the institution from one alumnus to another. News regarding the fundraising at a university can be indirectly informed to individuals (e.g. alumni). The use of social media, especially Facebook, in attracting contribution from alumni was demonstrated by the informants of this study, as reflected in the following statements for example:

> Of course, we will fully utilise it for the number plates.[134]
>
> Of course, several social media platforms exist. Therefore, we will leverage UTM's Facebook page and other such options.[135]

The role of social media (e.g. Facebook) is important in encouraging contributions from alumni. This notion was supported in the studies by scholars such as Dillon,[136] Zickar, Ron, and Arnold,[137] and Peruta and Helm.[138] To illustrate, Dillon stated that by merely 'liking' a university's Facebook page, the role of alumni becomes comparable to the alumni who attend the university's events. Therefore, social media including Facebook are highly important as they could improve the relationship between the alumni and the university. Moreover, the contribution from social media could be achieved easily and continuously.

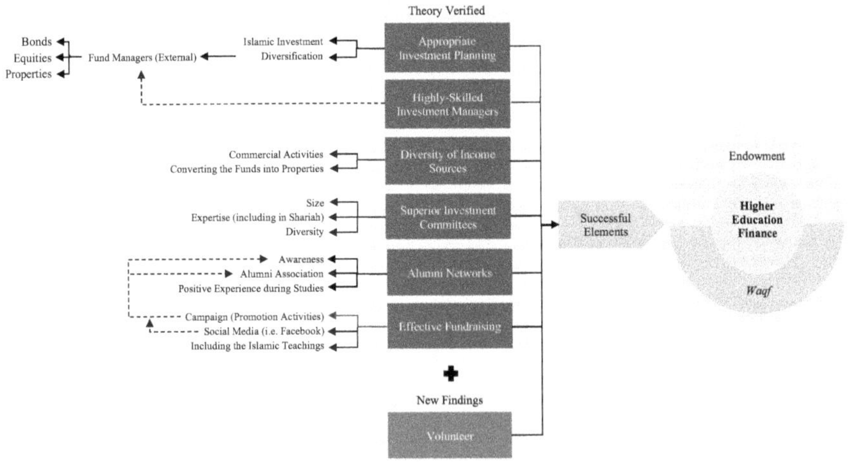

Figure 6.4 Link Between the Elements

Source: Developed by the authors.

Conclusion

In this chapter, several elements that contribute to the successful implementation of endowment and *waqf* funds were discussed. These elements were superior investment committees, highly skilled investment managers, alumni networks, diversity of income sources, effective fundraising, and volunteers. Each university examined in this study has strengths in certain elements. All universities may be deemed to have a superior investment committee given the committee size and the selection of members by the top management of the university in terms of expertise and diversity. Regarding skilled investment managers, UM and UKM have an advantage as these universities have appointed fund managers from financial institutions. Alumni networks are strong elements in UTM and UPM as the implementation of endowment and *waqf* funds occur along with their alumni. In terms of the diversity of income sources, UTM is highly active in regenerating the investment returns of its endowment. Besides reinvestment, various activities to regenerate the endowment income are performed to expand the endowment fund. This practice is also applied by other universities examined in this study. Furthermore, another important element that can increase endowment and *waqf* funds at the selected universities (e.g. UTM, UPM, USIM, and UniSZA) is the promotion activities under the campaign concept. All universities examined in this study utilised communication channels to promote their funds and seek potential donors. Islamic teachings should be incorporated into the promotion to encourage fund contributions by Muslim donors. Last but not least, the involvement of volunteers in the management of funds is also deemed important for universities analysed in this study as they could assist the universities in promotion activities and safeguard the property that is funded through endowment and *waqf*. This chapter found that appropriate investment planning might not be an element that drives the successful implementation of endowment and *waqf* funds as the diversification in the investment portfolios remains insufficient, although most of the investments comply with Shariah. While UM and UKM also invest in assets other than fixed deposits, their diversification has not reached a satisfactory level because of the relatively low number of funds managed by their fund managers.

Notes

1 B. Abdul Hamid, W. Hassan-Kamarudin, and S. Abdul Syahid Sowell, "The Endowment Fund as a Source of Sustainability for Higher Education in Malaysia: Maximising Investment Returns," *ISRA Research Paper*, no. 103 (2018): 1–32, 21.

2 J. Lerner, A. Schoar, and J. Wang, "Secrets of the Academy: The Drivers of University Endowment Success," *Journal of Economic Perspectives* 22, no. 3 (2008): 207–22, 214–15.

3 Shaleni a/p S. Muthiah (Financial Officer, Account & Investment Division, Bursar's Office, Universiti Malaya (UM), Kuala Lumpur), in an interview with the authors, 20 March 2020.

4 Mohd Akbal Qamas Abdul Basir (Assistant Bursar, Bursar's Office, Universiti Kebangsaan Malaysia (UKM), Bangi), in an interview with the authors, 23 March 2020.

5 Ahmad Mustaqim Zolkafali (Assistant Registrar, Chancellor Foundation, Universiti Kebangsaan Malaysia (UKM), Bangi), in an interview with the authors, 27 March 2020.

6 Norafitri Buradi (Accountant, Bursar's Office, Universiti Teknologi Malaysia (UTM), Skudai), interview with the authors, 27 March 2020.
7 Yusof Boon (Associate Professor, Director, Endowment Unit, Universiti Teknologi Malaysia, Skudai), in an interview with the authors, 23 February 2020.
8 Nur Asriati Jasmi (Financial Officer, Bursar's Office, Universiti Putra Malaysia (UPM), Serdang), in an interview with the authors, 3 April 2020.
9 Nuruliman Ibrahim (Head, Waqf Management Section, Centre for Management of Waqf, Zakat and Endowment (WAZAN), Universiti Putra Malaysia (UPM), Serdang), in an interview with the authors, 31 March 2020.
10 Noor Mizan Arifin (Assistant Registrar, Office of Waqf & Endowment, Universiti Sultan Zainal Abidin (UniSZA), Kuala Nerus), in an interview with the authors, 2 March 2020.
11 M. Leković, "Investment Diversification as a Strategy for Reducing Investment Risk," *Economic Horizons* 20, no. 2 (2018): 169–84, 169, https://doi.org/10.5937/ekonhor1802173l.
12 D. Jayeola, Z. Ismail, and S. F. Sufahani, "Effects of Diversification of Assets in Optimizing Risk of Portfolio," *Malaysian Journal of Fundamental and Applied Sciences* 13, no. 4 (2017): 584–87, 584, https://doi.org/10.11113/mjfas.v0n0.567.
13 I. Gurrib and S. Alshahrani, "Diversification in Portfolio Risk Management: The Case of the UAE Financial Market," *International Journal of Trade, Economics and Finance* 3, no. 6 (2012): 445–49, 449, https://doi.org/10.7763/ijtef.2012.v3.243.
14 M. Tuttle, *How Harvard and Yale Beat the Market* (Hoboken: John Wiley & Sons, Inc., 2009), 33.
15 Nuruliman Ibrahim (Head, Waqf Management Section, Centre for Management of Waqf, Zakat and Endowment, Universiti Putra Malaysia, Serdang), in an interview with the authors, 31 March 2020.
16 Razman Ibrahim (Assistant Registrar, Center for Awqaf and Zakat (PWZ), Universiti Sains Islam Malaysia (USIM), Nilai), in an interview with the authors, 3 March 2020.
17 Shaleni a/p S. Muthiah (Financial Officer, Account & Investment Division, Bursar's Office, Universiti Malaya, Kuala Lumpur), in an interview with the authors, 20 March 2020.
18 Mohd Akbal Qamas Abdul Basir (Assistant Bursar, Bursar's Office, Universiti Kebangsaan Malaysia, Bangi), in interview with the authors, 23 March 2020.
19 Ahmad Mustaqim Zolkafali (Assistant Registrar, Chancellor Foundation, Universiti Kebangsaan Malaysia (UKM), Bangi), in an interview with the authors, 27 March 2020.
20 Norafitri Buradi (Accountant, Bursar's Office, Universiti Teknologi Malaysia, Skudai), in an interview with the authors, 27 March 2020.
21 Yusof Boon (Associate Professor, Director, Endowment Unit, Universiti Teknologi Malaysia, Skudai), in an interview with the authors, 23 February 2020.
22 Nur Asriati Jasmi (Financial Officer, Bursar's Office, Universiti Putra Malaysia, Serdang), in an interview with the authors, 3 April 2020.
23 Noor Mizan Arifin (Assistant Registrar, Office of Waqf & Endowment, Universiti Sultan Zainal Abidin, Kuala Nerus), in an interview with the authors, 2 March 2020.
24 Shaleni a/p S. Muthiah (Financial Officer, Account & Investment Division, Bursar's Office, Universiti Malaya, Kuala Lumpur), in an interview with the authors, 20 March 2020.
25 Mohd Akbal Qamas Abdul Basir (Assistant Bursar, Bursar's Office, Universiti Kebangsaan Malaysia, Bangi), in interview with the authors, 23 March 2020.
26 Yusof Boon (Associate Professor, Director, Endowment Unit, Universiti Teknologi Malaysia, Skudai), in an interview with the authors, 23 February 2020.
27 Nuruliman Ibrahim (Head, Waqf Management Section, Centre for Management of Waqf, Zakat and Endowment, Universiti Putra Malaysia, Serdang), in an interview with the authors, 31 March 2020.
28 Noor Mizan Arifin (Assistant Registrar, Office of Waqf & Endowment, Universiti Sultan Zainal Abidin, Kuala Nerus), in an interview with the authors, 2 March 2020.
29 P. M. Bosse, D. M. Grim, and F. Chism, "Duty, Opportunity, Mastery: Investment Committee Best Practices," *Vanguard Research* (2017): 1–20, 18.

30 Shaleni a/p S. Muthiah (Financial Officer, Account & Investment Division, Bursar's Office, Universiti Malaya, Kuala Lumpur), in an interview with the authors, 20 March 2020.
31 Mohd Akbal Qamas Abdul Basir (Assistant Bursar, Bursar's Office, Universiti Kebangsaan Malaysia, Bangi), in an interview with the authors, 23 March 2020.
32 Norafitri Buradi (Accountant, Bursar's Office, Universiti Teknologi Malaysia, Skudai), in an interview with the authors, 27 March 2020.
33 Yusri Hashim (Deputy Bursar, Central Management Operation Financial Division, Bursar's Office, Universiti Putra Malaysia, Serdang), in an interview with the authors, 18 May 2020.
34 Noor Mizan Arifin (Assistant Registrar, Office of Waqf & Endowment, Universiti Sultan Zainal Abidin, Kuala Nerus), in an interview with the authors, 2 March 2020
35 Shaleni a/p S. Muthiah (Financial Officer, Account & Investment Division, Bursar's Office, Universiti Malaya, Kuala Lumpur), in an interview with the authors, 20 March 2020.
36 Mohd Akbal Qamas Abdul Basir (Assistant Bursar, Bursar's Office, Universiti Kebangsaan Malaysia, Bangi), in an interview with the authors, 23 March 2020.
37 Norafitri Buradi (Accountant, Bursar's Office, Universiti Teknologi Malaysia, Skudai), in an interview with the authors, 27 March 2020.
38 Yusri Hashim (Deputy Bursar, Central Management Operation Financial Division, Bursar's Office, Universiti Putra Malaysia, Serdang), in an interview with the authors, 18 May 2020.
39 Noor Mizan Arifin (Assistant Registrar, Office of Waqf & Endowment, Universiti Sultan Zainal Abidin, Kuala Nerus), in an interview with the authors, 2 March 2020.
40 Shaleni a/p S. Muthiah (Financial Officer, Account & Investment Division, Bursar's Office, Universiti Malaya, Kuala Lumpur), in an interview with the authors, 20 March 2020.
41 Mohd Akbal Qamas Abdul Basir (Assistant Bursar, Bursar's Office, Universiti Kebangsaan Malaysia, Bangi), in an interview with the authors, 23 March 2020.
42 Norafitri Buradi (Accountant, Bursar's Office, Universiti Teknologi Malaysia, Skudai), in an interview with the authors, 27 March 2020.
43 Noor Mizan Arifin (Assistant Registrar, Office of Waqf & Endowment, Universiti Sultan Zainal Abidin, Kuala Nerus), in an interview with the authors, 2 March 2020.
44 Shaleni a/p S. Muthiah (Financial Officer, Account & Investment Division, Bursar's Office, Universiti Malaya, Kuala Lumpur), in an interview with the authors, 20 March 2020.
45 Mohd Akbal Qamas Abdul Basir (Assistant Bursar, Bursar's Office, Universiti Kebangsaan Malaysia, Bangi), in an interview with the authors, 23 March 2020.
46 Norafitri Buradi (Accountant, Bursar's Office, Universiti Teknologi Malaysia, Skudai), in an interview with the authors, 27 March 2020.
47 Nur Asriati Jasmi (Financial Officer, Bursar's Office, Universiti Putra Malaysia, Serdang), in an interview with the authors, 3 April 2020.
48 Noor Mizan Arifin (Assistant Registrar, Office of Waqf & Endowment, Universiti Sultan Zainal Abidin, Kuala Nerus), in an interview with the authors, 2 March 2020.
49 Shaleni a/p S. Muthiah (Financial Officer, Account & Investment Division, Bursar's Office, Universiti Malaya, Kuala Lumpur), in an interview with the authors, 20 March 2020.
50 Ibid.
51 Mohd Akbal Qamas Abdul Basir (Assistant Bursar, Bursar's Office, Universiti Kebangsaan Malaysia, Bangi), in an interview with the authors, 23 March 2020.
52 Lerner, Schoar, and Wang, "Secrets of the Academy: The Drivers of University Endowment Success," 218.
53 Shaleni a/p S. Muthiah (Financial Officer, Account & Investment Division, Bursar's Office, Universiti Malaya, Kuala Lumpur), in an interview with the authors, 20 March 2020.
54 Mohd Akbal Qamas Abdul Basir (Assistant Bursar, Bursar's Office, Universiti Kebangsaan Malaysia, Bangi), in interview with the authors, 23 March 2020.
55 Shaleni a/p S. Muthiah (Financial Officer, Account & Investment Division, Bursar's Office, Universiti Malaya, Kuala Lumpur), in an interview with the authors, 20 March 2020.

56 Mohd Akbal Qamas Abdul Basir (Assistant Bursar, Bursar's Office, Universiti Kebangsaan Malaysia, Bangi), in an interview with the authors, 23 March 2020.
57 Shaleni a/p S. Muthiah (Financial Officer, Account & Investment Division, Bursar's Office, Universiti Malaya, Kuala Lumpur), in an interview with the authors, 20 March 2020.
58 Mohd Akbal Qamas Abdul Basir (Assistant Bursar, Bursar's Office, Universiti Kebangsaan Malaysia, Bangi), in an interview with the authors, 23 March 2020.
59 Yusof Boon (Associate Professor, Director, Endowment Unit, Universiti Teknologi Malaysia, Skudai), in an interview with the authors, 23 February 2020.
60 Nuruliman Ibrahim (Head, Waqf Management Section, Centre for Management of Waqf, Zakat and Endowment, Universiti Putra Malaysia, Serdang), in an interview with the authors, 31 March 2020.
61 Y. Wang, "What Influences Alumni Donations?" *Journal of Economics, Business and Management* 6, no. 4 (2018): 160–63, 160.
62 Yusof Boon (Associate Professor, Director, Endowment Unit, Universiti Teknologi Malaysia, Skudai), in an interview with the authors, 23 February 2020.
63 Nuruliman Ibrahim (Head, Waqf Management Section, Centre for Management of Waqf, Zakat and Endowment, Universiti Putra Malaysia, Serdang), in an interview with the authors, 31 March 2020.
64 Noor Mizan Arifin (Assistant Registrar, Office of Waqf & Endowment, Universiti Sultan Zainal Abidin, Kuala Nerus), in an interview with the authors, 2 March 2020.
65 Wang, "What Influences Alumni Donations?" 160.
66 U. N. Saraeh, N. I. Abdul Rahman, N. Noordin, S. N. Ramlan, R. Ahmad, and M. F. Sakdan, "The Influence of Students' Experience on Alumni Giving in Malaysian Public Educational Institution," *Paper presented, MATEC Web of Conferences, 150*, EDP Sciences, 2018, 1–6, 1.
67 D. D. Vidal and T. G. Pittz, "Educating Beyond the Classroom: Alumni Giving and the Value of Campus Culture," *Studies in Higher Education* (2018): 1–15, 11, https://doi.org/10.1080/03075079.2018.1482269.
68 Yusof Boon (Associate Professor, Director, Endowment Unit, Universiti Teknologi Malaysia, Skudai), in an interview with the authors, 23 February 2020.
69 Mahamood, Ab. Rahman, and Che Seman, "Cabaran Pelaksanaan Wakaf Universiti Awam Di Malaysia: Analisis Menurut Perundangan Di Malaysia," 387.
70 Noor Mizan Arifin (Assistant Registrar, Office of Waqf & Endowment, Universiti Sultan Zainal Abidin, Kuala Nerus), in an interview with the authors, 2 March 2020.
71 Yusof Boon (Associate Professor, Director, Endowment Unit, Universiti Teknologi Malaysia, Skudai), in an interview with the authors, 23 February 2020.
72 Nuruliman Ibrahim (Head, Waqf Management Section, Centre for Management of Waqf, Zakat and Endowment, Universiti Putra Malaysia, Serdang), in an interview with the authors, 31 March 2020.
73 Razman Ibrahim (Assistant Registrar, Center for Awqaf and Zakat, Universiti Sains Islam Malaysia, Nilai), in an interview with the authors, 3 March 2020.
74 Ahmad Mustaqim Zolkafali (Assistant Registrar, Chancellor Foundation, Universiti Kebangsaan Malaysia (UKM), Bangi), in an interview with the authors, 27 March 2020.
75 Yusof Boon (Associate Professor, Director, Endowment Unit, Universiti Teknologi Malaysia, Skudai), in an interview with the authors, 23 February 2020.
76 "Warta Endowmen," vol. 3 (Johor Bahru, 2019).
77 M. Munadi, "Pengelolaan Endowment Fund Di Perguruan Tinggi Malaysia: Studi Kasus Di Universitas Teknologi Malaysia," *Al-Ulum* 17, no. 2 (2017): 306–31, 306, https://doi.org/10.30603/au.v17i2.199.
78 S. Schaffer, N. Polissar, and M. Neradilek, *Exploratory Analysis of Nonprofit Success Factors* (Seattle, WA: Public Interest Management Group, 2015), 4.
79 S. I. Ceptureanu et al., "Sustainability Perceptions in Romanian Non-Profit Organizations: An Exploratory Study Using Success Factor Analysis," *Sustainability* 10, no. 297 (2018): 1–23, 16.

80 Ahmad Mustaqim Zolkafali (Assistant Registrar, Chancellor Foundation, Universiti Kebangsaan Malaysia (UKM), Bangi), in an interview with the authors, 27 March 2020.
81 Yusof Boon (Associate Professor, Director, Endowment Unit, Universiti Teknologi Malaysia, Skudai), in an interview with the authors, 23 February 2020.
82 N. Mohd Ali, R. Ahmad, and N. S. Ahmad Mahdzan, "The Need of an Effective Business Model for Waqf Land Development in Malaysia," *Paper presented, The 20th International Research Conference on Business, Economics, and Social Sciences*, Istanbul, Turkey, 2015, 1–12, 1.
83 M. Sulaiman and M. A. Zakari, "Efficiency and Effectiveness of Waqf Institutions in Malaysia: Toward Financial Sustainability," in *Access to Finance and Human Development—Essays on Zakah, Awqaf and Microfinance*, ed. H A El-Karanshawy et al. 43–53 (Doha, Qatar: Bloomsbury Qatar Foundation, 2015), 49.
84 Razman Ibrahim (Assistant Registrar, Center for Awqaf and Zakat, Universiti Sains Islam Malaysia, Nilai), in an interview with the authors, 3 March 2020.
85 Nuruliman Ibrahim (Head, Waqf Management Section, Centre for Management of Waqf, Zakat and Endowment, Universiti Putra Malaysia, Serdang), in an interview with the authors, 31 March 2020.
86 Yusof Boon (Associate Professor, Director, Endowment Unit, Universiti Teknologi Malaysia, Skudai), in an interview with the authors, 23 February 2020.
87 Ahmad Mustaqim Zolkafali (Assistant Registrar, Chancellor Foundation, Universiti Kebangsaan Malaysia (UKM), Bangi), in an interview with the authors, 27 March 2020.
88 Ahmad Yusof Boon (Associate Professor, Director, Endowment Unit, Universiti Teknologi Malaysia, Skudai), in an interview with the authors, 23 February 2020.
89 Nuruliman Ibrahim (Head, Waqf Management Section, Centre for Management of Waqf, Zakat and Endowment, Universiti Putra Malaysia, Serdang), in an interview with the authors, 31 March 2020.
90 Razman Ibrahim (Assistant Registrar, Center for Awqaf and Zakat, Universiti Sains Islam Malaysia, Nilai), in an interview with the authors, 3 March 2020.
91 Noor Mizan Arifin (Assistant Registrar, Office of Waqf & Endowment, Universiti Sultan Zainal Abidin, Kuala Nerus), in an interview with the authors, 2 March 2020.
92 R. Bekkers and P. Wiepking, "A Literature Review of Empirical Studies of Philanthropy: Eight Mechanisms That Drive Charitable Giving," *Nonprofit and Voluntary Sector Quarterly* 40, no. 5 (2011): 924–73, 924, https://doi.org/10.1177/0899764010380927.
93 A. Sargeant and L. Woodliffe, "Gift Giving: An Interdisciplinary Review," *International Journal of Nonprofit and Voluntary Sector Marketing* 12 (2007): 275–307, 293, https://doi.org/10.1002/nvsm.
94 V. C. H. Chua and C. M. Wong, "Tax Incentives, Individual Characteristics and Charitable Giving in Singapore," *International Journal of Social Economics* 26, no. 12 (1999): 1492 505, 1492.
95 Income Tax Act 1967 (ITA).
96 S. Weinstein and P. Barden, *The Complete Guide to Fundraising Management*, 4th ed. (Hoboken: John Wiley & Sons, Inc., 2017), 242–43.
97 Yusof Boon (Associate Professor, Director, Endowment Unit, Universiti Teknologi Malaysia, Skudai), in an interview with the authors, 23 February 2020.
98 Nuruliman Ibrahim (Head, Waqf Management Section, Centre for Management of Waqf, Zakat and Endowment, Universiti Putra Malaysia, Serdang), in an interview with the authors, 31 March 2020.
99 Razman Ibrahim (Assistant Registrar, Center for Awqaf and Zakat, Universiti Sains Islam Malaysia, Nilai), in an interview with the authors, 3 March 2020.
100 Noor Mizan Arifin (Assistant Registrar, Office of Waqf & Endowment, Universiti Sultan Zainal Abidin, Kuala Nerus), in an interview with the authors, 2 March 2020.
101 Ahmad Mustaqim Zolkafali (Assistant Registrar, Chancellor Foundation, Universiti Kebangsaan Malaysia (UKM), Bangi), in an interview with the authors, 27 March 2020.

102 J. Weerawardena, "Non-Profit Marketing Strategy," in *Transformational Leadership and Not for Profits and Social Enterprises*, ed. K. Wiltshire, A. Malhotra, and M. Axelsen, 1st ed. (New York: Routledge, 2018), 332.

103 Ahmad Mustaqim Zolkafali (Assistant Registrar, Chancellor Foundation, Universiti Kebangsaan Malaysia (UKM), Bangi), in an interview with the authors, 27 March 2020.

104 Yusof Boon (Associate Professor, Director, Endowment Unit, Universiti Teknologi Malaysia, Skudai), in an interview with the authors, 23 February 2020.

105 Nuruliman Ibrahim (Head, Waqf Management Section, Centre for Management of Waqf, Zakat and Endowment, Universiti Putra Malaysia, Serdang), in an interview with the authors, 31 March 2020.

106 Razman Ibrahim (Assistant Registrar, Center for Awqaf and Zakat, Universiti Sains Islam Malaysia, Nilai), in an interview with the authors, 3 March 2020.

107 Noor Mizan Arifin (Assistant Registrar, Office of Waqf & Endowment, Universiti Sultan Zainal Abidin, Kuala Nerus), in an interview with the authors, 2 March 2020.

108 P. Charseatd, "Role of Religious Beliefs in Blood Donation Behavior among the Youngster in Iran: A Theory of Planned Behavior Perspective," *Journal of Islamic Marketing* 7, no. 3 (2016): 1–20, 14.

109 Ahmad Mustaqim Zolkafali (Assistant Registrar, Chancellor Foundation, Universiti Kebangsaan Malaysia (UKM), Bangi), in an interview with the authors, 27 March 2020.

110 Yusof Boon (Associate Professor, Director, Endowment Unit, Universiti Teknologi Malaysia, Skudai), in an interview with the authors, 23 February 2020.

111 Nuruliman Ibrahim (Head, Waqf Management Section, Centre for Management of Waqf, Zakat and Endowment, Universiti Putra Malaysia, Serdang), in an interview with the authors, 31 March 2020.

112 Razman Ibrahim (Assistant Registrar, Center for Awqaf and Zakat, Universiti Sains Islam Malaysia, Nilai), in an interview with the authors, 3 March 2020.

113 Noor Mizan Arifin (Assistant Registrar, Office of Waqf & Endowment, Universiti Sultan Zainal Abidin, Kuala Nerus), in an interview with the authors, 2 March 2020.

114 Yusof Boon (Associate Professor, Director, Endowment Unit, Universiti Teknologi Malaysia, Skudai), in an interview with the authors, 23 February 2020.

115 Nuruliman Ibrahim (Head, Waqf Management Section, Centre for Management of Waqf, Zakat and Endowment, Universiti Putra Malaysia, Serdang), in an interview with the authors, 31 March 2020.

116 Razman Ibrahim (Assistant Registrar, Center for Awqaf and Zakat, Universiti Sains Islam Malaysia, Nilai), in an interview with the authors, 3 March 2020.

117 Noor Mizan Arifin (Assistant Registrar, Office of Waqf & Endowment, Universiti Sultan Zainal Abidin, Kuala Nerus), in an interview with the authors, 2 March 2020.

118 Yusof Boon (Associate Professor, Director, Endowment Unit, Universiti Teknologi Malaysia, Skudai), in an interview with the authors, 23 February 2020.

119 Nuruliman Ibrahim (Head, Waqf Management Section, Centre for Management of Waqf, Zakat and Endowment, Universiti Putra Malaysia, Serdang), in an interview with the authors, 31 March 2020.

120 Razman Ibrahim (Assistant Registrar, Center for Awqaf and Zakat, Universiti Sains Islam Malaysia, Nilai), in an interview with the authors, 3 March 2020.

121 Noor Mizan Arifin (Assistant Registrar, Office of Waqf & Endowment, Universiti Sultan Zainal Abidin, Kuala Nerus), in an interview with the authors, 2 March 2020.

122 L. Lysakowski, "The Importance of Volunteers in a Capital Campaign," *International Journal of Nonprofit and Voluntary Sector Marketing* 7, no. 4 (2002): 325–33, 325.

123 K. Bales, "Measuring the Propensity to Volunteer," *Social Policy & Administration* 30, no. 3 (1996): 206–26, https://doi.org/10.1111/j.1467-9515.1996.tb00555.x.

124 Shaleni a/p S. Muthiah (Financial Officer, Account & Investment Division, Bursar's Office, Universiti Malaya, Kuala Lumpur), in an interview with the authors, 20 March 2020.

125 Mohd Akbal Qamas Abdul Basir (Assistant Bursar, Bursar's Office, Universiti Kebangsaan Malaysia, Bangi), in an interview with the authors, 23 March 2020.
126 Tuttle, *How Harvard and Yale Beat the Market*, 33.
127 Yusof Boon (Associate Professor, Director, Endowment Unit, Universiti Teknologi Malaysia, Skudai), in an interview with the authors, 23 February 2020.
128 Nuruliman Ibrahim (Head, Waqf Management Section, Centre for Management of Waqf, Zakat and Endowment, Universiti Putra Malaysia, Serdang), in an interview with the authors, 31 March 2020.
129 Razman Ibrahim (Assistant Registrar, Center for Awqaf and Zakat, Universiti Sains Islam Malaysia, Nilai), in an interview with the authors, 3 March 2020.
130 Yusof Boon (Associate Professor, Director, Endowment Unit, Universiti Teknologi Malaysia, Skudai), in an interview with the authors, 23 February 2020.
131 Nuruliman Ibrahim (Head, Waqf Management Section, Centre for Management of Waqf, Zakat and Endowment, Universiti Putra Malaysia, Serdang), in an interview with the authors, 31 March 2020.
132 Razman Ibrahim (Assistant Registrar, Center for Awqaf and Zakat, Universiti Sains Islam Malaysia, Nilai), in an interview with the authors, 3 March 2020.
133 Wang, "What Influences Alumni Donations?" 160.
134 Ahmad Mustaqim Zolkafali (Assistant Registrar, Chancellor Foundation, Universiti Kebangsaan Malaysia (UKM), Bangi), in an interview with the authors, 27 March 2020.
135 Yusof Boon (Associate Professor, Director, Endowment Unit, Universiti Teknologi Malaysia, Skudai), in an interview with the authors, 23 February 2020.
136 J. L. R. Dillon, "Factors and Characteristics of Alumni Role Identity: Implications for Practice in Higher Education Fundraising and Alumni Relations," Ph.D. thesis, The Faculty of the Schools of Education, The University of San Francisco, 2017, ii.
137 M. J. Zickar, T. H. Ron, and C. Arnold, "Using Facebook Pages to Connect with Students, Faculty, Alumni, and Friends: An Empirical Analysis," *Teaching of Psychology* 45, no. 4 (2018): 358–62, 358, https://doi.org/10.1177/0098628318796923.
138 A. Peruta and C. Helm, "Engaging University Alumni through Social Media: Strategies for Creating Community," *The Journal of Social Media in Society* 7, no. 1 (2018): 123–50, 127.

7 Conclusion

This book discussed the sources of funding for HEIs, the concepts of endowment and *waqf* as sources of funding for HEIs, and the successful elements of endowment and *waqf* in HEIs. This book also elaborated on the application and elements that could drive the successful implementation of these funds at Malaysian public universities.

Discussion of these elements is important for the practitioners at HEIs who wish to implement endowment or/and *waqf* funds, as both funds are discussed in detail. Given that the application and elements that can successfully drive the implementation of endowment and *waqf* are discussed in this book, determining the appropriate method of implementation of these funds would be easier for other universities. Moreover, the book provided key insights into factors that lead to the successful implementation of both these funds at selected universities.

The book demonstrated that both public and private parties are responsible to provide the higher education finance because of the benefits they reap from the education provided. Given that the government has been granted a mandate to serve the country, it is responsible for managing the public fund and investing in the higher education sector. The funding from the government could provide equal opportunity for every individual, including the poor, to gain from the higher education system to create a better future. An educated generation would improve the well-being of the citizens and contribute to the country in terms of knowledge and skills.

The high demand for higher education has burdened the government in funding this sector. Therefore, the sources provided by private parties, who benefit directly from this sector, are crucial. This cost-sharing can benefit both parties. From the Islamic perspective, education is one of the basic needs not only for an individual but also for society. The categorisation of government funding for education as *fard kifayah* indicates that the government is not the only party to fund this sector. If the government is faced with the burden of funding the high demand for higher education, the private sector needs to supplement the funding to this sector.

Besides the previously discussed two parties, another party that contributes to the higher education finance is the group comprising foundations, business corporations, individuals, religious organisations, and alumni through voluntary donations. Although this party does not benefit directly from HEIs, it is strongly motivated

DOI: 10.4324/9781003435976-7

to contribute because of its values and beliefs. Notably, the party's contribution is significant and highly demanded by Islam. Various mediums that could be used by the party to channel contribution include endowment and *waqf* funds, which were emphasised in this book.

The implementation of endowment and *waqf* funds at HEIs is for the same purpose—to provide perpetual funding to these institutions. The institution implementing these funds gains the trust of the donors to manage them and is responsible for ensuring that the funds are sustained over the long term. Therefore, their benefits can be reaped from one generation to another. Generally, an endowment consists of three types of funds, namely true endowment, term endowment, and quasi-endowment while *waqf* consists of *waqf khas* and *waqf am*. Although the names of these funds differ, the objectives are similar. True endowment and *waqf khas* fall under the same category, which is specific, while quasi-endowment and *waqf am* are categorised as general. Another type of fund for endowment is known as term endowment, which comprises funds restricted by the donor for a certain time. Although *waqf* generally does not include this type of fund, its application in the *madhhab* of Maliki is known as *waqf mu'aqqat*, which is also allowed.

Although the endowment and *waqf* funds appear to have the same purpose and type, specific features distinguish them from each other. In terms of the philosophy of giving, both funds apply different philosophies, which influence the contribution from the donors to these funds. For donors who contribute their property to the endowment fund, humanity and generosity become the factors that motivate them to do so. In the case of *waqf*, the practice of giving is demanded in Islam and is considered one of the categories under the *Maqasid Shariah*, which implies the safeguarding of wealth; it becomes the main motivator for the donors, especially Muslims, to contribute their property to the *waqf* fund. The meanings of the general type of endowment and *waqf* funds also differs from each other. For endowment, the general product indicates that the university treats the unrestricted funds as an endowment, whereas the *waqf* funds donated by donors could be used for general purposes.

The presence of pillars in the practice of *waqf* also distinguishes this fund from an endowment fund. Meanwhile, failure to fulfil the pillars, which comprise *al-wāqif*, *al- mawqūf*, *al-mawqūf 'alayh*, and *ṣighah*, leads to the practice of the *waqf* becoming invalid. These funds differ in terms of a few elements, which are perpetuity, rights of ownership, and inalienability. An endowment has the element of perpetuity as the property contributing to this fund must be invested, whereas *waqf* must be preserved. In terms of the ownership element, endowment has flexible rights of ownership, in which the donors can determine whether the fund belongs to the university or should be returned. However, once the donors contribute their property to *waqf*, it would solely belong to Allah. The existence of an inalienable element in *waqf* also distinguishes this fund from an endowment fund as it cannot be transferred to another party once the donors have contributed their property to the *waqf* fund.

In discussing the successful elements of endowment and *waqf* funds in higher education finance, this book adopted the findings from the study by Lerner, Schoar, and Wang,[1] who found that asset allocation to alternative assets was the main investment choice of endowment funds at more selective universities, such as the Ivy League Schools. As the scholars noted that their findings might not be applicable for ordinary endowments, such as the top endowment fund where investing in alternative assets creates high returns, other studies revealed that asset diversification was an investment strategy that could enhance the risk-adjusted return related to investments. Therefore, this book applied the term appropriate investment planning as the first element to determine the success of endowment and *waqf* funds. In this element, the Shariah-compliant investments should be the main choice instead of conventional investments for the endowment and *waqf* funds at HEIs in Malaysia to ensure that the returns gained are halal in Islam.

This book also adopted other successful elements found in the same study, such as superior investment committee, highly skilled investment managers, and alumni networks. In evaluating the investment committee, some indicators listed in other studies—size, expertise, and diversity—were adopted in this study. In terms of size, the number of members in the investment committee was neither large nor small. In Malaysia, the minimum number of members required is six. In terms of expertise, this number is among the important basic features in ensuring that endowment and *waqf* funds have qualified members to make investment-related decisions. Having experts in the Shariah field is also an important factor, which determines whether or not the diversification of investment is legal as per Islam. The diversification of the members of the investment committee, especially in terms of experience, is another indicator determining whether the committee is superior, as the issues related to the group dynamics, such as groupthink, confirmation bias, and group polarisation, could be limited in a diversified committee.

Another successful element of endowment and *waqf* funds discussed in this book was highly skilled investment managers. The need for these skilled managers is inevitable based on their ability to manage investments and their experience, which enable wise decision-making. However, the absence of internal investment managers who possess investment skills is not an issue as external managers can be appointed for the endowment and *waqf* funds. They should still be selected carefully to avoid wrong selection. In Malaysia, the selection of external fund managers is based on criteria laid down by the SCM, which include them being duly licensed or authorised by the relevant authority, having adequate financial resources, and having an adequate performance track record.

Alumni are among the parties that could contribute to the the endowment and *waqf* funds at HEIs. Building relationships with the alumni is one of the successful elements of these funds, although indicators exist that encourage them to contribute to the funds, such as 'creating and sharing' the values. This indicator is important as the alumni consider contributing if they have a sense of belonging to the university. They would also contribute if they have a positive experience during their studies as it would create a sense of satisfaction towards the university. The aid from the alumni association is also essential in building relationships with the alumni, through which a sustainable relationship between the university and alumni can be established. Campus events are also important in encouraging the alumni to contribute to the funds at HEIs as they could motivate the alumni to initiate a life-long relationship with the university.

Besides all the elements discussed here, the diversity of income sources and effective fundraising can be the other two successful elements of endowment and *waqf* funds. In terms of diversity, income sources other than investments that can generate funds for the endowment and *waqf* should also be considered. To be specific, for the institutions with a passive investment portfolio of funds, the diversification of income sources is crucial in ensuring an expansion of their funds. One of the mechanisms to expand the funds is the involvement in commercial activities as it can effectively impact fundraising.

The last element is effective fundraising, which is important for philanthropic funds such as endowment and *waqf*, as it can ensure that these funds have sufficient income sources for the institution. In collecting the contributions from the public (e.g. individuals, foundations, corporations, and government), various communication channels should be utilised to implement the fundraising activities and ensure that the information regarding the funds reaches all segments of society. The implementation of the activities should be performed under the umbrella concept of a campaign as it is the strongest factor in determining success. Given the strong impact of social media on today's society, the implementation of fundraising activities through this channel is important, especially through social networks (e.g. Facebook) as they are the most effective medium to inspire people to contribute.

All Malaysian public universities have implemented the endowment fund to collect contributions from the public for funding the operations. The *waqf* fund has been implemented in 17 universities. Both funds are highly important as they can provide additional sources of income over and above the funds provided by the government. Despite the grouping of endowment and *waqf* funds under the same category, namely philanthropy, the application of both funds in Malaysian HEIs differs from each other.

The implementation of the endowment at public universities is under the management of the university itself, which is under the jurisdiction of the bursar. As the endowment funds need to be invested, all investment activities of the fund are also managed by the university bursar, as applied in the universities selected in this study such as UM, UKM, and UTM. The laws regulating the implementation of the endowment funds at HEIs in Malaysia are subject to local legislation, which is the Trustee Act 1949 (Act 208). However, the judiciary still refers to English law to decide cases. To acquire more information on how the endowment fund is implemented at Malaysian public universities, a few universities were selected based on fund collection.

For UM and UKM, the endowment funds were established based on the demand from Responsibility Centres (PTJ). Therefore, the purpose of establishing endowment chairs varied according to the objectives. Given that the endowment chairs at these universities were established based on demand from the PTJ, the PTJ is responsible for managing the endowment chair in terms of collection of donations and distribution of benefits. In the case of UTM, the endowment fund is under a special fund known as UTM Endowment Fund, which aims to provide welfare to students. Besides, the UTM Endowment Unit is responsible for managing the collection of donations and the distribution of benefits.

In terms of legal structure, the establishment of an endowment fund at the selected public universities is under the Deputy VC or Chancellor. The donation of funds from donors is accepted in both cash and non-cash forms. Three types of endowment have been applied at UM and UTM, namely true endowment, term endowment, and quasi-endowment while UKM has applied only two types of endowment—true endowment and term endowment. The funds donated by donors to the UTM Endowment Fund should not be returned. However, for UM and UKM, the fund may need to be returned based on the donor's agreement. Many active endowment chairs remain at UM (e.g. Kursi Dr Siti Hasmah Mohd Ali, Kursi Khazanah Nasional, Kursi Perlindungan Kewangan Warga Tua) and UKM (e.g. Kursi Tan Sri Noah, Kursi Pok Rafeah, Kursi Kecemerlangan RHB) since the inception of the endowment fund. In UTM, there are the following four types of endowment schemes: Tabung Endowment Merdeka, Tabung Endowment Azman Hashim, Tabung Endowment Alumni, and Tabung Endowment Ainuddin Wahid.

In contrast to the endowment fund, the *waqf* fund in Malaysia is under the jurisdiction of the MAIN. As a sole trustee of the *waqf* fund, the MAIN is responsible for managing the fund. The universities that attempt to implement the *waqf* fund at their institution are required to receive permission from the MAIN for *waqf* fund management. The consent from MAIN renders them eligible to collect, generate, and manage the *waqf* fund themselves (e.g. *waqf* unit). This approach has been adopted by the selected public universities, such as UPM, USIM, and UniSZA.

The *waqf* fund at UPM is known as Dana Wakaf Ilmu, and the funds at USIM and UniSZA are Dana Wakaf al-Abrar and Dana Wakaf UniSZA, respectively. The *waqf* fund at these universities was established mainly to fund the university infrastructure facilities and students' welfare. In terms of legal structure, the *waqf* fund at the universities is under the Deputy VC or VC while the governance model is based on the *waqf* governance models, as suggested by the government. The permissions granted by the MAIN to implement the *waqf* fund at universities vary from each other according to the signed agreement. For UPM, the status of *waqf* manager or *mutawalli* provided by the MAIS is based on a five-year contract. In the case of USIM, the status granted by MAINS is full autonomy while the permission to UniSZA is granted by MAIDAM under a JV. The donation received by the UPM and UniSZA is in the cash and non-cash forms, whereas that received by USIM is only in cash.

Given that the *waqf* donation in the form of cash can be invested to generate *waqf* income, universities including UPM and UniSZA have been leveraging the opportunity to generate cash *waqf* through investment activities. The investment matters of the cash *waqf* for UPM are managed by the bursar while they are managed by the investment committee known as the Financial and Investment Committee at UniSZA. All the universities selected in this study have two types of *waqf* funds, *waqf am* and *waqf khas*, which use their specific name.

As discussed earlier, the successful elements of endowment and *waqf* funds in the higher education finance are appropriate investment planning, superior investment committees, highly skilled investment managers, alumni networks, diversity of income sources, and effective fundraising. These elements are used as platforms to empirically examine the elements that can successfully drive the implementation of the funds at Malaysian public universities. The findings of this study revealed that each university has its strengths in certain elements. At the same time, only some elements contributed to the successful implementation of endowment and *waqf* in funding Malaysian public universities.

The first element found to contribute to the successful implementation of endowment and *waqf* funds was superior investment committees. In examining whether the investment committee in the universities selected in this study was superior, the basic aspects of size, expertise, and diversity were used. All investment committees at the selected universities passed the minimum number of members (i.e. 6) set by the MoHE in the Investment Guidelines. Although these members were selected by the top management of the university, it did not indicate whether all the members possessed expertise in the area of investment. Expertise, including in the area of Shariah, is the main qualifying factor for the members of the investment committee, in addition to two other factors, knowledge and experience. The investment committees at the universities consisted of diverse members in terms of experience and expertise. This diversification is important because of its ability to limit the issues related to group dynamics. Based on these findings, the investment committees at the universities selected in this study were demonstrated to be superior. However, these results did not represent USIM as they were yet to be involved in any investment activities.

The second element comprises the highly skilled investment manager. This element could be analysed only for UM and UKM as these were the only universities that have fund managers. Fund managers at these universities were said to be highly skilled as they were appointed by the financial institutions in Malaysia. Given that the fund managers have been established in this country, their ability to manage the investment activities of an endowment fund at universities has been proven. Moreover, they should also be considered professional investment managers because they are registered with the SCM. Both universities agreed that their fund managers exhibited excellent performance by providing desirable returns from the investments. The fund managers at UM and UKM position these universities favourably because they can invest in assets other than only fixed deposits, including bonds, equities, and properties. The diversification in the investment portfolios is important as it is an investment strategy for the endowment fund.

The third element was the alumni network, which could be analysed for only certain universities, UTM, UPM, USIM, and UniSZA, and could not be discussed at UM and UKM as the establishment of the endowment funds at these universities was based on the chair. In other words, the donor for each endowment chair was established. In the case of endowment and *waqf* funds at other universities, new contributions were constantly required to run a certain project. Alumni is one of the parties that can provide new contributions to these funds at these institutions, as acknowledged by the informants from UTM and UPM, where their alumni could increase the collection of their funds. The alumni association at both universities played a significant role in encouraging the alumni to contribute to the funds. Besides, internal factors, including the positive experience of alumni, drove the alumni to contribute, as revealed by the UTM informant. At the same time, awareness also had a role in increasing the funds as the informants of USIM and UniSZA stated that the lack of awareness might render achieving alumni contributions difficult.

To ensure the expansion in the size of the endowment and *waqf* funds, the return from investments should be regenerated to gain more income. Besides reinvestment, other income-generating sources should be explored, as proven through UKM, UTM, and UPM. As the *waqf* funds can be invested only in fixed deposits, involvement in other activities is recommended not only to expand the fund size but also to promote the name of the funds indirectly. Moreover, converting the funds into properties should also be considered, as practised by USIM, as it would secure the value of the fund in the long term, given that property value generally tended to increase rapidly. The properties were profitable in the form of rental income derived.

Effective fundraising is another element found to contribute to the successful implementation of endowment and *waqf* funds in this study. All the universities (i.e. UTM, UPM, USIM, and UniSZA) were highly active in promoting their endowment and *waqf* funds. The promotion activities under the campaign concept were performed through various communication channels, which were present to ensure that the information related to the funds could reach the community, especially the potential donors. These practices helped not only in creating awareness among the public but also in branding the funds. All the universities employed the most effective communication channel in the current time, specifically social media. This channel also appears to be important for the development of the alumni network to ensure the seamless acquisition of information about the funds at the university. To attract Muslim contributors, the aspect of Islamic teachings was included when communicating with them. In facilitating donors' contributions, various collection channels were employed by the universities, including sophisticated channels such as mobile apps/wallets.

Besides the previously discussed elements, the involvement of volunteers was another important element derived based on the interviews with universities. Although it might not be an element that directly contributed to the successful implementation of endowment and *waqf* funds, the informants recognised the contribution of their energy or involvement in the management of endowment and *waqf* funds. Besides, their presence could assist the endowment and *waqf* management units in promoting or safeguarding the properties related to the endowment or *waqf* funds.

This study found that the element of appropriate investment planning may not contribute to the successful implementation of endowment and *waqf* funds at Malaysian public universities. The diversification in the investment portfolios for a few cases in this study remained insufficient despite most investments being Shariah-compliant. Furthermore, none of the investments involved alternative investments as the investment included only traditional assets. Although the investment portfolio at UM and UKM was more diversified (e.g. fixed deposits, bonds, equities, and properties) compared to other universities that were investing only in fixed deposits because of the presence of fund managers, the diversification did not reach a satisfactory level given the low total number of funds managed—ten for UM and five for UKM. Based on international experience, the required number of fund managers to represent good diversification was 100 or more.

Besides the contribution to the literature in the area of endowment and *waqf* funds, this book also contributes in terms of three main aspects, namely theory, practice, and policymaking. The theoretical contributions are evident as this book combined the discussion of two types of funds—endowment and *waqf* funds. Therefore, readers could determine the concept of each fund through this book while identifying the differences between them and their application at the selected Malaysian public universities. Moreover, the theoretical contributions are also reflected in terms of the exposure of the readers to the elements that can lead to the successful implementation of endowment and *waqf* in funding Malaysian public universities. This is important because the government encourages the implementation of these funds by public universities through its education policy, the Malaysia Education Blueprint 2015–2025 (Higher Education).

This book also provides practical contributions by revealing the application of endowment and *waqf* funds in the selected Malaysian public universities. Therefore, it can be used as a reference by other universities in the country, including private universities (with an attempt to implement these funds) on how to implement these funds in their institutions. The findings of the study discussed in this book were related to the elements that can lead to the successful implementation of endowment and *waqf* funds. These findings could assist universities, including those in the progress of implementing these funds, to place focus on and enhance the efforts on each element. These results were presented to facilitate the success potential for the funds implemented in other institutions.

This book also has policy implications for the policymakers, including the MoHE, to consider. The discussion on the elements that can lead to the successful implementation of endowment and *waqf* funds can help provide solutions while policies can be formulated to empower these funds in HEIs, particularly public universities. One of the policies that the government can consider enacting is related to the appointment of fund managers. No specific provision currently exists for appointing fund managers to enable the involvement of the universities in the investment in assets such as bonds, equities, and properties. Therefore, the enactment of relevant policies to encourage the involvement of public universities to invest in these assets can be considered.

This study also had a few limitations. The first limitation was related to the literature. Despite many studies on *waqf*, studies on the endowment in the Malaysian context are limited. As a result, the authors faced difficulty in obtaining rich information on the endowment implementation in the country, especially at public universities. At the same time, studies related to the elements that led to the success of endowment and *waqf* funds at Malaysian public universities were highly limited. Therefore, a limited search was made on the works of literature discussing this matter in the context of Malaysia. In addressing these limitations, a reference was made to studies that were conducted by Western scholars abroad. Subsequently, the theoretical foundation related to this fund in terms of the concepts, applications, and elements leading to success could be established.

The second limitation was related to the informants in the endowment area. The endowment management at Malaysian public universities varied. Furthermore, some universities placed the endowment fund under the university bursar while other universities placed this fund under certain units. The PTJ was the responsible party to manage the endowment fund under the bursar, as it was created based on the application of the endowment chair. The university that practised this method comprised a variety of endowment funds, which were managed by a different PTJ. This variety of funds led to a diversity of chairs, resulting in the inability of the authors to conduct interviews because of time and money constraints. To address this limitation, an interview was conducted with the representatives of fund management centres at the university, such as the Chancellor Foundation at UKM. The data obtained from the centres related to the endowment fund could be regarded as sufficient, considering that other data were obtained by the authors through interviewing the representatives from the endowment unit and finance division.

Given the few limitations of this study as discussed earlier, several important points for improvements in future research can be identified. Given that the element of volunteers was discovered in the field studies and not previously discussed in detail in the chapter on theory, future research could discuss the theory in detail to provide a comprehensive view. The contribution of this element in determining the successful implementation of endowment and *waqf* funds at the higher education level was empirically confirmed in this study.

The second limitation focused on the scope of endowment chairs. Given that some universities developed the endowment fund through the establishment of chairs, future research could be conducted on the scope of chairs to provide deeper insights. At the same time, the research on this scope could also identify other universities that applied the endowment fund through this method.

In the case of practitioners of the endowment fund involved in investment activities, one of the recommendations of this study was the development of diversified portfolios. The diversification of the investment portfolios could be achieved by appointing fund managers from financial institutions in Malaysia. The appointment of more fund managers with different investment styles helped diversify the investment portfolio and expand the endowment fund; therefore, future research could do more discussion and study on that, especially in the Malaysian context so that it can emphasise the importance of appointing fund managers. Meanwhile, for *waqf*, future research on the involvement in other activities besides investments (i.e. only involved in fixed deposits) could be added so that its role in expanding the *waqf* fund can be emphasised by the *waqf* practitioners.

Note

1 J. Lerner, A. Schoar, and J. Wang, "Secrets of the Academy: The Drivers of University Endowment Success," *Journal of Economic Perspectives* 22, no. 3 (2008): 207–22.

Bibliography

Arabic References

Al-Bukhārī, M. I. *Ṣaḥīḥ al-Bukhārī*. 5th ed. Vol. 3. Bayrūt: Dār Ibn Kathīr, 1993.

———. *Ṣaḥīḥ al-Bukhārī*. Riyāḍ: Dār al-Salām, 1999.

Al-Dardīr, M. A. *Al-Sharḥ al-Ṣaghīr 'ala Aqrab al-Masālik ila Madhhab al-Imām Mālik*. Vol. 4. United Arabic Emirates (UAE): Wizārah al-'Adl wa al-Shu'ūn al-Islāmiyyah wa al-Awqāf, 1989.

———. *Al-Sharḥ al-Ṣaghīr 'ala Aqrab al-Masālik ila Madhhab al-Imām Mālik*. Vol. 4. Qāhirah: Dār al-Ma'ārif, 1986.

Al-Dussūqī, M. A., A. Al-Dardīr, and M. Alish. *Hāshiyah al-Dussūqī 'ala al-Sharḥ al-Kabīr*. Vol. 4. Qāhirah: Dār Ihyā' al-Kutub al-'Arabiyyah, n.d.

Al-Hammām, K. D. *Sharḥ Fatḥ al-Qadīr 'ala al-Hidāyah Sharḥ Bidāyah al-Mubtadi'*. 1st ed. Vol. 6. Bayrūt: Dār al-Kutub al-'Ilmiyyah, 2003.

Al-Kasānī, Abū Bakr Ibn Mas'ūd al-Ḥanāfī. *Baḍā'i' al-Ṣana'i' fī Tartīb al-Sharā'i'*. Vol. 8. Bayrūt: Dār al-Kutub al-'Ilmiyyah, 2003.

Al-Nasā'ī. *Sunan al-Nasā'ī: Bi Sharḥ al-Ḥafīẓ Jalāl al-Dīn al-Ṣuyūṭī*. Vol. 5. Bayrūt: Dār al-Kitāb al-'Alamiyah, n.d.

Al-Nawawī, Abī Zakariyyā Maḥy al-Dīn Ibn Sharf. *al-Majmū' Sharḥ al-Muhadhdhab li al-Shirāzī*. Vol. 16. Jeddah: Maktabah al-Irshād, 1980.

———. *Sharḥ Ṣaḥīḥ Muslim*. Vol. 11. Bayrūt: Dār al-Ma'rifah, 2005.

Al-Qurṭūbī, Abī Wālid Muḥammad Ibn Aḥmad Ibn Muḥammad Ibn Aḥmad Ibn Rushd. *al-Jāmi' li Aḥkām al-Qur'ān*. Vol. 5. Bayrūt: Al-Risālah Publishers, 2006.

Al-Rahaybānī, M. S. *Maṭālib Uli al-Nuhā fī Sharḥ Ghāyah al-Muntahā*. 3rd ed. Vol. 6. N.p.: N.p., 2000.

Al-Sarakhsī, Abū Bakr Muḥammad Shams al-Dīn. *Al-Mabsūṭ*. Vol. 12. Bayrūt: Dār al-Ma'rifah, 1989.

Al-Sharbīnī, Shams al-Dīn Muḥammad Ibn Muḥammad al-Khāṭib. *Mughnī al-Muḥtāj ilā Ma'rifātī Ma'ānī Alfāẓ al-Minhāj*. Vol. 2. Bayrūt: Dār al-Ma'rifah, 1997.

Al-Shāṭibī, Abī Isḥāq Ibrāhim Ibn Mūsā Ibn Muḥammad al-Lakhmī. *al-Muwāfaqāt*. Vol. 2. Bayrūt: Dār al-Kutub al-'Ilmiyah, 2005.

Al-Shawkānī, Muḥammad Ibn 'Alī Ibn Muḥammad. *Fatḥ al-Qādir*. Vol. 5. Qāhirah: Dār al-Ḥadīth, 2007.

Al-Ṭabarī, M. J. *Jamī' al-Bayān 'an Ta'wīl al-Qur'ān*. Vol. 3. N.p.: Maktabah Muṣṭafā al-Bābī al-Ḥalābī, 1968.

Al-Tirmidhī. *al-Jāmi' al-Ṣaḥīḥ wa Huwa Sunan al-Tirmidhī*. Vol. 3. Bayrūt: Dār al-Kitāb al-'Alamiyah, n.d.

———. *Al-Jāmi' al-Ṣaḥīḥ wa Huwa Sunan al-Tirmidhī*. Vol. 5. Riyāḍ: al-Maktabah al-Islāmiyyah, 1938.

Dāwud, Abū. *Sunan Abū Dāwud*. Vol. 4. Bayrūt: Dār al-Risālah al-'Alamiyah, 2009.

Ibn 'Ābidīn, Muḥammad Amīn. *Radd al-Muḥtār 'ala al-Durr al-Mukhtār Sharḥ Tanwīr al-Abṣār*. Vol. 6. Bayrūt: Dār al-Ma'rifah, 2000.

———. *Radd al-Muḥtār 'ala al-Durr al-Mukhtār Sharḥ Tanwīr al-Abṣār*. Vol. 6. Riyāḍ: Dār 'Alīm al-Kutub, 2003.

Ibn Kathīr, Abū Fidā' Ismā'il Ibn 'Umar, al-Qurshī al-Damashqī. *Tafsīr al-Qur'ān al-'Aẓīm. Tafsir Al-Qur'an Al-'Azmi*. 1st ed. Vol. 2. Qāhirah: Dār al-Ghad al-Gadīd, 2007.

———. *Tafsīr al-Qur'ān al- 'Aẓīm*. Vol. 2. Riyāḍ: Dār Taybah li al-Nashr wa al-Tawzī', 2009.

Ibn Mājah, Abū 'Abd Allāh Muḥammad Ibn Yazid al-Qazwinī. *Sunan Ibn Mājah*. Vol. 2. Bayrūt: Dār Iḥyā' al-Turāth al-'Arabī, 1975.

———. *Sunan Ibn Mājah*. Vol. 1. N.p.: Dār Ihyā' al-Kutub al-'Arabiyah, 2009.

Ibn Qudāmah, Abī Muḥammad 'Abd Allāh Ibn Aḥmad Ibn Muḥammad al-Maqdisī. *Mughnī*. Vol. 8. Qāhirah: Hajr, 1992.

Nazīḥ Ḥammād. *Mu'jam al-Muṣṭalaḥāt al-Iqtiṣādiyyah fī Lughah al-Fuqahā'*. 3rd ed. Riyāḍ: Dār al-'Alamiyyah li al-Kitāb al-Islāmī, 1995.

Niẓām. *al-Fatawā al-Hindiyah*. 1st ed. Vol. 2. Bayrūt: Dār al-Kutub al-'Ilmiyyah, 2000.

Ṣabrī, I. S. *Al-Waqf al-Islāmī bayna al-Naẓariyyah wa al-Taṭbīq*. 1st ed. Al-'Urdūn: Dār al-Nafā'is, 2008.

Wahbah al-Zuḥaylī. *al-Fiqh al-Islāmī wa Adillatuh*. Vol. 8. Dimashq: Dār al-Fikr, 2010.

Malay and English References Books

Bennett, R. *Nonprofit Marketing and Fundraising*. London and New York: Routledge: Taylor & Francis Group, 2019.

Bray, M. *New Resources for Education: Community Management and Financing of Schools in Less Developed Countries*. London: Commonwealth Secretariat, 1987.

Buchanan, J. M., and M. R. Flowers. *The Public Finance: An Introductory Textbook*. 5th ed. Homewood, IL: Richard D. Irwin, Inc., 1980.

Cascione, G. L. *Philanthropists in Higher Education: Institutional, Biographical, and Religious Motivations for Giving*. New York: Routledge Falmer, 2003.

Longman Dictionary of Contemporary English. 4th ed. London: Pearson Education Limited, 2003.

Donnelly, A. S. *The Three Rs of Investing*. Homewood, IL: Dow Jones-Irwin, 1985.

Franz, R., and S. Kranner. *University Endowments: A Primer*. Charlottesville, VA: CFA Institute Research Foundation, 2019.

Johnstone, B. *Sharing the Costs of Higher Education: Student Financial Assistance in the United Kingdom, the Federal Republic of Germany, France, Sweden, and the United States*. New York: The College Board, 1986.

Johnstone, D. B. *Financing Higher Education: Cost-Sharing in International Perspective*. Rotterdam: Sense Publishers, 2006.

Kotler, P., and A. Andreasen. *Strategic Marketing for Nonprofit Organizations*. 4th ed. Hoboken, NJ: Prentice Hall, 1991.

List of Shariah-Compliant Securities by the Shariah Advisory Council of the Securities Commission Malaysia. Kuala Lumpur: Securities Commission Malaysia, 2019.

Ministry of Education Malaysia. *Malaysia Education Blueprint 2015–2025 (Higher Education)*. Putrajaya: Ministry of Education Malaysia, 2015.

Ministry of Higher Education Malaysia. *University Transformation Programme, Purple Book: Enhancing University Income Generation, Endowment & Waqf.* Putrajaya: Kementerian Pendidikan Tinggi Malaysia, 2016.

The New International Webster's Comprehensive Dictionary of the English Language. Deluxe Enc. Naples, FL: Trident Press International, 1996.

Panduan Pengurusan Wakaf Institusi Pendidikan. Putrajaya: Jabatan Wakaf, Zakat dan Haji (JAWHAR), 2018.

Salamon, S. *Ekonomi Islam: Pengenalan Sistem dan Kemungkinan.* Petaling Jaya: al- Rahmaniah, 1989.

Schaffer, S., N. Polissar, and M. Neradilek. *Exploratory Analysis of Nonprofit Success Factors.* Seattle, WA: Public Interest Management Group, 2015.

Securities Commission Malaysia (SC). *Guidelines on Unit Trust Funds.* Kuala Lumpur: SC, 2008.

Siddiqi, M. N. *Teaching Economics in Islamic Perspective.* 1st ed. Jeddah: Scientific Publishing Centre, 1996.

Swensen, D. *Pioneering Portfolio Management: An Unconventional Approach to Institutional Investment.* New York: Free Press, 2009.

Tuttle, M. *How Harvard and Yale Beat the Market.* Hoboken: John Wiley & Sons, Inc., 2009.

Weinstein, S., and P. Barden. *The Complete Guide to Fundraising Management.* 4th ed. Hoboken: John Wiley & Sons, Inc., 2017.

Chapter in Books

Alias, M., F. Johari, and A. Abdul Rahman. "Waqf Financing for Islamic Higher Education: USIM's Perspectives." In *Waqf Financing for Higher Education: Issues, Challenges and the Way Forward,* edited by M. R. Ab. Aziz, M. Alias, F. Johari, A. Abdul Rahman, and Z. Shafii, 27–42. Bandar Baru Nilai: USIM Publisher, 2014.

Amran, A., and J. Muhammad. "Changes and Challenges in Financial Autonomy." In *Governance Reforms in Public Universities of Malaysia,* edited by F. Md. Taib and M. N. L. Y. Abdullah, 59–77. Pulau Pinang: Penerbit Universiti Sains Malaysia, 2015.

Chan, R. Y. "Studying Philanthropy and Fundraising in the Field of Higher Education: A Proposed Conceptual Model." In *Facilitating Higher Education Growth through Fundraising and Philanthropy,* edited by H. C. Alphin, J. Lavine, S. Stark, and A. Hocker, 1–27. Hershey, PA: Information Science Reference (an imprint of IGI Global), 2016.

Che Wan Ismail, C. W. M., H. Wahid, and M. A. Mohd Noor. "Pola Perbelanjaan Dan Cadangan Penentuan Haddul Kifayah Mahasiswa Institusi Pengajian Tinggi: Kajian Di Kuala Terengganu, Terengganu." In *Pengurusan Zakat Di Malaysia: Isu Dan Cabaran Kontemporari,* edited by H. Wahid and M. A. Mohd Noor, 29–50. Bangi: Pusat Penyelidikan Ekonomi dan Kewangan Islam (EKONIS-UKM), 2018.

Cizakca, M. "Waqf in History and Its Implications for Modern Islamic Economies." In *Essential Readings in Contemporary Waqf Issues,* edited by M. Kahf and S. M. Mahamood, 3–42. Kuala Lumpur: CERT Publications Sdn. Bhd., 2011.

Haneef, M. A. "Funding of Higher Education in Malaysia: The Potential Role of Awqaf and Endowment." In *International Symposium on Waqf and Higher Education (ISWHE 2016),* edited by S. Kayadibi and S. Alimova, 20–25. Kuala Lumpur: Centre for Islamic Economics (CIE), IIUM, 2016.

Hussin, R., S. Z. Syed Abdul Kader, R. Abdul Rashid, and N. A. Suhaili. "The Approaches Adopted by the Selected States in Appointing Universities as Waqf Managers." In *Islamic*

Development Management: Recent Advancements and Issues, edited by N. Z. Mohd Sidek, R. Said, and W. N. Wan Hasan, 239–48. Singapore: Springer, 2019.

Johnstone, D. B., A. Arora, and W. Experton. "The Financing and Management of Higher Education: A Status Report on Worldwide Reforms." In *UNESCO World Conference on Higher Education*, 1–33. Paris, France: The World Bank, 1998.

Johnstone, D. B., and P. N. Marcucci. "Worldwide Trends in Higher Education Finance: Cost-Sharing, Student Loans, and the Support of Academic Research." In *UNESCO Forum on Higher Education, Research and Knowledge*, 1–36. N.p.: UNESCO, 2007.

Kamarudin, K. A., Z. Shafii, A. E. Abdul Kadir, and M. Haji Alias. "Konsep Dan Pembangunan Wakaf Di Negeri Sembilan Daripada Perspektif Majlis Agama Islam Negeri Sembilan." In *Waqf Financing for Higher Education: Issues, Challenges and the Way Forward*, 55–72. Bandar Baru Nilai: USIM Publisher, 2014.

Mohd Ramli, A., and M. O. Mohamed. "Cabaran Pembiayaan Sektor Pengajian Tinggi Awam Di Malaysia: Potensi Instrumen Wakaf Tunai." In *Sinergisme Wakaf Pendidikan Tinggi Di Malaysia*, edited by M. S. Shahruddin, B. Sayin, M. A. Mat Rani, M. M. Khalid, M. Y. Abdullah, A. Bhari, and A. Husin, 57–73. Shah Alam: Institut Kajian Zakat Malaysia (IKaZ), UiTM, 2016.

Skloot, E. "Should Not-for-Profits Go into Business?" In *Public & Nonprofit Marketing: Cases & Readings*, edited by C. H. Lovelock and C. B. Weinberg, 361–65. Canada: The Scientific Press and John Wiley & Sons, 1984.

Sulaiman, M., and M. A. Zakari. "Efficiency and Effectiveness of Waqf Institutions in Malaysia: Toward Financial Sustainability." In *Access to Finance and Human Development—Essays on Zakah, Awqaf and Microfinance*, edited by H. A. El- Karanshawy et al. 43–53. Doha, Qatar: Bloomsbury Qatar Foundation, 2015.

Tomczak, T., S. Reinecke, and A. Kuss. "Planning the Marketing Mix." In *Strategic Marketing*, 171–221. Wiesbaden: Springer Gabler, 2018.

Weerawardena, J. "Non-Profit Marketing Strategy." In *Transformational Leadership and Not for Profits and Social Enterprises*, edited by K. Wiltshire, A. Malhotra, and M. Axelsen. 1st ed., 332. New York: Routledge, 2018.

Reports

Asian Development Bank (ADB). *Good Practice in Cost Sharing and Financing in Higher Education*. Metro Manila: ADB, 2009.

Bynner, J., P. Dolton, L. Feinstein, G. Makepeace, L. Malmberg, and L. Woods. *Revisiting the Benefits of Higher Education*. London: Bedford Group for Lifecourse and Statistical Studies, Institute of Education, 2003.

Bynner, J., and M. Egerton. *The Wider Benefits of Higher Education*. London: Higher Education Funding Council for England, 2001.

Callan Associates. *Cost of Doing Business Survey: Executive Summary*. San Francisco: Callan Associates, 2013.

Commondfund Institute. *Counting the Cost: A Commonfund Viewpoint*. Wilton, CT: Commondfund Institute, 2017.

Financial Accounting Standards Board (FASB). *Statement of Financial Accounting Standards No. 117: Financial Statements of Not-for-Profit Organizations*. N.p.: FASB, 2010.

Flannery, H., R. Harris, and C. Rhine. *2008 DonorCentrics Internet Giving Benchmarking Analysis*. Charleston, SC: Target Analytics, 2009.

Kaplan, A. E. *Voluntary Support of Education*. London, Mexico City, Singapore, and Washington, DC: Council for Advancement and Support of Education (CASE), 2020.

Kementerian Kewangan Malaysia. *Anggaran Perbelanjaan Persekutuan*. Kuala Lumpur: Percetakan Nasional Malaysia Berhad, 2015.

———. *Anggaran Perbelanjaan Persekutuan*. Kuala Lumpur: Percetakan Nasional Malaysia Berhad, 2018.

———. *Laporan Kajian Pengesanan Graduan 2018*. Putrajaya: KPM, 2019.

———. *Anggaran Perbelanjaan Persekutuan*. Kuala Lumpur: Percetakan Nasional Malaysia Berhad, 2020.

Lawson, M. and M. Martin. *The Commitment to Reducing Inequality Index*. Oxford: Oxfam International and Development Finance International, 2017.

Mitchell, M., M. Leachman, and K. Masterson. *Funding Down, Tuition Up: State Cuts to Higher Education Threaten Quality and Affordability at Public Colleges*. Washington, DC: Center on Budget and Policy Priorities, 2016.

National Association of College and University Business Officers (NACUBO) and Commonfund Institute. *NACUBO—Commonfund Study of Endowments*. Washington, DC: NACUBO, 2017.

National Association of College and University Business Officers (NACUBO) & Teachers Insurance and Annuity Association of America (TIAA). *NACUBO—TIAA Study of Endowments: Summary Results and Key Insights*. N.p.: NACUBO & TIAA, 2023.

Nonprofit Tech for Good. *2018 Global Trends in Giving Report*. N.p.: Nonprofit Tech for Good, 2018.

Organisation for Economic Co-operation and Development (OECD). *On the Edge: Securing a Sustainable Future for Higher Education*. France: OECD Publications, 2004.

Taback, A., J. Sweetman, J. Lenarcic, and T. Mcmillion. *Alternative Thinking-Alternative Investments: The Missing Piece in Portfolios?* New York: Wells Fargo Investment Institute, 2018.

UK Science & Innovation Network. *Kingdom of Saudi Arabia*. N.p.: UK Science & Innovation Network, 2018.

Yale University. *The Yale Endowment*. New Haven: Yale University, 2016.

———. *The Yale Endowment*. New Haven: Yale University, 2017.

Journals

Abdul Hamid, B., W. Hassan-Kamarudin, and S. Abdul Syahid Sowell. "The Endowment Fund as a Source of Sustainability for Higher Education in Malaysia: Maximising Investment Returns." *ISRA Research Paper*, no. 103 (2018): 1–32.

Abdul Razak, D., N. A. Che Embi, M. Che Mohd Salleh, and F. Fakhrunnas. "A Study on Sources of Waqf Funds for Higher Education in Selected Countries." *Adam Akademi* 6, no. 1 (2016): 113–28.

Ahmad, A. R., A. Baharudin, W. Z. Wan Yusoff, S. M. D. Syed Abdullah, and N. K. Soon. "Transformation of Waqf Implementation at Malaysian Public Universities." *Advanced Science Letters* 22, no. 9 (2016): 2184–86. https://doi.org/10.1166/asl.2016.7560.

Ahmed, S. "Public and Private Higher Education Financing in Nigeria." *European Scientific Journal* 11, no. 7 (2015): 92–109.

Ali Hamdan, S. U., and S. M. Mahamood. "Aplikasi Prinsip Berkekalan Wakaf di Institusi Pengajian Tinggi Terpilih: Perspektif Perundangan." *Journal of Shariah Law Research* 1, no. 2 (2016): 229–50.

"Alternative Investments 2020: An Introduction to Alternative Investments." *World Economic Forum*. Cologny/Geneva, 2015. http://www3.weforum.org/docs/WEF_Alternative_Investments_2020_An_Introdu ction_to_AI.pdf.

Azlen, M. W., and I. Zermati. "Investing Like the Harvard and Yale Endowment Funds." *Alternative Investment Analyst Review* 6, no. 3 (2017): 7–13.

Bahari, Z., and A. S. A. Ahmad Shukor. "Pemerkasaan Tadbir Urus Wakaf Pendidikan Tinggi Malaysia." *Proceeding Strengthening Local Communities Facing the Global Era* 1 (2017): 28–44. http://jurnal.unmuhjember.ac.id/index.php/pslcf/article/view/886.

Bales, K. "Measuring the Propensity to Volunteer." *Social Policy & Administration* 30, no. 3 (1996): 206–26. https://doi.org/10.1111/j.1467-9515.1996.tb00555.x.

Barber, B. M., and G. Wang. "Do (Some) University Endowments Earn Alpha?" *Financial Analysts Journal* 69, no. 5 (2013): 26–44.

Bekkers, R., and P. Wiepking. "A Literature Review of Empirical Studies of Philanthropy: Eight Mechanisms That Drive Charitable Giving." *Nonprofit and Voluntary Sector Quarterly* 40, no. 5 (2011): 924–73. https://doi.org/10.1177/0899764010380927.

Beneito, P., J. E. Bosca, and J. Ferri. "Tuition Fees and Students' Effort at University." *Economics of Education Review* 64 (2018): 114–28.

Black, K. H. "Risk Management for Endowment and Foundation Portfolios." *The Journal of Alternative Investments* 15, no. 4 (2013): 87–96.

Bosse, P. M., D. M. Grim, and F. Chism. "Duty, Opportunity, Mastery: Investment Committee Best Practices." *Vanguard Research* (2017): 1–20.

Brady, H. E., K. L. Schlozman, and S. Verba. "Prospecting for Participants: Rational Expectations and the Recruitment of Political Activists." *American Political Science Review* 93, no. 1 (1999): 153–68.

Brown, J. R., S. Dimmock, J. K. Kang, D. Richardson, and S. Weisbenner. "The Governance of University Endowments: Insights from a TIAA-CREF Institute Survey." *Research Dialogue*, no. 102 (2012): 1–15.

Cejnek, G., R. Franz, O. Randl, and N. Stoughton. "A Survey of University Endowment Management Research." *SSRN Electronic Journal* (2013): 1–39. https://doi.org/10.2139/ssrn.2205207.

Ceptureanu, S. I., E. G. Ceptureanu, V. L. Bogdan, and V. Radulescu. "Sustainability Perceptions in Romanian Non-Profit Organizations: An Exploratory Study Using Success Factor Analysis." *Sustainability* 10, no. 297 (2018): 1–23. https://doi.org/10.3390/su10020294.

Chapman, C. M., B. M. Masser, and W. R. Louis. "The Champion Effect in Peer-to-Peer Giving: Successful Campaigns Highlight Fundraisers More Than Causes." *Nonprofit and Voluntary Sector Quarterly* (2018): 1–21. https://doi.org/10.1177/0899764018805196.

Charseatd, P. "Role of Religious Beliefs in Blood Donation Behavior among the Youngster in Iran: A Theory of Planned Behavior Perspective." *Journal of Islamic Marketing* 7, no. 3 (2016): 1–20.

Chua, V. C. H., and C. M. Wong. "Tax Incentives, Individual Characteristics and Charitable Giving in Singapore." *International Journal of Social Economics* 26, no. 12 (1999): 1492–505.

Dahalan, N. F., R. Ramli, R. Hashim, N. Y. Ismon, and S. Romli. "Risiko Pengurusan Dana Wakaf Untuk Institusi Pendidikan Tinggi di Malaysia: Satu Kerangka Konseptual." *Jurnal 'Ulwan* 1 (2016): 164–78.

Dhillon, G., N. Mohammed, and N. Y. Min. "Equity & Trust's Law Applications in Malaysia, UK and US—In Tandem or Apart?" *Current Law Journal* 1, no. Ixxiv (2011).

Dimmock, S. G. "Background Risk and University Endowment Funds." *The Review of Economics and Statistics* 94, no. 3 (2012): 789–99.

Dimmock, S. G., N. Wang, and J. Yang. "The Endowment Model and Modern Portfolio Theory." *NBER Working Paper Series*, no. 25559 (2019): 1–62. https://doi.org/10.2139/ssrn.3330919.

Drezner, N. D. "Philanthropic Mirroring: Exploring Identity-Based Fundraising in Higher Education." *The Journal of Higher Education* (2017): 1–35.

Ehrenberg, R. G. "Demystifying Endowments." *School of Industrial and Labor Relations, Cornell University*, no. 132 (2009): 1–13. http://digitalcommons.ilr.cornell.edu/workingpapers/132/%0ARequired.

Ellis, C. D. "Best Practice Investment Committees." *The Journal of Portfolio Management* 37, no. 2 (2011): 139–47.

Fadhilah, A. A., S. Zurina, A. Mohammad, and A. Nursilah. "The Effort of Selected Public and Private Universities to Develop Awqaf Property in Malaysia." *Pertanika Journal of Social Sciences and Humanities* 25, no. Special Issue (2017): 267–80.

Fielden, J. "Global Trends in University Governance." *Education Working Paper Series*, no. 9 (2008): 1–65.

Fishman, J. J. "What Went Wrong: Prudent Management of Endowment Funds and Imprudent Endowment Investing Policies." *The Journal of College and University Law* 40, no. 2 (2014): 199–246.

Gallo, M. L. "How Are Graduates and Alumni Featured in University Strategic Plans? Lessons from Ireland." *Perspectives: Policy and Practice in Higher Education* 22, no. 3 (2018): 92–97. https://doi.org/10.1080/13603108.2017.1397065.

Getz, Malcolm. "Endowment." *The Bottom Line* 4, no. 2 (2007): 37–41. https://doi.org/10.1108/eb025286.

Grant, J. H., and D. L. Lindauer. "The Economics of Charity Life-Cycle Patterns of Alumnae Contributions." *Eastern Economic Journal* 12, no. 2 (1986): 129–41.

Gurrib, I., and S. Alshahrani. "Diversification in Portfolio Risk Management: The Case of the UAE Financial Market." *International Journal of Trade, Economics and Finance* 3, no. 6 (2012): 445–49. https://doi.org/10.7763/ijtef.2012.v3.243.

Harjoto, M. A., I. Laksmana, and Y. Yang. "Board Diversity and Corporate Investment Oversight." *Journal of Business Research* 90 (2018): 40–47. https://doi.org/10.1016/j.jbusres.2018.04.033.

Harrison, W. B. "College Relations and Fund-Raising Expenditures: Influencing the Probability of Alumni Giving to Higher Education." *Economics of Education Review* 14, no. 1 (1995): 73–84. https://doi.org/10.1016/0272-7757(94)00035-5.

Harun, F. M., B. T. Possumah, M H. Mohd Shafiai, and A. H. Mohd Nor. "Issues and Economic Role of Waqf in Higher Education Institution: Malaysian Experience." *Al-Iqtishad: Journal of Islamic Economics* 8, no. 1 (2016): 149–68. https://doi.org/10.15408/aiq.v8i1.2514.

Harun, R., H. Abd Mutalib, R. Abdul Rashid, A. Murat, and N. I. Yaakub. "Promotion as a Determinant for Waqf Awareness Among University Students." *International Academic Research Journal* 2, no. 1 (2016): 95–99.

Hasan, R., and S. A. Siraj. "Toward Developing a Model of Stakeholder Trust in Waqf Institutions." *Islamic Economic Studies* 25, no. Special Issue (2017): 85–109. https://doi.org/10.12816/0036187.

Hassan, W., N. Mazlan, and A. Lahsasna. "Malaysian Higher Education Institutions: Is the Endowment Fund the Way Forward?" *IF HUB* (2017): 16–21. https://ikr.inceif.org/handle/INCEIF/2674.

Hübner, M. "Do Tuition Fees Affect Enrollment Behavior? Evidence from a 'Natural Experiment' in Germany." *Economics of Education Review* 31 (2012): 949–60. https://doi.org/10.1016/j.econedurev.2012.06.006.

Hussin, R. "Waqf Implementation in Malaysian Universities: Overview and Way Forward." *The Social Sciences* 13, no. 1 (2018): 145–49.

Hussin, R., R. Abdul Rashid, and N. I. Yaakub. "Exploratory Study on Waqf Implementation in Malaysian Public and Private Universities: With Special Reference to Turkish Universities." *International Journal of Business, Economics and Law* 9, no. 4 (2016): 16–23.

Jacob, W. J., and V. Gokbel. "Global Higher Education Learning Outcomes and Financial Trends: Comparative and Innovative Approaches." *International Journal of Educational Development* 58 (2018): 5–17. https://doi.org/10.1016/j.ijedudev.2017.03.001.

Jalbout, M. "The Case for Engaging Arab Donors in Financing Global Education." *Global Economy & Development*, no. 80 (2014): 1–25.

Jayeola, D., Z. Ismail, and S. F. Sufahani. "Effects of Diversification of Assets in Optimizing Risk of Portfolio." *Malaysian Journal of Fundamental and Applied Sciences* 13, no. 4 (2017): 584–87. https://doi.org/10.11113/mjfas.v0n0.567.

Johari, F., M. Alias, S. Abdul Shukor, K. Abd. Wahab, M. R. AB. Aziz, N. Ahmad, Z. Kefeli-Zulkefli, F. Abu Hussin, and P. Ibrahim. "Factors That Influence Repeat Contribution of Cash Waqf in Islamic Philanthropy." *Malaysian Accounting Review* 14, no. 2 (2015): 55–78.

Johnstone, B. "Challenges of Financial Austerity: Imperatives and Limitations of Revenue Diversification in Higher Education." *The Welsh Journal of Education* 11, no. 1 (2002): 18–36. https://doi.org/10.16922/wje.11.1.3.

Johnstone, D. Bruce. "The Economics and Politics of Cost Sharing in Higher Education: Comparative Perspectives." *Economics of Education Review* 23, no. 4 (2004): 403–10. https://doi.org/10.1016/j.econedurev.2003.09.004.

Kaffe, C. "Peer Effects in Investment Manager Selection: Evidence from University Endowments." *Judge Business School, University of Cambridge* (2019): 1–38.

Kahf, M. "Suwar Mustajida Min Al-Waqf." (2004): 1–75. http://monzer.kahf.com/papers/arabic/sowar_mustajida_min_al-waqf.pdf.

Lagazio, C., and F. Querci. "Exploring the Multi-Sided Nature of Crowdfunding Campaign Success." *Journal of Business Research* 90 (2018): 318–24. https://doi.org/10.1016/j.jbusres.2018.05.031.

Lee, H. "The Growth and Stratification of College Endowments in the United States." *International Journal of Educational Advancement* 8, no. 3/4 (2008): 136–51. https://doi.org/10.1057/ijea.2009.10.

Lee, Y. J., and J. Shon. "What Affects the Strategic Priority of Fundraising? A Longitudinal Study of Art, Culture and Humanity Organizations' Fundraising Expenses in the USA." *Voluntas* (2018). https://doi.org/10.1007/s11266-018-9982-1.

Leković, M. "Investment Diversification as a Strategy for Reducing Investment Risk." *Economic Horizons* 20, no. 2 (2018): 169–84. https://doi.org/10.5937/ekonhor1802173l.

Lerner, J., A. Schoar, and J. Wang. "Secrets of the Academy: The Drivers of University Endowment Success." *Journal of Economic Perspectives* 22, no. 3 (2008): 207–22.

Lin, T. C. "The Role of Higher Education in Economic Development: An Empirical Study of Taiwan Case." *Journal of Asian Economics* 15, no. 2 (2004): 355–71.

Lord, M. "Smaller University Endowments: Team Characteristics, Portfolio Composition and Performance." *Qualitative Research in Financial Markets* 6, no. 1 (2014): 4–32. https://doi.org/10.1108/QRFM-07-2012-0021.

———. "University Endowment Committees: How a Learning Orientation and Knowledge Factors Contribute to Portfolio Diversification and Performance." *The European Journal of Finance* (2014): 1–25. https://doi.org/10.1080/1351847X.2013.879536.

Lund, B. "Universities Engaging Social Media Users: An Investigation of Quantitative Relationships between Universities' Facebook Followers/Interactions and University Attributes." *Journal of Marketing for Higher Education* (2019): 1–17. https://doi.org/10.1080/08841241.2019.1641875.

Lysakowski, L. "The Importance of Volunteers in a Capital Campaign." *International Journal of Nonprofit and Voluntary Sector Marketing* 7, no. 4 (2002): 325–33.

Madanchi, M., S. Shahverdiani, and F. Hamidifar. "Endowment and Charity Financing Model to Develop Science and Technology." *International Journal of Finance and Managerial Accounting* 1, no. 4 (2016): 55–70.

Mahamood, S. M., and A. Ab Rahman. "Financing Universities through Waqf, Pious Endowment: Is It Possible?" *Humanomics* 31, no. 4 (2015): 430–53. https://doi.org/10.1108/H-02-2015-0010.

Mahamood, S. M., A. Ab Rahman, and A. Che Seman. "Cabaran Pelaksanaan Wakaf Universiti Awam Di Malaysia: Analisis Menurut Perundangan Di Malaysia." *Kanun* 30, no. 2 (2018): 383–409.

Mariana, D. R. "Education as a Determinant of the Economic Growth. The Case of Romania." *Procedia—Social and Behavioral Sciences* 197 (2015): 404–12. https://doi.org/10.1016/j.sbspro.2015.07.156.

Martin, C. "Should Students Have to Borrow? Autonomy, Wellbeing and Student Debt." *Journal of Philosophy of Education* (2015): 1–20.

McClure, K. R., L. Frierson, A. W. Hall, and K. L. Ostlund. "Philanthropic Giving by Foundations to Higher Education Institutions: A State-Level Social Network Analysis." *Philanthropy & Education* 1, no. 1 (2017): 1–28. https://doi.org/10.2979/phileduc.1.1.02.

Milosevic, M. "Skills or Networks? Success and Fundraising Determinants in a Low Performing Venture Capital Market." *Research Policy* 47, no. 1 (2018): 49–60. https://doi.org/10.1016/j.respol.2017.09.009.

Mohamed Nor, S., and N. I. Yaakub. "Educational Endowments Governance for Institutions of Higher Education in Malaysia: A Preliminary Study." *Advanced Science Letters* X, no. XXX–XXX (2015): 1–4. https://doi.org/10.1166/asl.2017.7266.

Mohammad, M. T. S., and A. H. Mar Iman. "Obstacles of the Current Concept of Waqf to the Development of Waqf Properties and the Recommended Alternative." *Malaysian Journal of Real Estate* 1, no. 1 (2006): 27–38. https://doi.org/10.1108/H-02-2015-0010.

Mohammad Aslam, M. M., and W. M. D. H. Wan Mohar. "Kelestarian Program Akademik Dan Kewangan Dalam Pengajian Tinggi Islam." *Journal of Asian Islamic Higher Institutions (JAIHI)* 1, no. 1 (2015): 1–6.

Mohiddin, M. N. "Kredibiliti Wakaf Dalam Menangani Isu Pembiayaan Pengajian Tinggi." *International Research Journal of Shariah, Muamalat and Islam (IRJSMI)* 2, no. 4 (2020): 9–21. https://doi.org/10.35631/IRJSMI.24002.

Mokthar, M. Z. "Perceptions of Universiti Sains Malaysia Muslim Staff on Factors Influencing Their Intention to Perform Cash Waqf." *Journal of Islamic Studies and Culture* 4, no. 2 (2016): 101–09. https://doi.org/10.15640/jisc.v4n2a11.

Mujani, W. K., M. S. Mohd Taib, M. K. I. Rifin, and K. Aboo Talib Khalid. "The History of the Development of Higher Education Waqf in Malaysia." *International Journal of Civil Engineering and Technology (IJCIET)* 9, no. 3 (2018): 549–57.

Mujani, W. K., and N. I. Yaakub. "Waqf for Higher Education in Malaysia: Overview on Challenges." *European Journal of Multidisciplinary Studies* 5, no. 1 (2017): 455–61.

Munadi, M. "Pengelolaan Endowment Fund Di Perguruan Tinggi Malaysia: Studi Kasus Di Universitas Teknologi Malaysia." *Al-Ulum* 17, no. 2 (2017): 306–31. https://doi.org/10.30603/au.v17i2.199.

Mustaffa, N., and M. Z. Muda. "Pengurusan Wakaf Pendidikan Di Institusi Pengajian Tinggi Malaysia: Satu Sorotan Literatur." *International Journal of Management Studies* 21, no. 2 (2014): 63–81. https://doi.org/10.11113/umran2014.1n1.5.

Neill, C. "Tuition Fees and the Demand for University Places." *Economics of Education Review* 28 (2009): 561–70. https://doi.org/10.1016/j.econedurev.2009.01.002.

Oladapo, H. B., R. A. Oseni, and M. O. Mohammed. "A Comparative Analysis of Waqf Institution and Endowment Foundation: Determinants of Sustainability." *International Journal of Novel Research in Humanity and Social Sciences* 3, no. 4 (2016): 151–62.

Ortiz, R. A., S. Witte, A. Gouw, A. Sanfilippo, R. Tsai, D. Fumagalli, C. Yu, et al. "Engaging a Community for Rare Genetic Disease: Best Practices and Education From Individual Crowdfunding Campaigns." *Interactive Journal of Medical Research* 7, no. 1 (2018): 1–11.

Ozturk, I. "The Role of Education in Economic Development: A Theoretical Perspective." *Journal of Rural Development and Administration* XXXIII, no. 1 (2001): 39–47.

Pérez-Esparrells, C., and E. M. Torre. "The Challenge of Fundraising in Universities in Europe." *International Journal of Higher Education* 1, no. 2 (2012): 55–66. https://doi.org/10.5430/ijhe.v1n2p55.

Peruta, A., and C. Helm. "Engaging University Alumni through Social Media: Strategies for Creating Community." *The Journal of Social Media in Society* 7, no. 1 (2018): 123–50.

Rohayati, M. I., Y. Najdi, and J. C. Williamson. "Philanthropic Fundraising of Higher Education Institutions: A Review of the Malaysian and Australian Perspectives." *Sustainability* 8, no. 541 (2016): 1–20. https://doi.org/10.3390/su8060541.

Rolfe, H. "The Effect of Tuition Fees on Students' Demands and Expectations: Evidence from Case Studies of Four Universities." *Discussion Paper*, no. 190 (2001): 1–24.

Rosen, H. S., and A. J. W. Sappington. "What Do University Endowment Managers Worry About? An Analysis of Alternative Asset Investments and Background Income." *NBER Working Paper Series*, no. 21271 (2015): 1–34.

Sá, F. "The Effect of Tuition Fees on University Applications: Evidence from the UK." *IZA Discussion Paper*, no. 8364 (2014): 1–26.

Sargeant, A., and L. Woodliffe. "Gift Giving: An Interdisciplinary Review." *International Journal of Nonprofit and Voluntary Sector Marketing* 12 (2007): 275–307. https://doi.org/10.1002/nvsm.

Sazonov, S., E. Kharlamova, I. Chekhovskaya, and E. Polyanskaya. "Mechanism of Determination of Effectiveness of Spending Assets of Endowment Funds on the Basis of Mathematical Models." *International Journal of Educational Management* 31, no. 1 (2017): 21–29. https://doi.org/10.1108/IJEM-02-2016-0040.

Sherlock, M. F., J. G. Gravelle, M. L. Crandall-Hollick, and J. M. Stupak. "College and University Endowments: Overview and Tax Policy Options." *Congressional Research Service* (2015): 1–27. http://search.ebscohost.com/login.aspx?direct=true&db=tsh&AN=111387593&site=ehost-live.

Siddiqi, M. N. "Shariah, Economics and the Progress of Islamic Finance: The Role of Shariah Experts." *Seventh Harvard Forum on Islamic Finance* (2006): 1–7. www.siddiqi.com/mns/Role_of_Shariah_Experts.htm.

Singh, S. "Higher Education Practices Worldwide for Sustainable Financing." *Working Paper Series* (2014): 1–19.

Souad, M., T. Ramdane, and M. S. Khan. "Fātimah Al-Fihrīand Religious Fraternity in Al-Qarawiyy in University: A Case Study." *International Journal of Humanities and Social Science* 7, no. 10 (2017): 177–83. https://doi.org/10.1108/17504971211236308.

Sulaiman, S., and A. Hasan. "Strategi Pembangunan dan Pelaburan Wakaf Secara Lestari Menurut Perspektif Syariah." *Jurnal Syariah* 24, no. 2 (2016): 237–70.

Sulaiman, S., A. Hasan, and A. A. Sulaiman-Mohamad. "Pembangunan dan Pelaburan Lestari Harta Wakaf dari Perspektif Islam." *Kanun* 28, no. 1 (2016): 68–100.

Terry, N., and A. Macy. "Determinants of Alumni Giving Rates." *Journal of Economics and Economic Education Research* 8, no. 3 (2007): 3–17.

Tulip, Peter. "Financing Higher Education in the United States." *OECD Economics Department Working Papers*, no. 584 (2007): 1–38. http://search.proquest.com/docview/56601248?accountid=17248.

Vidal, D. D., and T. G. Pittz. "Educating Beyond the Classroom: Alumni Giving and the Value of Campus Culture." *Studies in Higher Education* (2018): 1–15. https://doi.org/10.1080/03075079.2018.1482269.

Wang, Y. "What Influences Alumni Donations?" *Journal of Economics, Business and Management* 6, no. 4 (2018): 160–63. https://doi.org/10.18178/joebm.2018.6.4.567.

Wang, Y., and S. Liu. "Education, Human Capital and Economic Growth: Empirical Research on 55 Countries and Regions (1960–2009)." *Theoretical Economics Letters* 6 (2016): 347–55. https://doi.org/10.4236/tel.2016.62039.

Webb, J. "A Path to Sustainability: How Revenue Diversification Helps Colleges and Universities Survive Tough Economic Conditions." *Journal of International & Interdisciplinary Business Research* 2, no. 7 (2015): 69–97.

Weerts, D. J., and J. M. Ronca. "Profiles of Supportive Alumni: Donors, Volunteers, and Those Who 'Do It All'." *International Journal of Educational Advancement* 7, no. 1 (2007): 20–34. https://doi.org/10.1057/palgrave.ijea.2150044.

Wolanin, T. R. "Financing Higher Education in the United States: An Overview." *International Higher Education*, no. 19 (2015): 8–10. https://ejournals.bc.edu/ojs/index.php/ihe/article/download/6875/6092.

Zhimin, L., C. Chunlian, and W. Xian. "Alumni Relations in Chinese HEIs: Case Studies of Three Major Universities." *Front. Educ. China* 11, no. 1 (2016): 74–101.

Zhou, H., and S. Ye. "Fundraising in the Digital Era: Legitimacy, Social Network, and Political Ties Matter in China." *Voluntas: International Journal of Voluntary and Nonprofit Organizations* (2019). https://doi.org/10.1007/s11266-019-00112-9.

Zickar, M. J., T. H. Ron, and C. Arnold. "Using Facebook Pages to Connect with Students, Faculty, Alumni, and Friends: An Empirical Analysis." *Teaching of Psychology* 45, no. 4 (2018): 358–62. https://doi.org/10.1177/0098628318796923.

Theses/Dissertations

Dillon, J. L. R. "Factors and Characteristics of Alumni Role Identity: Implications for Practice in Higher Education Fundraising and Alumni Relations." Ph.D. thesis, the Faculty of the School of Education, The University of San Francisco, 2017.

McElhaney, R. L. S. "The Effects of Higher Education Endowment Management Practices on Endowment Performance." Ph.D. thesis, the University of Southern Mississippi, 2010.

Seminar/Conferences/Proceeding

Binfarè, M., R. S. Harris, G. W. Brown, and C. T. Lundblad. "How Important Are Investment Committees? Evidence from University Endowments." *Paper presented, UNC Alternative Investments Conference*, Chapel Hill, 2017, 1–49.

Bulut, M., and C. Korkut. "Cash Waqfs (CWs) and Financing of Education at Ottoman Experience." *Paper presented, International Symposium on Waqf and Higher Education (ISWHE 2016)*, Istanbul, Turkey, 2016, 16–19.

Gustina, and Hidayatul Ihsan. "Financing Higher Education through Waqf Assets." *Paper presented, International Conference of Applied Science on Engineering, Business, Linguistics and Information Technology (ICo-ASCNITech)*, Padang, Indonesia, 2017, 89–94.

Hashim, R., R. Ramli, N. F. Dahalan, N. Y. Ismon, and S. Romli. "Prospek Penjanaan Dana Wakaf Institusi Pengajian Tinggi." *Paper presented, International Conference on Waqf*, Kuala Terengganu, 2015, 1–13.

Hong, Y., Y. Hu, and G. Burtch. "How Does Social Media Affect Contribution to Public versus Private Goods in Crowdfunding Campaigns?" *Paper presented, Thirty Sixth International Conference on Information Systems*, Fort Worth, 2015, 1–15.

Kahf, M. "Financing the Development of Awqaf Property." *Paper presented, Seminar on Development of Awqaf*, Kuala Lumpur, 1998, 1–45.

Mohd Ali, N., R. Ahmad, and N. S. Ahmad Mahdzan. "The Need of an Effective Business Model for Waqf Land Development in Malaysia." *Paper presented, The 20th International Research Conference on Business, Economics, and Social Sciences*, Istanbul, Turkey, 2015, 1–12.

Mujani, W. K., M. S. Mohd Taib, and M. K. I. Rifin. "Waqf Higher Education in Malaysia." *Paper presented, International Conference on Education, E-Learning and Management Technology*, Atlantis Press, 2016, 519–22.

Raja Ramli, R. N. A., and N. A Abd Hamid. "Kelestarian Wakaf dalam Membangunkan Institusi Pendidikan: Kajian Awal." *Paper presented, International Conference on Postgraduate Research*, Kuala Lumpur, 2014, 45–465.

Saraeh, U. N., N. I. Abdul Rahman, N. Noordin, S. N. Ramlan, R. Ahmad, and M. F. Sakdan. "The Influence of Students' Experience on Alumni Giving in Malaysian Public Educational Institution." *Paper presented, MATEC Web of Conferences, 150*, EDP Sciences, 2018, 1–6.

Wang, B., B. Osatuyi, and W. Hou. "Effects of Donor- and Supporter-Based Campaign Networks on Crowdfunding Campaign Success." *Proceedings of the 50th Hawaii International Conference on System Sciences*, ed. T. X. Bui and R. Sprague. 2017, 5589–98. IEEE Computer Society.

Websites

"The 20 Richest Colleges in the United States in FY 2021, by Endowment Funds Market Value." *Statista*, 2021. Accessed on 29 March 2023. www.statista.com/statistics/221147/the-20-richest-colleges-in-the-us/

"50 Richest Universities in the World: University Endowment Rankings." *Nonprofit Colleges Online*, n.d. Accessed on 29 March 2023. www.nonprofitcollegesonline.com/wealthiest-universities-in-the-world/.

Abu Hasan, A., N. A. Hamzah, and A. I. Ismail. "Dana Endowmen: Malaysia Jauh Ketinggalan." *Sinar Harian Online*, August 13, 2019. Accessed on 24 October 2020. www.sinarharian.com.my/article/42648/BERITA/Nasional/Dana- endowmen-Malaysia-jauh-ketinggalan%0D.

"Acts 20:35." *Bible Hub*. Accessed on 21 July 2020. https://biblehub.com/acts/20-35.htm.

"Asia Marketing Research, Internet Usage, Population Statistics and Facebook Subscribers." *Ipiosnternet World Stats*, 2019. Accessed on 19 November 2019. www.internetworldstats.com/asia.htm.

"Asset Class Explained." *UniSuper*. Accessed on 3 October 2019. www.unisuper.com.au/investments/investment-basics/asset-classes- explained#Asset class characteristics.

"Awqaf and Minors Affairs Foundation Raises Asset Value to Dh2.8 Billion, Increase Profits by 11 Percent." *Albawaba Business*, 2018. Accessed on 24 October 2020. www.albawaba.com/business/pr/awqaf-and-minors-affairs-foundation- raises-asset-value-dh28-billion-increases-profits-11

Batrawy, A. "UAE Tycoon Launches Largest Arab Education Fund with $1.14B." *The San Diego Union-Tribune*, April 20, 2016. Accessed on 25 October 2020. www.sandiegouniontribune.com/sdut-uae-tycoon-launches-largest-arab-education-fund-2016apr20-story.html.

"Cash Waqf Scheme." *Centre for Management of Waqf, Zakat and Endowment (WAZAN)*, 2018. Accessed 23 October 2018. www.wazan.upm.edu.my/waqf/upm_trust_fund_for_knowledge/cash_waqf_ scheme-38933

"Direktori Universiti Awam." *Kementerian Pendidikan Malaysia (Jabatan Pendidikan Tinggi)*, 2017. Accessed on 27 September 2018. http://jpt.mohe.gov.my/index.php/ipta/institusi-pendidikan-tinggi-awam/direktori-universiti-awam.

"Employment Rate." *OECD*, 2020. Accessed on 17 October 2020. https://data.oecd.org/emp/employment-rate.htm.

"Endowment Costs: The Secret History." *Charles Skorina & Company*, 2017. Accessed on 4 February 2020. www.charlesskorina.com/?p=5211%0D.

Fong, F. "RM23m for 'Wakaf' Collected by 13 Public Universities." *New Straits Times*, August 7, 2017. Accessed on 19 October 2019. www.nst.com.my/news/nation/2017/08/264977/rm23m-wakaf-collected-13- public-universities-date.

"Governor's Speech at the 2nd IFSB Summit: The Rise and Effectiveness of Corporate Governance in the Islamic Financial Services Industry." *Bank Negara Malaysia*, 2005. Accessed on 1 November 2019. www.bnm.gov.my/index.php?ch=en_speech&pg=en_speech&ac=170&lang=en%0 D.

"Introduction." *Centre for Management of Waqf, Zakat and Endowment (WAZAN)*, 2018. Accessed on 23 October 2018. www.wazan.upm.edu.my/waqf/upm_trust_fund_for_knowledge/introduction-38931.

"Kategori UA." *Ministry of Higher Education*. Accessed on 19 October 2018. www.mohe.gov.my/institusi/universiti-awam/kategori-ua.

Kazemi, H., and K. Wilkens. "A Simple Approach to the Management of Endowments." *All About Alpha*, 2017. Accessed on 19 October 2018. www.allaboutalpha.com/blog/2017/08/07/a-simple-approach-to-the-management-of-endowments/.

Kerr, E. "10 Universities with the Biggest Endowments," *U.S. News & World Report*, 2019. Accessed on 25 October 2020. www.usnews.com/education/best-colleges/the-short-list-college/articles/10-universities-with-the-biggest- endowments%0D.

Kyodo. "Japan's Public and Private Universities Face Major Shake-Ups and Mergers as Student Numbers Fall." *The Japan Times*, April 12, 2016. Accessed on 25 October 2020. www.japantimes.co.jp/news/2016/04/12/national/japans-public- private-universities-face-major-shakeup-mergers-student-numbers-fall/#.W6xHcUBMTIU.

Lederman, D. "The Culling of Higher Ed Begins." *Inside Higher Ed*, July 19, 2017. Accessed on 26 October 2020. www.insidehighered.com/news/2017/07/19/number-colleges-and- universities-drops-sharply-amid-economic-turmoil.

"List of Islamic Fund Management Companies." *Securities Commission Malaysia*, 2019. Accessed on 18 October 2020. www.sc.com.my/development/icm- v2/statistics/list-of-islamic-fund-management-companies.

Monti, F. A. "The Surprisingly Complex ABCs of Endowment Funds." *Inside Philanthropy*, 2015. Accessed on 24 February 2020. www.insidephilanthropy.com/the-gift-adviser/2015/3/4/the-surprisingly- complex-abcs-of-endowment-funds.html.

Moody, J. "10 Schools Where Alumni Donate." *U.S. News & World Report*, December 18, 2018. Accessed on 26 October 2020. www.usnews.com/education/best- colleges/the-short-list-college/articles/universities-where-the-most-alumni-donate.

Morse, R., and E. Brooks. "Best Colleges Ranking Criteria and Weights." *U.S. News & World Report*, September 9, 2018. Accessed on 26 October 2020. www.usnews.com/education/best-colleges/articles/ranking-criteria-and- weights.

"Pengenalan." *Wakaf UniSZA*. Accessed on 27 February 2020. https://wakaf.unisza.edu.my/pengenalan/%0D.

"Peranan Unit Endowmen." *UTM Endowment*, n.d. Accessed on 25 October 2020. https://endowmen.utm.my/fungsi/

"Pusat Wakaf Dan Zakat (PWZ)." *Pusat Wakaf dan Zakat (PWZ)*. Accessed on 27 November 2019. http://pwz.usim.edu.my/.

"QS Arab Region University Rankings 2023." *QS Quacquarelli Symonds Limited*, 2023. Accessed on 29 March 2023. www.topuniversities.com/university-rankings/arab-region-university-rankings/2023.

"QS World University Rankings 2023." *QS Quacquarelli Symonds Limited*, 2023. Accessed on 24 March 2023. www.topuniversities.com/university-rankings/world-university-rankings/2023.

Rosenberg, J. S. "Harvard Campaign Totals $9.62 Billion." *Harvard Magazine*, September 20, 2018. Accessed on 4 November 2019. https://harvardmagazine.com/campaigntotal-18%0D.

Rose-Smith, I. "KAUST's Edgar Nehme Said to Leave for a Bass Family Office." *Institutional Investors*, 2017. Accessed on 25 October 2020. www.institutionalinvestor.com/article/b1505qcns6p6jw/kausts-edgar- nehme-said-to-leave-for-a-bass-family-office

Ryan, G. "Harvard's Endowment Manager Cutting Half Its Staff." *Boston Business Journal*, 2017. Accessed on 3 February 2020. www.bizjournals.com/boston/news/2017/01/25/harvards-endowment- manager-cutting-half-its-staff.html

Ryder, K. "The University Endowment Model: Cracked, Not Broken." *CNN Money*, July 12, 2010. Accessed on 2 October 2019. https://money.cnn.com/2010/07/06/news/economy/university_endowments.fortune/index.htm

"School Enrolment, Tertiary (% Gross)." *The World Bank*, 2018. Accessed on 19 March 2020. https://data.worldbank.org/indicator/SE.TER.ENRR?end=2018&start=1970.

"Sharing the Harvard Experience." *Harvard Alumni*, 2012. Accessed on 22 October 2019. https://alumni.harvard.edu/stories/sharing-harvard-experience.

"Social Media Giving Statistics." *Nonprofits Source*, 2018. Accessed on 4 November 2019. https://nonprofitssource.com/online-giving-statistics/#Social.

"Statistics for Islamic Capital Market in Malaysia." *Securities Commission Malaysia*. Accessed on 19 July 2022. www.sc.com.my/analytics/islamic-capital-market.

"Statistik Institusi Pendidikan Tinggi Swasta (IPTS) sehingga 31 Ogos 2018." *Kementerian Pendidikan Malaysia (Jabatan Pendidikan Tinggi)*, 2018. Accessed on 27 September 2018. https://drive.google.com/drive/folders/18w0PWQnD7DV2W1Dspio3zHm5Up5-AC3l.

"Sustainable and Responsible Investments." *Capital Markets Malaysia*. Accessed on 22 November 2019. www.capitalmarketsmalaysia.com/islamic-capital-market/sustainable-and-responsible-investments/.

"Trustees of UPM Waqf Fund." *Centre for Management of Waqf, Zakat and Endowment (WAZAN)*, 2018. Accessed on 25 October 2020. https://wazan.upm.edu.my/about_us/trustees_committees/trustees_of_upm_waqf_f und-38935

"UniSZA Waqf Fund Committee." *UniSZA Waqf*. Accessed on 28 February 2020. https://wakaf.unisza.edu.my/jawatankuasa-dana-wakaf-unisza/.

"Waqf Distribution." *Centre for Management of Waqf, Zakat and Endowment (WAZAN)*, 2018. Accessed on 25 October 2020. https://wazan.upm.edu.my/about_us/trustees_committees/waqf_disbursement-44095?L=en.

Newspaper

Sabri, M. F. "Geran Permudah Pembiayaan Pendidikan." *Utusan Malaysia*, September 19, 2017.

Appendices

Appendix I: List of Interview Questions

Element/ Elemen	*Question/Soalan*		*Informant*
	Endowment/Endowmen	*Waqf /Wakaf*	
Appropriate Investment Planning *Perancangan Pelaburan yang Sesuai*	1) What are the types of endowment funds (i.e. true, term, or quasi-endowment) currently implemented in this institution? *Apakah jenis-jenis tabung endowmen (iaitu, endowmen sebenar, jangka atau separa) yang sedang dilaksanakan di institusi ini?* 2) What proportion of the endowment fund is allowed to be invested? *Apakah bahagian daripada tabung endowmen yang dibenarkan untuk dilaburkan?* 3) What types of conventional investments (e.g. real estate, cash, fixed deposit) are offered as options for the endowment fund of this institution to invest in? *Apakah jenis-jenis pelaburan konvensional (iaitu, hartanah, wang tunai, deposit tetap dan lain-lain) yang ditawarkan sebagai pilihan bagi tabung endowmen di institusi ini untuk melabur?* 4) Is this institution's endowment fund also involved in alternative assets (e.g. hedge funds and private capital funds) investment? *Adakah tabung endowmen di institusi ini juga terlibat dalam aset alternatif (iaitu, tabung lindung nilai dan modal persendirian)?*	1) What are the types of *waqf* funds (i.e. *waqf am* or *waqf khas*) currently implemented in this institution? *Apakah jenis-jenis tabung wakaf (iaitu, wakaf am atau waqf khas) yang yang sedang dilaksanakan di institusi ini?* 2) What proportion of the *waqf* fund is allowed to be invested? *Apakah bahagian daripada tabung wakaf yang dibenarkan untuk dilaburkan?* 3) What types of conventional investments (e.g. real estate, cash, fixed deposit) are offered as options for the *waqf* fund of this institution to invest in? *Apakah jenis-jenis pelaburan konvensional (iaitu, hartanah, wang tunai, deposit tetap dan lain-lain) yang ditawarkan sebagai pilihan bagi tabung wakaf di institusi ini untuk melabur?* 4) What are the Shariah-compliant investments chosen by the *waqf* fund to invest in? *Apakah pelaburan-pelaburan patuh Syariah yang dipilih oleh tabung wakaf untuk melabur?*	Finance Division

(*Continued*)

(Continued)

Element/ Elemen	*Question/Soalan*		*Informant*
	Endowment/Endowmen	*Waqf /Wakaf*	
	5) Which types of assets (i.e. conventional or alternative) the endowment fund of this institution is likely to invest in? *Apakah jenis-jenis pelaburan tabung endowmen di institusi ini yang cenderung untuk melabur?*		
	6) How does this institute ensure that its endowment fund's investment activities are Shariah-compliant? *Bagaimanakah institusi ini memastikan bahawa aktiviti pelaburan tabung endowmen adalah patuh Syariah?*		
	7) What are the Shariah-compliant investments chosen by the endowment fund to invest in? *Apakah pelaburan-pelaburan patuh Syariah yang dipilih oleh tabung endowmen untuk melabur?*		
Superior Investment Committees *Jawatankuasa Pelaburan yang Unggul*	1) What are the roles of the investment committee in managing the institution's endowment fund? *Apakah peranan-peranan jawatankuasa pelaburan dalam menguruskan tabung endowmen di institusi ini?*	1) What are the roles of the investment committee in managing the institution's *waqf* fund? *Apakah peranan-peranan jawatankuasa pelaburan dalam menguruskan tabung wakaf di institusi ini?*	Finance Division
	2) How many members are present in the endowment investment committee? *Berapakah bilangan ahli yang wujud dalam jawatankuasa pelaburan endowmen?*	2) How many members are present in the *waqf* investment committee? *Berapakah bilangan ahli yang wujud dalam jawatankuasa pelaburan wakaf?*	
	3) On what basis are the members appointed? *Atas dasar apakah ahli-ahli tersebut dilantik?*	3) On what basis are the members appointed? *Atas dasar apakah ahli-ahli tersebut dilantik?*	

	4) How can we ensure that the issues related to the group dynamics (e.g. groupthink, confirmation bias, group polarisation) can be limited in the investment committee? *Bagaimana untuk memastikan isu-isu yang berkaitan dengan kumpulan dinamik (seperti kumpulan berfikir, pengesahan berat sebelah, polarisasi kumpulan dll.) dapat dihadkan dalam jawatankuasa pelaburan?*	4) How can we ensure that the issues related to the group dynamics (e.g. groupthink, confirmation bias, group polarisation) can be limited in the investment committee? *Bagaimana untuk memastikan isu-isu yang berkaitan dengan kumpulan dinamik (seperti kumpulan berfikir, pengesahan berat sebelah, polarisasi kumpulan dll.) dapat dihadkan dalam jawatankuasa pelaburan?*	
Highly Skilled Investment Managers *Pengurus Pelaburan yang Berkemahiran Tinggi*	1) What are the roles of the investment manager in managing the institution's endowment fund? *Apakah peranan-peranan pengurus pelaburan dalam menguruskan tabung endowmen di institusi ini?* 2) On what basis is the investment manager appointed? *Atas dasar apakah pengurus pelaburan tersebut dilantik?* 3) Does your institution have an external investment manager as well? *Adakah institusi anda mempunyai pengurus pelaburan luaran juga?* 4) How much does this institution spend every month to pay the internal investment manager as well as the external investment manager (if any)? *Berapa banyakkah institusi ini membelanjakan setiap bulan untuk membayar pengurus pelaburan dalaman dan juga pengurus pelaburan luaran (jika ada)?*	1) What are the roles of the investment manager in managing the institution's *waqf* fund? *Apakah peranan-peranan pengurus pelaburan dalam menguruskan tabung wakaf di institusi ini?* 2) On what basis is the investment manager appointed? *Atas dasar apakah pengurus pelaburan tersebut dilantik?* 3) Does your institution have an external investment manager as well? *Adakah institusi anda mempunyai pengurus pelaburan luaran juga?* 4) How much does this institution spend every month to pay the internal investment manager as well as the external investment manager (if any)? *Berapa banyakkah institusi ini membelanjakan setiap bulan untuk membayar pengurus pelaburan dalaman dan juga pengurus pelaburan luaran (jika ada)?*	Finance Division
Alumni Networks *Rangkaian Alumni*	1) How active is the institution's alumni in contributing to the endowment fund? *Sejauh mana keaktifan alumni di institusi ini dalam menyumbang kepada tabung endowment?*	1) How active is the institution's alumni in contributing to the *waqf* fund? *Sejauh mana keaktifan alumni di institusi ini dalam menyumbang kepada tabung wakaf?*	Fund Management Unit and Fund

(*Continued*)

(Continued)

Element/ Elemen	*Question/Soalan*		*Informant*
	Endowment/Endowmen	*Waqf /Wakaf*	
	2) How does the institution ensure that its alumni contribute continuously to the endowment fund? *Bagaimanakah institusi ini memastikan bahawa alumni menyumbang secara berterusan kepada tabung endowmen?*	2) How does the institution ensure that its alumni contribute continuously to the *waqf* fund? *Bagaimanakah institusi ini memastikan bahawa alumni menyumbang secara berterusan kepada tabung wakaf?*	Management Centre
	3) Does this institution use its alumni to attract contributions to the endowment fund from the public? *Adakah institusi ini menggunakan alumni untuk menarik sumbangan kepada tabung endowmen daripada orang awam?*	3) Does this institution use its alumni to attract contributions to the *waqf* fund from the public? *Adakah institusi ini menggunakan alumni untuk menarik sumbangan kepada tabung wakaf daripada orang awam?*	
Diversity of Income Sources *Kepelbagaian Sumber Pendapatan*	1) Besides returns on investments, are there any other sources of income for this institution's endowment fund? *Selain daripada pulangan pelaburan, adakah terdapat sumber-sumber pendapatan lain bagi tabung endowmen di institusi ini?*	1) Besides returns on investments, are there any other sources of income for this institution's *waqf* fund? *Selain daripada pulangan pelaburan, adakah terdapat sumber-sumber pendapatan lain bagi tabung wakaf di institusi ini?*	Fund Management Unit and Fund Management Centre
	2) What is the most profitable activity among the various income sources? *Apakah aktiviti yang paling menguntungkan dalam kalangan mereka?*	2) What is the most profitable activity among the various income sources? *Apakah aktiviti yang paling menguntungkan dalam kalangan mereka?*	
	3) Are there any conditions that must be adhered to by the endowment fund to allow this fund to engage in such activities? *Adakah terdapat sebarang syarat yang mesti dipatuhi oleh tabung endowmen untuk membenarkan tabung ini terlibat dalam aktiviti-aktiviti tersebut?*	3) Are there any conditions that must be adhered to by the *waqf* fund to allow this fund to engage in such activities? *Adakah terdapat sebarang syarat yang mesti dipatuhi oleh tabung wakaf untuk membenarkan tabung ini terlibat dalam aktiviti-aktiviti tersebut?*	

Effective Fundraising *Peningkatan Dana Berkesan*	1) What are the best ways to attract people to contribute to the endowment fund? *Apakah cara-cara terbaik untuk menarik orang ramai untuk menyumbang kepada tabung endowmen?* 2) What is the most effective method for attracting people to contribute? *Apakah kaedah yang paling berkesan dalam menarik orang ramai untuk menyumbang?* 3) What are the communication channels (e.g. radio, television, newspapers) used to inform potential donors in executing such a method? *Apakah saluran-saluran komunikasi (iaitu, radio, televesyen, surat khabar dll.) yang digunakan untuk memaklumkan kepada bakal penderma dalam melaksanakan kaedah tersebut?* 4) What is the most effective communication channel for persuading a larger number of people (including alumni) to contribute? *Apakah saluran komunikasi yang paling berkesan dalam memujuk lebih ramai orang (termasuk alumni) untuk menyumbang?* 5) How frequently is the method implemented? *Berapa kerapkah pelaksanaan kaedah tersebut?* 6) How can we ensure that the communication is effective in persuading Muslims to contribute? *Bagaimana untuk memastikan bahawa komunikasi tersebut adalah berkesan dalam memujuk umat Islam untuk menyumbang?* 7) What are the collection channels provided to facilitate people's contribution? *Apakah saluran-saluran kutipan yang disediakan bagi memudahkan orang ramai untuk menyumbang?*	1) What are the best ways to attract people to contribute to the *waqf* fund? *Apakah cara-cara terbaik untuk menarik orang ramai untuk menyumbang kepada tabung wakaf?* 2) What is the most effective method for attracting people to contribute? *Apakah kaedah yang paling berkesan dalam menarik orang ramai untuk menyumbang?* 3) What are the communication channels (e.g. radio, television, newspapers) used to inform potential donors in executing such a method? *Apakah saluran-saluran komunikasi (iaitu, radio, televesyen, surat khabar dll.) yang digunakan untuk memaklumkan kepada bakal penderma dalam melaksanakan kaedah tersebut?* 4) What is the most effective communication channel for persuading a larger number of people (including alumni) to contribute? *Apakah saluran komunikasi yang paling berkesan dalam memujuk lebih ramai orang (termasuk alumni) untuk menyumbang?* 5) How frequently is the method implemented? *Berapa kerapkah pelaksanaan kaedah tersebut?* 6) How can we ensure that the communication is effective in persuading Muslims to contribute? *Bagaimana untuk memastikan bahawa komunikasi tersebut adalah berkesan dalam memujuk umat Islam untuk menyumbang?* 7) What are the collection channels provided to facilitate people's contribution? *Apakah saluran-saluran kutipan yang disediakan bagi memudahkan orang ramai untuk menyumbang?*	Fund Management Unit and Fund Management Centre

Appendix II

List of Shariah-Compliant Securities—
May 2019

BARANGAN PENGGUNA & PERKHIDMATAN
CONSUMER PRODUCTS & SERVICES

Bil/ *No.*	Kod Stok/ *Stock code*	Nama Sekuriti / *Name of Securities*
1.	7120	Acoustech Bhd
2.	1481	Advance Synergy Bhd
3.	6599	AEON Co. (M) Bhd
4.	7315	AHB Holdings Bhd
5.	5238	AirAsia X Bhd
6.	2658	Ajinomoto (Malaysia) Bhd
7.	6351	Amway (Malaysia) Holdings Bhd
8.	5194	APFT Bhd
9.	6432	Apollo Food Holdings Bhd
10.	7722	Asia Brands Bhd
11.	7129	Asia File Corporation Bhd
12.	8885	Avillion Bhd
13.	5248	Bermaz Auto Bhd
14.	9288	Bonia Corporation Bhd
15.	9474	Brahim's Holdings Bhd
16.	7174	CAB Cakaran Corporation Bhd
17.	7154	Caely Holdings Bhd
18.	7128	CAM Resources Bhd
19.	7035	CCK Consolidated Holdings Bhd
20.	7209	Cheetah Holdings Bhd
21.	7202	Classic Scenic Bhd
22.	5104	CNI Holdings Bhd
23.	7205	Cocoaland Holdings Bhd
24.	9423	CWG Holdings Bhd
25.	7179	D.B.E. Gurney Resources Bhd
26.	7119	DeGem Bhd
27.	5908	DKSH Holdings (Malaysia) Bhd
28.	1619	DRB-HICOM Bhd
29.	3026	Dutch Lady Milk Industries Bhd
30.	2097	Eastland Equity Bhd
31.	7182	EKA Noodles Bhd
32.	9091	Emico Holdings Bhd
33.	7149	Eng Kah Corporation Bhd
34.	5081	Esthetics International Group Bhd
35.	7208	Euro Holdings Bhd
36.	7094	Eurospan Holdings Bhd
37.	8605	Federal International Holdings Bhd
38.	6939	Fiamma Holdings Bhd
39.	9172	Formosa Prosonic Industries Bhd

BARANGAN PENGGUNA & PERKHIDMATAN
CONSUMER PRODUCTS & SERVICES

Bil/ *No.*	Kod Stok/ *Stock code*	Nama Sekuriti / *Name of Securities*
1.	7120	Acoustech Bhd
2.	1481	Advance Synergy Bhd
3.	6599	AEON Co. (M) Bhd
4.	7315	AHB Holdings Bhd
5.	5238	AirAsia X Bhd
6.	2658	Ajinomoto (Malaysia) Bhd
7.	6351	Amway (Malaysia) Holdings Bhd
8.	5194	APFT Bhd
9.	6432	Apollo Food Holdings Bhd
10.	7722	Asia Brands Bhd
11.	7129	Asia File Corporation Bhd
12.	8885	Avillion Bhd
13.	5248	Bermaz Auto Bhd
14.	9288	Bonia Corporation Bhd
15.	9474	Brahim's Holdings Bhd
16.	7174	CAB Cakaran Corporation Bhd
17.	7154	Caely Holdings Bhd
18.	7128	CAM Resources Bhd
19.	7035	CCK Consolidated Holdings Bhd
20.	7209	Cheetah Holdings Bhd
21.	7202	Classic Scenic Bhd
22.	5104	CNI Holdings Bhd
23.	7205	Cocoaland Holdings Bhd
24.	9423	CWG Holdings Bhd
25.	7179	D.B.E. Gurney Resources Bhd
26.	7119	DeGem Bhd
27.	5908	DKSH Holdings (Malaysia) Bhd
28.	1619	DRB-HICOM Bhd
29.	3026	Dutch Lady Milk Industries Bhd
30.	2097	Eastland Equity Bhd
31.	7182	EKA Noodles Bhd
32.	9091	Emico Holdings Bhd
33.	7149	Eng Kah Corporation Bhd
34.	5081	Esthetics International Group Bhd
35.	7208	Euro Holdings Bhd
36.	7094	Eurospan Holdings Bhd
37.	8605	Federal International Holdings Bhd
38.	6939	Fiamma Holdings Bhd
39.	9172	Formosa Prosonic Industries Bhd

(*Continued*)

(Continued)

40	3689	Fraser & Neave Holdings Bhd
41	5079	GETS Global Bhd
42	0136	Greenyield Bhd
43	5160	Homeritz Corporation Bhd
44	5024	Hup Seng Industries Bhd
45	8478	Hwa Tai Industries Bhd
46	7243	Impiana Hotel Bhd
47	5107	IQ Group Holdings Bhd
48	7223	Jadi Imaging Holdings Bhd
49	7152	Jaycorp Bhd
50	7167	Johore Tin Bhd
51	8672	Kamdar Group (M) Bhd
52	7216	Kawan Food Bhd
53	6203	Khee San Bhd
54	7062	Khind Holdings Bhd
55	4847	Konsortium Transnasional Bhd
56	8303	Kuantan Flour Mills Bhd
57	7130	Kumpulan Powernet Bhd
58	7006	Latitude Tree Holdings Bhd
59	9385	Lay Hong Bhd
60	8079	Lee Swee Kiat Group Bhd
61	7089	Lii Hen Industries Bhd
62	7085	LTKM Bhd
63	7087	Magni-Tech Industries Bhd
64	5983	MBM Resources Bhd
65	7234	MESB Bhd
66	7935	Milux Corporation Bhd
67	5166	Minda Global Bhd
68	5886	Mintye Bhd
69	5202	MSM Malaysia Holdings Bhd
70	4707	Nestle (Malaysia) Bhd
71	7060	New Hoong Fatt Holdings Bhd
72	7215	Ni Hsin Resources Bhd
73	7139	Niche Capital Emas Holdings Bhd
74	5066	NTPM Holdings Bhd
75	5533	OCB Bhd
76	0049	Oceancash Pacific Bhd
77	7107	Oriental Food Industries Holdings Bhd
78	7052	Padini Holdings Bhd
79	4081	Pan Malaysia Corporation Bhd
80	1287	Pan Malaysia Holdings Bhd
81	5022	Paos Holdings Bhd
82	9407	Paragon Union Bhd
83	5657	Parkson Holdings Bhd
84	6068	PCCS Group Bhd
85	5231	Pelikan International Corporation Bhd
86	0186	Perak Transit Bhd
87	7080	Permaju Industries Bhd
88	5681	Petronas Dagangan Bhd
89	7088	Poh Huat Resources Holdings Bhd
90	5080	Poh Kong Holdings Bhd
91	7237	Power Root Bhd
92	4065	PPB Group Bhd
93	7168	PRG Holdings Bhd
94	8966	Prolexus Bhd

(Continued)

95	7134	PWF Consolidated Bhd
96	7084	QL Resources Bhd
97	9946	Rex Industry Bhd
98	0183	Salutica Bhd
99	9113	Sanbumi Holdings Bhd
100	7943	Sand Nisko Capital Bhd
101	5157	Saudee Group Bhd
102	9792	SEG International Bhd
103	7180	Sern Kou Resources Bhd
104	7412	SHH Resources Holdings Bhd
105	7246	Signature International Bhd
106	4197	Sime Darby Bhd
107	9776	Sinmah Capital Bhd
108	8532	Sinotop Holdings Bhd
109	5242	Solid Automotive Bhd
110	7103	Spritzer Bhd
111	9865	Suiwah Corporation Bhd
112	7186	SWS Capital Bhd
113	7082	SYF Resources Bhd
114	7211	Tafi Industries Bhd
115	4405	Tan Chong Motor Holdings Bhd
116	7200	Tek Seng Holdings Bhd
117	9369	Teo Guan Lee Corporation Bhd
118	0012	Three-A Resources Bhd
119	7176	TPC Plus Bhd
120	4588	UMW Holdings Bhd
121	7757	UPA Corporation Bhd
122	7240	Vertice Bhd
123	7121	Xian Leng Holdings Bhd
124	5584	Yee Lee Corporation Bhd
125	5159	Yoong Onn Corporation Bhd
126	5131	Zhulian Corporation Bhd

BARANGAN INDUSTRI & PERKHIDMATAN
INDUSTRIAL PRODUCTS & SERVICES

Bil/ *No.*	**Kod Stok/** ***Stock code***	**Nama Sekuriti /** ***Name of Securities***
1	7086	Ablegroup Bhd
2	5198	ABM Fujiya Bhd
3	9148	Advanced Packaging Technology (M) Bhd
4	7609	Ajiya Bhd
5	2674	Alcom Group Bhd
6	2682	Amalgamated Industrial Steel Bhd
7	7083	Analabs Resources Bhd
8	4758	Ancom Bhd
9	6556	Ann Joo Resources Bhd
10	9342	Anzo Holdings Bhd
11	5568	APB Resources Bhd
12	5015	APM Automotive Holdings Bhd
13	7214	A-Rank Bhd
14	7181	ARB Bhd
15	7162	Astino Bhd
16	8176	ATA IMS Bhd
17	7099	Atta Global Group Bhd
18	7579	AWC Bhd
19	5021	AYS Ventures Bhd
20	7005	B.I.G. Industries Bhd

(*Continued*)

(Continued)

21	6998	Bintai Kinden Corporation Bhd
22	0168	Boilermech Holdings Bhd
23	7036	Borneo Oil Bhd
24	2771	Boustead Holdings Bhd
25	5100	BP Plastics Holding Bhd
26	7221	BSL Corporation Bhd
27	7188	BTM Resources Bhd
28	2852	Cahya Mata Sarawak Bhd
29	5105	Can-One Bhd
30	7076	CB Industrial Product Holding Bhd
31	8052	Central Industrial Corporation Bhd
32	2879	Chemical Company of Malaysia Bhd
33	5273	Chin Hin Group Bhd
34	5007	Chin Well Holdings Bhd
35	5797	Choo Bee Metal Industries Bhd
36	7016	Chuan Huat Resources Bhd
37	7018	CME Group Bhd
38	7986	CN Asia Corporation Bhd
39	2127	Comfort Gloves Bhd
40	5037	Compugates Holdings Bhd
41	8044	Computer Forms (Malaysia) Bhd
42	8435	Concrete Engineering Products Bhd
43	5094	CSC Steel Holdings Bhd
44	7157	CYL Corporation Bhd
45	5082	Cymao Holdings Bhd
46	5184	Cypark Resources Bhd
47	8125	Daibochi Bhd
48	5276	Dancomech Holdings Bhd
49	7212	Destini Bhd
50	5265	Dolphin International Bhd
51	7169	Dominant Enterprise Bhd
52	7233	Dufu Technology Corp Bhd
53	7165	DWL Resources Bhd
54	8907	EG Industries Bhd
55	5208	EITA Resources Bhd
56	9016	Eksons Corporation Bhd
57	5056	Engtex Group Bhd
58	7217	Eonmetall Group Bhd
59	7773	EP Manufacturing Bhd
60	5101	Evergreen Fibreboard Bhd
61	7229	Favelle Favco Bhd
62	3107	Fima Corporation Bhd
63	9318	Fitters Diversified Bhd
64	5277	FoundPac Group Bhd
65	7197	Ge-Shen Corporation Bhd
66	5220	Globaltec Formation Bhd
67	5649	Golden Pharos Bhd
68	7192	Goodway Integrated Industries Bhd
69	3247	GUH Holdings Bhd
70	5151	Halex Holdings Bhd
71	5095	Heveaboard Bhd
72	5072	Hiap Teck Venture Bhd
73	9601	Ho Wah Genting Bhd
74	5165	Hock Heng Stone Industries Bhd

(*Continued*)

131	5219	Pestech International Bhd
132	5183	Petronas Chemicals Group Bhd
133	7163	PJBumi Bhd
134	7172	PMB Technology Bhd
135	6637	PNE PCB Bhd
136	8117	Poly Glass Fibre (M) Bhd
137	8869	Press Metal Aluminium Holdings Bhd
138	9873	Prestar Resources Bhd
139	7123	Priceworth International Bhd
140	7201	Progressive Impact Corporation Bhd
141	8273	Public Packages Holdings Bhd
142	7544	Quality Concrete Holdings Bhd
143	7498	Ralco Corporation Bhd
144	7232	Resintech Bhd
145	9954	RGT Bhd
146	9741	Rohas Tecnic Bhd
147	7803	Rubberex Corporation (M) Bhd
148	9822	Sam Engineering & Equipment (M) Bhd
149	7811	Sapura Industrial Bhd
150	5170	Sarawak Cable Bhd
151	9237	Sarawak Consolidated Industries Bhd
152	7239	Scanwolf Corporation Bhd
153	7247	SCGM Bhd
154	4731	Scientex Bhd
155	7073	Seacera Group Bhd
156	5181	SIG Gases Bhd
157	7115	SKB Shutters Corporation Bhd
158	7155	SKP Resources Bhd
159	7248	SLP Resources Bhd
160	7132	SMIS Corporation Bhd
161	5134	Southern Acids (M) Bhd
162	6904	Subur Tiasa Holdings Bhd
163	7207	Success Transformer Corporation Bhd
164	5211	Sunway Bhd
165	7235	Superlon Holdings Bhd
166	4448	Tasek Corporation Bhd
167	5289	Techbond Group Bhd
168	7034	Thong Guan Industries Bhd
169	7854	Timberwell Bhd
170	7285	Tomypak Holdings Bhd
171	5010	Tong Herr Resources Bhd
172	7173	Toyo Ink Group Bhd
173	7100	Uchi Technologies Bhd
174	1368	UEM Edgenta Bhd
175	7137	UMS Holdings Bhd
176	7227	UMS-Neiken Group Bhd
177	7091	Unimech Group Bhd
178	7133	United U-Li Corporation Bhd
179	6963	V.S. Industry Bhd
180	4995	Versatile Creative Bhd
181	7226	Watta Holding Bhd
182	7231	Wellcall Holdings Bhd
183	5009	White Horse Bhd
184	7050	Wong Engineering Corporation Bhd

(*Continued*)

(Continued)

185	7025	Woodlandor Holdings Bhd
186	4243	WTK Holdings Bhd
187	7245	WZ Satu Bhd
188	7020	YKGI Holdings Bhd
189	7014	YLI Holdings Bhd

TENAGA
ENERGY

Bil/ ***No.***	**Kod Stok/** ***Stock code***	**Nama Sekuriti /** ***Name of Securities***
1	5115	Alam Maritim Resources Bhd
2	7251	Barakah Offshore Petroleum Bhd
3	5257	Carimin Petroleum Bhd
4	5141	Dayang Enterprise Holdings Bhd
5	5132	Deleum Bhd
6	7277	Dialog Group Bhd
7	7253	Handal Resources Bhd
8	4324	Hengyuan Refining Company Bhd
9	5199	Hibiscus Petroleum Bhd
10	5255	Icon Offshore Bhd
11	7164	KNM Group Bhd
12	5186	Malaysia Marine and Heavy Engineering Holdings Bhd
13	7108	Perdana Petroleum Bhd
14	5133	Petra Energy Bhd
15	3042	Petron Malaysia Refining & Marketing Bhd
16	5256	Reach Energy Bhd
17	5218	Sapura Energy Bhd
18	7045	Scomi Energy Services Bhd
19	7158	Scomi Group Bhd
20	5279	Serba Dinamik Holdings Bhd
21	2739	Sino Hua An International Bhd
22	1201	Sumatec Resources Bhd
23	7228	T7 Global Bhd
24	7206	TH Heavy Engineering Bhd
25	7250	Uzma Bhd
26	5243	Velesto Energy Bhd
27	5142	Wah Seong Corporation Bhd
28	7293	Yinson Holdings Bhd

PEMBINAAN
CONSTRUCTION

Bil/ ***No.***	**Kod Stok/** ***Stock code***	**Nama Sekuriti /** ***Name of Securities***
1	5281	Advancecon Holdings Bhd
2	7078	Ahmad Zaki Resources Bhd
3	5932	Bina Puri Holdings Bhd
4	8761	Brem Holding Bhd
5	8591	Crest Builder Holdings Bhd
6	7528	DKLS Industries Bhd
7	5253	Econpile Holdings Bhd
8	8877	Ekovest Bhd

(Continued)

9	5205	Eversendai Corporation Bhd
10	7047	Fajarbaru Builder Group Bhd
11	5226	Gabungan AQRS Bhd
12	9261	Gadang Holdings Bhd
13	5398	Gamuda Bhd
14	3204	George Kent (Malaysia) Bhd
15	5169	Ho Hup Construction Company Bhd
16	6238	Hock Seng Lee Bhd
17	3336	IJM Corporation Bhd
18	5268	Ikhmas Jaya Group Bhd
19	0192	Inta Bina Group Bhd
20	8834	Ireka Corporation Bhd
21	4723	Jaks Resources Bhd
22	7161	Kerjaya Prospek Group Bhd
23	5171	Kimlun Corporation Bhd
24	9628	Lebtech Bhd
25	5129	Melati Ehsan Holdings Bhd
26	8192	Mercury Industries Bhd
27	5006	Merge Energy Bhd
28	7595	MGB Bhd
29	9571	Mitrajaya Holdings Bhd
30	5924	MTD ACPI Engineering Bhd
31	5085	Mudajaya Group Bhd
32	5703	Muhibbah Engineering (M) Bhd
33	7071	OCR Group Bhd
34	8311	Pesona Metro Holdings Bhd
35	9598	Pintaras Jaya Bhd
36	7145	Prinsiptek Corporation Bhd
37	5070	Protasco Bhd
38	6807	Puncak Niaga Holdings Bhd
39	5263	Sunway Construction Group Bhd
40	5054	TRC Synergy Bhd
41	5042	TSR Capital Bhd
42	7070	Vizione Holdings Bhd
43	3565	WCE Holdings Bhd
44	9679	WCT Holdings Bhd
45	7028	Zecon Bhd
46	2283	Zelan Bhd

PENGANGKUTAN & LOGISTIK
TRANSPORTATION & LOGISTICS

Bil/ *No.*	**Kod Stok/** *Stock code*	**Nama Sekuriti /** *Name of Securities*
1	5032	Bintulu Port Holdings Bhd
2	8133	Boustead Heavy Industries Corporation Bhd
3	7187	Chin Hin Group Property Bhd
4	7117	CJ Century Logistics Holdings Bhd
5	5136	Complete Logistic Services Bhd
6	5259	E.A. Technique (M) Bhd
7	7210	Freight Management Holdings Bhd

(*Continued*)

(Continued)

8	0078	GD Express Carrier Bhd
9	2062	Harbour-Link Group Bhd
10	7013	Hubline Bhd
11	6645	Lingkaran Trans Kota Holdings Bhd
12	3816	MISC Bhd
13	2194	MMC Corporation Bhd
14	9806	Nationwide Express Holdings Bhd
15	6254	PDZ Holdings Bhd
16	8346	Perak Corporation Bhd
17	4634	Pos Malaysia Bhd
18	5145	Sealink International Bhd
19	7053	See Hup Consolidated Bhd
20	5173	Shin Yang Shipping Corporation Bhd
21	6521	Suria Capital Holdings Bhd
22	5149	TAS Offshore Bhd
23	7218	Transocean Holdings Bhd
24	5246	Westports Holdings Bhd
25	5267	Xin Hwa Holdings Bhd

HARTANAH
PROPERTY

Bil/ *No.*	**Kod Stok/ *Stock code***	**Nama Sekuriti / *Name of Securities***
1	7131	Acme Holdings Bhd
2	1007	Amcorp Properties Bhd
3	5959	Amverton Bhd
4	7007	ARK Resources Holdings Bhd
5	4057	Asaan Pac Holdings Bhd
6	2305	Ayer Holdings Bhd
7	9814	Bertam Alliance Bhd
8	6173	Bina Darulaman Bhd
9	5049	Country View Bhd
10	6718	Crescendo Corporation Bhd
11	3484	Damansara Realty Bhd
12	7198	DPS Resources Bhd
13	3417	Eastern & Oriental Bhd
14	8206	Eco World Development Group Bhd
15	3557	Ecofirst Consolidated Bhd
16	8613	ENRA Group Bhd
17	6815	EUPE Corporation Bhd
18	7249	Ewein Bhd
19	5020	Glomac Bhd
20	7010	Grand Hoover Bhd
21	9962	Gromutual Bhd
22	7105	HCK Capital Group Bhd
23	5062	Hua Yang Bhd
24	4251	I-Berhad
25	5084	Ibraco Bhd
26	9687	Ideal United Bintang International Bhd
27	5249	IOI Properties Group Bhd
28	1589	Iskandar Waterfront City Bhd
29	5175	Ivory Properties Group Bhd
30	8923	Jiankun International Bhd

(*Continued*)

31	6769	JKG Land Bhd
32	7323	Ken Holdings Bhd
33	5038	KSL Holdings Bhd
34	3174	Land & General Bhd
35	5789	LBS Bina Group Bhd
36	7617	Magna Prima Bhd
37	8583	Mah Sing Group Bhd
38	1651	Malaysian Resources Corporation Bhd
39	6181	Malton Bhd
40	5236	Matrix Concepts Holdings Bhd
41	7189	MB World Group Bhd
42	5182	MCT Bhd
43	1694	Menang Corporation (M) Bhd
44	5040	Meridian Bhd
45	8893	MK Land Holdings Bhd
46	6114	MKH Bhd
47	3913	MUI Properties Bhd
48	9539	Multi Usage Holdings Bhd
49	5073	Naim Holdings Bhd
50	5827	Oriental Interest Bhd
51	1724	Paramount Corporation Bhd
52	6912	Pasdec Holdings Bhd
53	4464	Pegasus Heights Bhd
54	8664	S P Setia Bhd
55	4596	Sapura Resources Bhd
56	5207	SBC Corporation Bhd
57	4286	Seal Incorporated Bhd
58	2224	Selangor Dredging Bhd
59	5213	Sentoria Group Bhd
60	6017	SHL Consolidated Bhd
61	5288	Sime Darby Property Bhd
62	4375	South Malaysia Industries Bhd
63	3743	Sunsuria Bhd
64	1538	Symphony Life Bhd
65	4022	Tadmax Resources Bhd
66	2259	Talam Transform Bhd
67	5191	Tambun Indah Land Bhd
68	2429	Tanco Holdings Bhd
69	7889	Thriven Global Bhd
70	7079	Tiger Synergy Bhd
71	5239	Titijaya Land Bhd
72	5401	Tropicana Corporation Bhd
73	5148	UEM Sunrise Bhd
74	5200	UOA Development Bhd
75	6378	WMG Holdings Bhd
76	7003	Y&G Corporation Bhd
77	7066	Yong Tai Bhd

PERLADANGAN
PLANTATION

Bil/ *No.*	**Kod Stok/** ***Stock code***	**Nama Sekuriti /** ***Name of Securities***
1	7054	Astral Asia Bhd
2	1899	Batu Kawan Bhd
3	5069	BLD Plantation Bhd
4	5254	Boustead Plantations Bhd
5	8982	Cepatwawasan Group Bhd
6	5029	Far East Holdings Bhd
7	5222	FGV Holdings Bhd
8	2291	Genting Plantations Bhd

(*Continued*)

(Continued)

9.	2135	Gopeng Bhd
10	5138	Hap Seng Plantations Holdings Bhd
11.	7501	Harn Len Corporation Bhd
12.	2216	IJM Plantations Bhd
13.	2607	Inch Kenneth Kajang Rubber PLC
14	6262	Innoprise Plantations Bhd
15	1961	IOI Corporation Bhd
16	4383	Jaya Tiasa Holdings Bhd
17.	5027	Kim Loong Resources Bhd
18	1996	Kretam Holdings Bhd
19	2445	Kuala Lumpur Kepong Bhd
20.	6572	Kwantas Corporation Bhd
21	5026	MHC Plantations Bhd
22.	5047	NPC Resources Bhd
23.	1902	Pinehill Pacific Bhd
24.	9695	PLS Plantations Bhd
25.	5113	Rimbunan Sawit Bhd
26.	2542	Riverview Rubber Estates Bhd
27	5126	Sarawak Oil Palms Bhd
28	5135	Sarawak Plantation Bhd
29.	5285	Sime Darby Plantation Bhd
30.	4316	Sin Heng Chan (Malaya) Bhd
31	5012	Ta Ann Holdings Bhd
32	5112	TH Plantations Bhd
33	9059	TSH Resources Bhd
34.	2593	United Malacca Bhd
35.	2089	United Plantations Bhd

TEKNOLOGI
TECHNOLOGY

Bil/ ***No.***	**Kod Stok/** ***Stock code***	**Nama Sekuriti /** ***Name of Securities***
1.	5195	Censof Holdings Bhd
2.	0051	Cuscapi Bhd
3.	7204	D&O Green Technologies Bhd
4.	4456	Dagang Nexchange Bhd
5.	8338	Dataprep Holdings Bhd
6.	5216	Datasonic Group Bhd
7.	5036	Edaran Bhd
8.	0090	Elsoft Research Bhd
9	0065	Excel Force MSC Bhd
10	0128	Frontken Corporation Bhd
11	0021	GHL Systems Bhd
12	7022	Globetronics Technology Bhd
13	0056	Grand-Flo Bhd
14	5028	HeiTech Padu Bhd
15	0166	Inari Amertron Bhd
16	9393	Industronics Bhd
17	5161	JCY International Bhd
18	0143	Key Asic Bhd
19	5011	Mesiniaga Bhd
20	5286	Mi Technovation Bhd
21	0113	MMS Ventures Bhd
22	0041	MSCM Holdings Bhd
23	0138	My E.G. Services Bhd
24	0083	Notion Vtec Bhd
25	9008	Omesti Bhd
26	7160	Pentamaster Corporation Bhd
27	5204	Prestariang Bhd

(*Continued*)

28	9075	Theta Edge Bhd
29	0118	Trive Property Group Bhd
30	4359	Turiya Bhd
31	5005	Unisem (M) Bhd
32	0097	Vitrox Corporation Bhd
33	5162	VSTECS Bhd
34	0008	Willowglen MSC Bhd

UTILITI
UTILITIES

Bil/ *No.*	Kod Stok/ *Stock code*	Nama Sekuriti / *Name of Securities*
1	5209	Gas Malaysia Bhd
2	5264	Malakoff Corporation Bhd
3	3069	Mega First Corporation Bhd
4	5041	PBA Holdings Bhd
5	6033	Petronas Gas Bhd
6	5272	Ranhill Holdings Bhd
7	8567	Salcon Bhd
8	8524	Taliworks Corporation Bhd
9	5347	Tenaga Nasional Bhd

PERKHIDMATAN KEWANGAN
FINANCIAL SERVICES

Bil/ *No.*	Kod Stok/ *Stock code*	Nama Sekuriti / *Name of Securities*
1	5258	BIMB Holdings Bhd
2	1818	Bursa Malaysia Bhd
3	6139	Syarikat Takaful Malaysia Keluarga Bhd

PENJAGAAN KESIHATAN
HEALTH CARE

Bil/ *No.*	Kod Stok/ *Stock code*	Nama Sekuriti / *Name of Securities*
1	7191	Adventa Bhd
2	7090	Apex Healthcare Bhd
3	7148	Duopharma Biotech Bhd
4	5168	Hartalega Holdings Bhd
5	5225	IHH Healthcare Bhd
6	7153	Kossan Rubber Industries Bhd
7	0002	Kotra Industries Bhd
8	5878	KPJ Healthcare Bhd
9	7081	Pharmaniaga Bhd
10	7106	Supermax Corporation Bhd
11	7113	Top Glove Corporation Bhd
12	7178	Y.S.P. Southeast Asia Holding Bhd

TELEKOMUNIKASI & MEDIA
TELECOMMUNICATIONS & MEDIA

Bil/ *No.*	Kod Stok/ *Stock code*	Nama Sekuriti / *Name of Securities*
1	0159	Asia Media Group Bhd
2	6888	Axiata Group Bhd

(*Continued*)

(Continued)

3.	6947	Digi.Com Bhd
4.	6012	Maxis Bhd
5.	5090	Media Chinese International Ltd
6.	0172	OCK Group Bhd
7.	7190	Pelangi Publishing Group Bhd
8.	5252	Sasbadi Holdings Bhd
9.	9431	Seni Jaya Corporation Bhd
10.	6084	Star Media Group Bhd
11.	4863	Telekom Malaysia Bhd
12.	5031	TIME dotCom Bhd
13.	5754	Utusan Melayu (Malaysia) Bhd

PASARAN ACE
ACE MARKET

BARANGAN PENGGUNA & PERKHIDMATAN
CONSUMER PRODUCTS & SERVICES

Bil/ *No.*	Kod Stok/ *Stock code*	Nama Sekuriti / *Name of Securities*
1.	0098	Bahvest Resources Bhd
2.	0179	Bioalpha Holdings Bhd
3.	0157	Focus Point Holdings Bhd
4.	0074	Green Ocean Corporation Bhd
5.	0170	Kanger International Bhd
6.	0140	Macpie Bhd
7.	0197	Wegmans Holdings Bhd

BARANGAN INDUSTRI & PERKHIDMATAN
INDUSTRIAL PRODUCTS & SERVICES

Bil/ *No.*	Kod Stok/ *Stock code*	Nama Sekuriti / *Name of Securities*
1.	0105	Asia Poly Holdings Bhd
2.	0072	AT Systematization Bhd
3.	0187	BCM Alliance Bhd
4.	0102	Connectcounty Holdings Bhd
5.	0190	Eversafe Rubber Bhd
6.	0039	GFM Services Bhd
7.	0160	Hiap Huat Holdings Bhd
8.	0188	HLT Global Bhd
9.	0024	JAG Bhd
10.	0193	Kejuruteraan Asastera Bhd
11.	0167	MClean Technologies Bhd
12.	0081	Mega Sun City Holdings Bhd
13.	0177	Pasukhas Group Bhd
14.	0038	Plastrade Technology Bhd
15.	0028	Scope Industries Bhd
16.	0055	Sersol Bhd
17.	0001	Supercomnet Technologies Bhd
18.	0084	Techfast Holdings Bhd
19.	0089	Tex Cycle Technology (M) Bhd
20.	0025	YBS International Bhd

(*Continued*)

3.	6947	Digi Com Bhd
4.	6012	Maxis Bhd
5.	5090	Media Chinese International Ltd
6.	0172	OCK Group Bhd
7.	7190	Pelangi Publishing Group Bhd
8.	5252	Sasbadi Holdings Bhd
9.	9431	Seni Jaya Corporation Bhd
10.	6084	Star Media Group Bhd
11.	4863	Telekom Malaysia Bhd
12.	5031	TIME dotCom Bhd
13.	5754	Utusan Melayu (Malaysia) Bhd

PASARAN ACE
ACE MARKET

BARANGAN PENGGUNA & PERKHIDMATAN
CONSUMER PRODUCTS & SERVICES

Bil/ *No.*	Kod Stok/ *Stock code*	Nama Sekuriti / *Name of Securities*
1.	0098	Bahvest Resources Bhd
2.	0179	Bioalpha Holdings Bhd
3.	0157	Focus Point Holdings Bhd
4.	0074	Green Ocean Corporation Bhd
5.	0170	Kanger International Bhd
6.	0140	Macpie Bhd
7.	0197	Wegmans Holdings Bhd

BARANGAN INDUSTRI & PERKHIDMATAN
INDUSTRIAL PRODUCTS & SERVICES

Bil/ *No.*	Kod Stok/ *Stock code*	Nama Sekuriti / *Name of Securities*
1	0105	Asia Poly Holdings Bhd
2.	0072	AT Systematization Bhd
3	0187	BCM Alliance Bhd
4	0102	Connectcounty Holdings Bhd
5.	0190	Eversafe Rubber Bhd
6	0039	GFM Services Bhd
7	0160	Hiap Huat Holdings Bhd
8	0188	HLT Global Bhd
9	0024	JAG Bhd
10	0193	Kejuruteraan Asastera Bhd
11	0167	MClean Technologies Bhd
12	0081	Mega Sun City Holdings Bhd
13	0177	Pasukhas Group Bhd
14	0038	Plastrade Technology Bhd
15	0028	Scope Industries Bhd
16	0055	Sersol Bhd
17	0001	Supercomnet Technologies Bhd
18	0084	Techfast Holdings Bhd
19	0089	Tex Cycle Technology (M) Bhd
20	0025	YBS International Bhd

(*Continued*)

(Continued)

PEMBINAAN
CONSTRUCTION

Bil/ *No.*	**Kod Stok/** *Stock code*	**Nama Sekuriti /** *Name of Securities*
1	0206	Gagasan Nadi Cergas Bhd
2	0198	GDB Holdings Bhd
3	0109	SC Estate Builder Bhd
4	0162	Widad Group Bhd

PENGANGKUTAN & LOGISTIK
TRANSPORTATION & LOGISTICS

Bil/ *No.*	**Kod Stok/** *Stock code*	**Nama Sekuriti /** *Name of Securities*
1	0048	Ancom Logistics Bhd
2	0080	Straits Inter Logistics Bhd
3	0199	TRI-Mode System (M) Bhd

TEKNOLOGI
TECHNOLOGY

Bil/ *No.*	**Kod Stok/** *Stock code*	**Nama Sekuriti /** *Name of Securities*
1	0181	Aemulus Holdings Bhd
2	0119	AppAsia Bhd
3	0068	Asdion Bhd
4	0191	Cabnet Holdings Bhd
5	0152	DGB Asia Bhd
6	0131	Diversified Gateway Solutions Bhd
7	0154	EA Holdings Bhd
8	0107	Eduspec Holdings Bhd
9	0045	G Neptune Bhd
10	0104	Genetec Technology Bhd
11	0174	iDimension Consolidated Bhd
12	0023	IFCA MSC Bhd
13	0094	INIX Technologies Holdings Bhd
14	0010	IRIS Corporation Bhd
15	0146	JF Technology Bhd
16	0127	JHM Consolidation Bhd
17	0036	Key Alliance Group Bhd
18	0111	K-One Technology Bhd
19	0176	Kronologi Asia Bhd
20	0075	LYC Healthcare Bhd
21	0126	Microlink Solutions Bhd
22	0112	Mikro MSC Bhd
23	0070	MQ Technology Bhd
24	0108	N2N Connect Bhd
25	0026	Nova MSC Bhd
26	0040	OpenSys (M) Bhd
27	0079	Orion IXL Bhd
28	0006	Pineapple Resources Bhd
29	0202	Radiant Globaltech Bhd
30	0200	Revenue Group Bhd
31	0203	Securemetric Bhd
32	0117	SMRT Holdings Bhd
33	0169	SMTrack Bhd

Appendix III

List of Shariah-Compliant Securities on the LEAP Market*

No.	*Stock Code*	*Name of Securities*	*Sector*
1	03001	Cloudaron Group Berhad	Technology
2	03016	CRG Incorporated Berhad	Consumer Products and Services
3	03003	JM Education Group Berhad	Consumer Products and Services
4	03015	Manforce Group Berhad	Consumer Products and Services
5	03006	Nova Pharma Solutions Berhad	Healthcare
6	03007	Polymer Link Holdings Berhad	Industrial Products and Services
7	03018	Supreme Consolidated Resources Berhad	Consumer Products and Services

**Note:* For sophisticated investors as prescribed under the Capital Market and Services Act 2007.
Source: SCM.

Appendix IV

List of Islamic Real Estate Investment Trusts (I-REITs)

No.	*Fund*	*Fund Management Company*
1	Al-'Aqar Healthcare REIT	Damansara REIT Managers Sdn Bhd
2	Al-Salam Real Estate Investment Trust	Damansara REIT Managers Sdn Bhd
3	Axis-REIT	Axis REIT Managers Bhd
4	KLCC Property & REIT—Stapled Securities	KLCC REIT Management Sdn Bhd

Source: SCM.

Appendix V

List of Islamic Exchange-Traded Funds (I-ETFs)

No.	*Fund*	*Fund Management Company*
1	MyETF Dow Jones Islamic Market Malaysia Titans 25	i-VCAP Management Sdn Bhd
2	MyETF MSCI Malaysia Islamic Dividend	i-VCAP Management Sdn Bhd Affin
3	MyETF MSCI SEA Islamic Dividend	i-VCAP Management Sdn Bhd
4	MyETF Thomson Reuters Asia Pacific Ex-Japan Islamic Agribusiness	i-VCAP Management Sdn Bhd Affin
5	MyETF Dow Jones U.S. Titans 50	i-VCAP Management Sdn Bhd
6	Tradeplus Shariah Gold Tracker	Affin Hwang Asset Management Bhd

Source: SCM.

Appendix VI

List of Licensed Financial Institutions

Licensed Financial Institutions	
Commercial Banks	• Affin Bank Berhad • Alliance Bank Malaysia Berhad • AmBank (M) Berhad • BNP Paribas Malaysia Berhad • Bangkok Bank Berhad • Bank of China (Malaysia) Berhad • CIMB Bank Berhad • China Construction Bank (Malaysia) Berhad • Citibank Berhad • Deutsche Bank (Malaysia) Berhad • HSBC Bank Malaysia Berhad • Hong Leong Bank Berhad • India International Bank (Malaysia) Berhad • Industrial and Commercial Bank of China (Malaysia) Berhad • J.P. Morgan Chase Bank Berhad • MUFG Bank (Malaysia) Berhad • Malayan Banking Berhad • Mizuho Bank (Malaysia) Berhad • OCBC Bank (Malaysia) Berhad • Public Bank Berhad • RHB Bank Berhad • Standard Chartered Bank Malaysia Berhad • Sumitomo Mitsui Banking Corporation Malaysia Berhad • The Bank of Nova Scotia Berhad • United Overseas Bank (Malaysia) Bhd
Islamic Banks	• Affin Islamic Bank Berhad • Al Rajhi Banking & Investment Corporation (Malaysia) Berhad • Alliance Islamic Bank Berhad • AmBank Islamic Berhad • Bank Islam Malaysia Berhad • Bank Muamalat Malaysia Berhad • CIMB Islamic Bank Berhad • HSBC Amanah Malaysia Berhad • Hong Leong Islamic Bank Berhad • Kuwait Finance House (Malaysia) Berhad

Licensed Financial Institutions	
	• MBSB Bank Berhad • Maybank Islamic Berhad • OCBC Al-Amin Bank Berhad • Public Islamic Bank Berhad • RHB Islamic Bank Berhad • Standard Chartered Saadiq Berhad
International Islamic Banks	• PT. Bank Muamalat Indonesia, Tbk
Investment Banks	• Affin Hwang Investment Bank Berhad • Alliance Investment Bank Berhad • Am Investment Bank Berhad • CIMB Investment Bank Berhad • Hong Leong Investment Bank Berhad • KAF Investment Bank Berhad • Kenanga Investment Bank Berhad • MIDF Amanah Investment Bank Berhad • Maybank Investment Bank Berhad • Public Investment Bank Berhad • RHB Investment Bank Berhad
Other Financial Institutions	• ERF Sdn. Bhd. • Pengurusan Danaharta Nasional Berhad (now managed under Prokhas Sdn. Bhd.)
Licensed Insurance Companies and Takaful Operators	
Life Business	• AIA Berhad • AXA Affin Life Insurance Berhad • Allianz Life Insurance Malaysia Berhad • AmMetLife Insurance Berhad • Etiqa Life Insurance Berhad • Gibraltar BSN Life Berhad • Great Eastern Life Assurance (Malaysia) Berhad • Hong Leong Assurance Berhad • MCIS Insurance Berhad • Manulife Insurance Berhad • Prudential Assurance Malaysia Berhad • Sunlife Malaysia Assurance Berhad • Tokio Marine Life Insurance Malaysia Bhd • Zurich Life Insurance Malaysia Berhad
General Business	• AIA General Berhad • AIG Malaysia Insurance Berhad • AXA Affin General Insurance Berhad • Allianz General Insurance Company (Malaysia) Berhad • AmGeneral Insurance Berhad • Berjaya Sompo Insurance Berhad • Chubb Insurance Malaysia Berhad • Danajamin Nasional Berhad • Etiqa General Insurance Berhad • Great Eastern General Insurance (Malaysia) Berhad • Liberty Insurance Berhad • Lonpac Insurance Berhad • MPI Generali Insurans Berhad

(*Continued*)

(Continued)

Licensed Financial Institutions	
	• MSIG Insurance (Malaysia) Bhd • Pacific & Orient Insurance Co. Berhad • Pacific Insurance Berhad • Progressive Insurance Berhad • QBE Insurance (Malaysia) Berhad • RHB Insurance Berhad • Tokio Marine Insurance (Malaysia) Berhad • Tune Insurance Malaysia Berhad • Zurich General Insurance Malaysia Berhad
Life and General Reinsurance Business	• Hannover Rueck SE
Life Reinsurance Business	• Malaysian Life Reinsurance Group Berhad
General Reinsurance Business	• Ambra Versicherung AG • Asia Capital Reinsurance Malaysia Sdn. Bhd • Malaysian Reinsurance Berhad • Munchener Ruckversicherungs-Gesellschaft • Swiss Reinsurance Company Ltd. • Toa Reinsurance Company Ltd.
Takaful Operators	• AIA PUBLIC Takaful Bhd • AmMetLife Takaful Berhad • Etiqa Family Takaful Berhad • Etiqa General Takaful Berhad • FWD Takaful Berhad • Great Eastern Takaful Berhad • Hong Leong MSIG Takaful Berhad • Prudential BSN Takaful Berhad • Sun Life Malaysia Takaful Berhad • Syarikat Takaful Malaysia Am Berhad • Syarikat Takaful Malaysia Keluarga Berhad • Takaful Ikhlas Family Berhad • Takaful Ikhlas General Berhad • Zurich General Takaful Malaysia Berhad • Zurich Takaful Malaysia Berhad
Retakaful Operators	• ACR Retakaful Berhad • Malaysian Reinsurance Berhad • Munchener Ruckversicherungs-Gesellschaft (Munich Re Retakaful) • Swiss Reinsurance Company Ltd. (Swiss Re Retakaful)

Source: Bank Negara Malaysia.

Index

Note: Page numbers in *italics* indicate a figure and page numbers in **bold** indicate a table on the corresponding page.

For Product Safety Concerns and Information please contact our EU representative GPSR@taylorandfrancis.com
Taylor & Francis Verlag GmbH, Kaufingerstraße 24, 80331 München, Germany

www.ingramcontent.com/pod-product-compliance
Ingram Content Group UK Ltd.
Pitfield, Milton Keynes, MK11 3LW, UK
UKHW020007200926
475702UK00015B/2513
* 9 7 8 1 0 3 2 5 6 5 3 1 6 *